FIVE MINUTES WITH GOD

FIVE MINUTES WITH GOD
Rusty Hills

WALKING WITH THE SAVIOR

ISBN-10: 1941972187
ISBN-13: 978-1941972182

Library of Congress Control Number: 2014950104

Published by Start2Finish Books
PO Box 660675 #54705
Dallas, TX 75266-0675
www.start2finish.org

Printed in the United States of America

Cover Design: Josh Feit, Evangela.com

INTRODUCTION

How many of us have made the commitment to begin a daily Bible reading program with the goal of reading through the Bible in a year, only to forget, fall behind, get discouraged, and give up? Sound familiar? We all want to study the Bible more, but our busy lives and hectic schedules make it difficult to devote time to personal Bible study. Likewise, every church understands the importance of Bible study and prayer in the lives of her members, and most have, at some point, attempted to implement some kind of daily Bible reading program, probably with disappointing results. It was out of this dilemma that *Five Minutes with God* was born.

Five Minutes with God is a different concept in daily Bible reading. It doesn't challenge the reader to complete the entire Bible (or even the New Testament) in a year's time. Instead, it encourages the reader to focus on shorter passages of Scripture and to read them intentionally and with greater understanding. It, in essence, narrows the field of vision to one particular idea or thought and helps the reader to see that portion of God's Word more clearly. By focusing on the gospels this year, readers can journey through the life of the Savior to learn about Him and from Him in a way that will deepen their faith and strengthen their resolve to live for Jesus. The accompanying devotional thoughts are designed to help further clarify the reading and encourage deeper thought into the meaning of each passage. Some of the thoughts are intended to instruct, while others have the purpose of motivating, but all of the readings and thoughts will hopefully inspire in the reader a greater appreciation for God's marvelous plan of redemption and a greater love for our Lord and Savior, Jesus Christ.

THE GREATEST LIFE EVER LIVED

In all of the history of humankind, no life has had a greater impact on the world than the life of Jesus Christ, not to mention the eternal impact of His death and resurrection. In His short time in this world, Jesus forever changed our view of God, the world, eternity, and salvation. He gave us a glimpse into the heart and mind of God and allowed us to approach God, to know Him in a way that had never been possible before. Through His perfect example of a life, He showed us how to live, how to love, how to serve, how to pray, and how to humbly submit to God's perfect will. He truly is the Master Teacher, Great Physician, Lion of Judah, Lamb of God, our Shepherd, Friend, Messiah, Savior, and Lord.

So important and life-changing was the life, influence, and saving work of Jesus that God saw fit to preserve, not one or two, but four eye-witness accounts for us to learn from. Each of those four gospel accounts is written to a specific audience and for a specific person. As these men tell the story of Jesus through the guidance of the Holy Spirit and from their perspective, they each add a new and different dimension to our understanding of the life of Christ. While they do not record every word or action of Jesus during His time in this world, these four accounts come together to paint for us a beautiful picture of the perfect life, atoning death, and victorious resurrection of Jesus Christ. Toward the end of his account of Jesus' life, the apostle John wrote concerning the many signs and works of Jesus that were recorded for us: "These are written so that you may believe that Jesus is the Christ, the Son of God, and that by believing you may have life in His name" (John 20:31). The four gospel accounts provide not only a beautiful story of God's love, but are also a powerful testament to the wisdom of God and to His desire for us to know His Son in a deep and meaningful way.

This daily devotional book represents an earnest attempt to combine all four gospel accounts in order to examine fully the recorded life of Christ in chronological order from beginning to end. While no assurances are made that every event is in exactly the right place in the timeline of Jesus' life, the readings are placed in such an order that will allow the reader to gain a greater understanding of the relationship between the gospels as they relate to the events of the life of our Lord.

HOW TO USE THIS BOOK

This book is different from other daily devotional books that you may be familiar with. In most of those books, there is a reading from the Bible that is suggested for each day, but that text is not crucial to understanding or benefitting from the day's devotional thought, which typically stands alone as an independent reading to give inspiration or motivation for the day. Not so, with *Five Minutes with God*. In reality, this book is part devotional book, part Bible study. This daily reading program was designed so that the Word of God is at the core of it, and that the reading of that word is crucial to it. The writings contained in this book were never intended to overshadow or replace the reading of God's word, but rather to illuminate and point the reader to it. As you spend time with these devotionals each day, understand that the reading of the biblical text is essential to understanding the thought, because it is directly related and connected to it. The assigned verses for the day will be short (only a few verses) and are prominently displayed at the top of each page. Please take the time to read that passage before reading the accompanying thought. Because the thought is often designed to shed light on the meaning of some portion of the biblical reading, you might find that it is helpful to re-read the verses after considering the day's thought.

Finally, it is my desire that these daily devotionals serve as a springboard to launch you into more and deeper Bible study. While some might view the brevity of these readings as a shortcoming of this system, I am of the belief that the short passages allow the reader to explore the text in more detail and glean nuggets of truth and understanding that might otherwise be overlooked. Likewise, the thoughts that are given in this book are just that—thoughts—and they are wholly mine. Read them, consider them, and then meditate on the passage with the intent of increasing your understanding of its purpose and teaching. Most of all, remember that this daily devotional is about Jesus. My prayer is that, through this study, you will come to know Him, appreciate Him, love Him, and follow Him in a fuller and better way.

To God be the glory!

DAY 1

 Today's Reading:
John 1:1-5

When we think of Jesus, we often limit our thinking to His earthly life—a teacher, a servant, a miracle-worker, an example, and a sacrifice. But John introduces Jesus to us as being much more than just a man. As "the Word," Christ is described as being eternal in nature, one with God, involved in creation, and the life-giving light to the world. He is God, life, light, and salvation; the eternal, perfect in every way, infinitely powerful, all-knowing, ever-present Son of God. And yet, He willingly took on flesh and came to this world to become our Savior! The Son of God became the Son of Man and experienced humanity with all of its trials and temptations. What an amazing testament to the great love of God and oh, what a Savior!

How would you describe Jesus to someone
who knew nothing about Him?

DON'T FORGET TO PRAY AND HAVE A GREAT DAY!

⏳ **THINGS TO PRAY FOR TODAY:**

DAY 2

Today's Reading:
John 1:6–13

Not much has changed in this old world. Jesus still offers light, love, forgiveness, and salvation to a dark and dying world, and the majority of the world still will not receive Him. He came to show us God and many still refuse to recognize Him. He came to show the Way and most still prefer to be lost. But it is also true that Jesus' invitation remains open. To those who are willing to believe in Him and receive Him, He still gives the right to be called children of God and to take part in all the wonderful blessings that come with that relationship. What a loving and patient God, and what a Savior!

Why do you think so many people refuse to accept God's love?

DON'T FORGET TO PRAY AND HAVE A GREAT DAY!

 THINGS TO PRAY FOR TODAY:

Day 3

 Today's Reading:
John 1:14–18

It is a thought unlike any that has been dreamed of by man—often thought of as preposterous or ridiculous. The very idea that deity, in all of His power, wisdom, glory, and would lay it all down and take on flesh. No god ever dreamed up by mankind would do such a thing. And yet, one of the great differences between God and any mythical god devised by the mind of men is that God loves! He is not only the all-powerful, all-knowing, all-present Creator and Ruler of the universe, but He is also a loving Father. Thus, His Son came into the world and took on flesh in order to show us God and bring grace and truth to mankind. He came because He loved us!

How does Jesus coming into the world prove the love of God?

DON'T FORGET TO PRAY AND HAVE A GREAT DAY!

 THINGS TO PRAY FOR TODAY:

DAY 4

Today's Reading:
Luke 1:26-38

F or nothing will be impossible with God." How can it be that Jesus would be conceived and born of a virgin? How can it be that Elizabeth would bear a son in her old age, having been barren? The answer to these and other questions concerning the birth, life, death, or resurrection of Christ is simply that nothing is impossible with God. Every aspect of the life of Christ, even the way in which He came into this world, demonstrates the power and ability of God. By that same power, God is still able to change our lives, answer our prayers, cleanse us of our sins, and help us overcome our shortcomings and past. For with God, nothing will be impossible.

Why is it important for us that God is all-powerful?

DON'T FORGET TO PRAY AND HAVE A GREAT DAY!

⏳ **THINGS TO PRAY FOR TODAY:**

Day 5

 Today's Reading:
Matthew 1:18–25

There is not much of a spotlight cast on Joseph in the story of Jesus, but this passage is very telling in understanding what kind of man he was. He was an honorable man, one who feared God and was concerned with doing right. For these reasons, God chose him and entrusted him with great honor and responsibility—providing care and training for Jesus during His childhood years. What an experience it must have been to have known Jesus so intimately and have had that special relationship with Him. While much different than that of Joseph, God has chosen each of us and has given us the opportunity to have a special relationship with Jesus as well. If we will, we can find in Jesus a friend, teacher, Savior, and Lord. What a privilege and blessing!

How has your relationship with Jesus been a blessing to you?

DON'T FORGET TO PRAY AND HAVE A GREAT DAY!

 THINGS TO PRAY FOR TODAY:

Day 6

 Today's Reading:
Luke 2:1–7

What if the residents of Bethlehem had known and believed who Jesus was? Do you think that there would have been a room found for Him? Would there have been a more suitable environment to be born into? Would there have been a bed provided to lay Him in? Presumably, the answer to these questions is a resounding "yes." Yet we live in a world that still does not make much room for Jesus. More and more often in our world and culture today, Jesus is not recognized or welcome. But we all must remember that we each have the opportunity to make room for Jesus in our lives. We can welcome Him in and allow Him to occupy the most prominent place in our hearts. But will we? Will there be room found for Jesus in you?

How can we make room for Jesus in our lives today?

DON'T FORGET TO PRAY AND HAVE A GREAT DAY!

⏳ **THINGS TO PRAY FOR TODAY:**

Day 7

Today's Reading:
Luke 2:8-20

Much has been made of the glorious news of the birth of Christ being proclaimed to these shepherds, but notice an aspect of this story that is often overlooked—their reaction to the news. First, they came to Jesus without delay (vv. 15-16). Second, they shared the news of Jesus with others (vv. 17-18). Finally, they glorified and praised God for all that they had seen and heard (v. 20). Today, there is still no better news that can be heard than the good news of Jesus Christ. It is news of love and atoning sacrifice, of redemption and relationship, of mercy and salvation. It is good news, great news, the best news! Surely, our reaction to the good news of Christ should be the same as that of the shepherds who were told of the Savior's birth. So, let us draw near to Him, tell others about Him, and praise and glorify God because of Him!

What are some good ways to respond to Christ today?

DON'T FORGET TO PRAY AND HAVE A GREAT DAY!

 THINGS TO PRAY FOR TODAY:

Day 8

Today's Reading:
Luke 2:25–35

Throughout Jesus' life, many would deny, question, and reject Him, ultimately leading to His death on the cross. Simeon is a wonderful example of someone who recognized and accepted Jesus as the Son of God and promised Messiah, and glorified God because of Him, despite the fact that Jesus came in a form that was much different than many (possibly including Simeon) expected. What a wonderful example of faith and acceptance of God's will and plan. In our lives today, God's will and plan still does not always come in the form that we expect. His blessings and answers to our prayers may look much different than we anticipated. Yet God's plan is always perfect and best for our lives. May God help us to have the faith to trust in His wisdom and accept His will for our lives.

Why does God's plan so often differ from our own?

DON'T FORGET TO PRAY AND HAVE A GREAT DAY!

 THINGS TO PRAY FOR TODAY:

Day 9

Today's Reading:
Luke 2:36–40

The Child grew"—what an amazing statement! Not because Jesus grew, for that is the normal process of human development. What is amazing is the fact that God sent His only Son to this world to take on flesh, and that he was born as all humanity is born. He came into the world as a weak and helpless baby to be cared for by Joseph and Mary. He had to be fed, bathed, clothed, and taught. He experienced human life from its earliest moments, and thus understands us with a sympathy that comes only from experience. When the Hebrews writer says that He is a High Priest who can "sympathize with our weaknesses" (4:15), it is true because He experienced every facet of humanity. It is a plan that could only be conceived in the mind of an all-knowing and loving God. What an amazing God and wonderful Savior we have!

How is it comforting to know that Jesus experienced human life?

DON'T FORGET TO PRAY AND HAVE A GREAT DAY!

 THINGS TO PRAY FOR TODAY:

DAY 10

Today's Reading:
Matthew 2:1–12

One of the things that stands out to me in this story is the trouble, expense, and determination with which the wise men came to find and worship Jesus. They made the long, difficult journey to see Him, they brought expensive gifts to offer Him, they searched for Him until they found Him, and they did all this for the opportunity to worship Him (v. 2). Too often, we take our worship for granted. It is easy, comfortable, convenient, and without risk. We have much to be thankful for. Yet we often find it burdensome, tiresome, and unrewarding. One of the great lessons of this story, and of the New Testament altogether, is that Jesus is worthy of our praise and worship. He deserves the very best that we have to offer Him. Let us rejoice in the opportunity to give Him the glory due His name and never take for granted the wonderful blessing of worship!

What blessings or rewards do you gain from worshipping God?

DON'T FORGET TO PRAY AND HAVE A GREAT DAY!

 THINGS TO PRAY FOR TODAY:

Day 11

 Today's Reading:
Matthew 2:13-23

It is hard to imagine the unspeakable means by which Herod tried to destroy Jesus and the overwhelming fear and hatred that must have motivated that cruel act. But Herod was just the first in a never-ending line of people and forces that have tried to rid the world of Jesus and His influence. There will always be those who, out of fear and hatred for a God that they don't even know, will try to dismiss, dispel, or destroy Him and His Word. But try though they may, they will never be able to rid the world of God. He has promised us that His Word will never pass away, and as long as there are faithful Christians who are living for Christ, He will continue to live on in this world and change lives for good.

*What can you do today to influence someone
for Christ and help further His cause?*

DON'T FORGET TO PRAY AND HAVE A GREAT DAY!

 THINGS TO PRAY FOR TODAY:

DAY 12

Today's Reading:
Luke 2:41–52

From the early age of twelve years old, Jesus demonstrated a remarkable understanding of the importance of doing the will of God. Throughout His life, He never wavered from that same determination—to do God's will and fulfill His purpose. As in every aspect of His life, Jesus is, in this passage, a wonderful and perfect example for us! Certainly, we understand that, as the Son of God, Jesus had a very special relationship with God and a unique purpose on this earth. Nevertheless, His example is powerful, and we should learn from Him that our primary and greatest purpose and motivation in life should be to be about our Father's business.

What are some things that your family
can do to be about the Father's business?

DON'T FORGET TO PRAY AND HAVE A GREAT DAY!

⏳ **THINGS TO PRAY FOR TODAY:**

DAY 13

 Today's Reading:
Mark 1:1–8

Can you imagine being John the Baptizer and having the enormous task of preparing the way for Jesus? How important his work was! As the forerunner of Christ, he laid the groundwork for Jesus' teaching to be received and for the repentance and change that Jesus would call for. In a way, we all have the same calling as John. As those who know Christ and have given our lives to Him, we are called to use our lives, influence, and teaching to prepare the hearts of those around us to receive the teachings of Christ and, ultimately, to give themselves to Him in faith and obedience. What a great opportunity and blessing it is to be involved in the work of the Lord!

Who in your life can you influence for Christ today?

DON'T FORGET TO PRAY AND HAVE A GREAT DAY!

⏳ THINGS TO PRAY FOR TODAY:

DAY 14

Today's Reading:
John 1:19-28

Two things stand out to me about John from this passage: his commitment to his calling and the humility with which he approached his work. John never wavered in his preaching. He endured the hardships and was wholly committed to fulfilling his purpose. He also never allowed the notoriety or success that he experienced to affect his character. He was constantly downplaying his own importance and pointing to the greatness of the coming Christ. What an example! As we approach our Christian lives, the commitment and character with which we live will have a great impact, either positive or negative, on those around us. Let us strive to draw people to Christ, rather than turn them away.

How can your commitment and character help the cause of Christ?

DON'T FORGET TO PRAY AND HAVE A GREAT DAY!

⏳ **THINGS TO PRAY FOR TODAY:**

DAY 15

 Today's Reading:
Matthew 3:13–17

In speaking of His baptism, Jesus says to John that "it is fitting for us to fulfill all righteousness." If it was right and good for Jesus to fulfill the righteousness of God and to leave nothing undone that would honor God and His will, the same can certainly be said for us. As we search the pages of God's word and learn of the will of God for our lives, our determination and commitment should be to do His will and leave undone nothing that God desires. It is interesting and troublesome that so many in today's world want to argue with the Scriptures in an attempt to avoid doing all that God commands. Instead, it ought to be our desire to be obedient to God in every way and, in the words of Jesus, "to fulfill all righteousness."

What are some things that you can do to fulfill all righteousness?

DON'T FORGET TO PRAY AND HAVE A GREAT DAY!

⧗ THINGS TO PRAY FOR TODAY:

DAY 16

Today's Reading:
John 1:29-34

It is interesting that, at this initial introduction of Jesus by John, he refers to Him not as a King and Conqueror, as so many of the Jews were looking for, or as the glorious Son of God as had been previously revealed to Him at Jesus' baptism, but as the sacrificial Lamb sent by God to take away the sins of the world. It was this picture of Jesus that was the hope of Israel and the supreme purpose of Jesus' coming into this world. And it is that great identity of Jesus as the Lamb of God that continues to offer hope and salvation to a lost and dying world, for it is only by His atoning death that we can find the redemption and forgiveness that we so desperately need. Thanks be to God for His incredible love and the wonderful gift of His Son who willingly died for us!

How has your life been changed by the sacrifice of Christ?

DON'T FORGET TO PRAY AND HAVE A GREAT DAY!

⏳ THINGS TO PRAY FOR TODAY:

DAY 17

 Today's Reading:
Matthew 4:1–11

These temptations of Jesus were surely not the first, last, or only times that Satan attempted to lure Jesus into sin. So why are these temptations recorded as they are? The simple answer to this question is that they are given to us for our learning. Through this event from Jesus' life, we learn about Satan—his cunning, his deception, his knowledge of us and our weaknesses, fears, and desires. We also learn how to deal with temptation—being strong and determined, using the truth of God's Word to ward off Satan's attacks, and caring more about faithfulness than about physical needs and desires. Most of all, it teaches us that we can win over Satan and temptation! Yes, Satan is powerful, and temptation is strong, but we do not face them alone! As our helper, we have the almighty God of the universe. With His word to guide us and His Son as our strength, we can overcome!

How will you deal with the temptations that you face today?

DON'T FORGET TO PRAY AND HAVE A GREAT DAY!

 THINGS TO PRAY FOR TODAY:

Day 18

Today's Reading:
John 1:35–42

Andrew, one of the first disciples of Jesus and later called to be an apostle, is not one of the most talked-about or well-known of the Lord's apostles. Yet in this text, and almost every time he is mentioned, Andrew gives us a great example and lesson in bringing others to Jesus. Upon meeting Jesus, Andrew's first and immediate action is to find his brother, Peter, to share the news of Christ with him. When you think of the tremendous impact Peter had on the early church, remember that it was Andrew who introduced him to Jesus. We often focus our evangelistic attention on faraway places while often overlooking those who are closest to us. While there is certainly a great need to take the good news of Christ to the whole world, let us remember that each of us probably has close friends and family who also need the gospel. Why not follow the example of Andrew by going to those people and telling them about Christ?

How can you reach out to your friends and family with the gospel?

DON'T FORGET TO PRAY AND HAVE A GREAT DAY!

 THINGS TO PRAY FOR TODAY:

Day 19

 Today's Reading:
John 1:43–51

F ollow Me." Two simple words, and yet a command that had a life-changing effect on anyone who heard and obeyed it. To follow Jesus meant to leave the world behind and give Him your life. It meant to make sacrifices and endure hardships. It meant to put Christ before everyone and everything else. It also meant to have the wonderful opportunity to sit at His feet and learn, to witness His compassion, forgiveness, and power, and to reap all the spiritual benefits of a relationship with the Son of God. Jesus still invites us to follow Him today, and to follow Him still means the same things— commitment, devotion, sacrifice. But the blessings continue to outweigh the challenges, and accepting Jesus' invitation still has the power to change lives.

Have you accepted the Lord's invitation?
If so, how has it changed your life?

DON'T FORGET TO PRAY AND HAVE A GREAT DAY!

⌛ THINGS TO PRAY FOR TODAY:

Day 20

Today's Reading:
John 2:1–11

An unusual situation, an unusual request, an unusual miracle. Why did Jesus choose this moment and this miracle to begin to demonstrate His power? Maybe we don't know for sure, but as you read through the life of Christ, keep this in mind: Jesus never did anything—a miracle, a teaching, an interaction with someone—without having a purpose. In this case, notice the result of the miracle: "and His disciples believed in Him." The effect of this act of power by Jesus at the very beginning of His ministry was that those who were already following Him were furthered convinced of His identity, and their faith was strengthened. And hopefully, as we read of His life and witness His power, compassion, and holiness, our faith is strengthened as well.

Why do you think that miracles were such
an important part of Jesus' ministry?

DON'T FORGET TO PRAY AND HAVE A GREAT DAY!

⧗ **THINGS TO PRAY FOR TODAY:**

Day 21

 Today's Reading:
John 2:13–22

The scene at the temple, though it had become commonplace for the day, was a shameful and disgusting one—merchants making a profit from people's worship; people thoughtlessly buying sacrificial animals instead of bringing their best to God. When Jesus saw the mockery and abuse with which some were treating the temple and the worship of God, He was filled with righteous indignation. In His authority and power as the Son of God, after taking the time to fashion a whip, He rid the temple of the merchants and money-changers and, in the process, made a powerful point about the importance of proper worship. God has always been concerned about how we approach Him in worship. What we bring to God in worship, and how we bring it, is vital to our relationship with Him and to the acceptance of our worship by Him. Let us always strive to give Him our very best!

Why do you think proper worship is so important to God?

DON'T FORGET TO PRAY AND HAVE A GREAT DAY!

 THINGS TO PRAY FOR TODAY:

DAY 22

Today's Reading:
John 3:1-12

To be born again—to start over, a new beginning, a second chance. It was a strange concept to Nicodemus, who could only conceive of the impossibility of a second physical birth. But the rebirth of which Jesus spoke was not a physical one but spiritual. That spiritual rebirth is still offered today, and it is still difficult for many to understand. We don't often get the chance to erase the failures and mistakes of the past and have a fresh start, but God gives us that opportunity through Christ. But being born again is not just an opportunity; it is a necessity. Notice that Jesus says that, in order to see the kingdom of God, we "*must* be born again" of water and the Spirit (for more on being born again, see Romans 6:1-7). It is such a simple act of obedience and submission, and yet it opens up so many wonderful blessings to us in Christ. What an amazing thought, that God allows us to be born again!

Have you been born again? If so, how has it changed your life?

DON'T FORGET TO PRAY AND HAVE A GREAT DAY!

⧗ **THINGS TO PRAY FOR TODAY:**

DAY 23

 Today's Reading:
John 3:13–21

"T he golden text of the Bible." That is the label that many have attached to John 3:16. That short verse does contain the core message of God's Word—that God loved us so much that He was willing to give His Son for us to die in our place so that we could be saved. Every facet of that verse amazes and overwhelms us as we consider our desperate need that required such a great sacrifice, the limitless love of God that motivated Him to give the very best of heaven for us, and the wonderful promise that is made to us because of that gift. It is truly an amazing thought! And yet, even as we savor those great truths, we are reminded by Jesus that many in the world will love darkness, rather than light, and will reject the greatest gift ever offered to them. But knowing that many would not accept Him, Jesus still came and died anyway, even for them. I am not sure that any of us can truly comprehend the depth of God's love or the greatness of the sacrifice that was offered for us. Thanks be to God!

Why do you think so many are unwilling to accept Jesus?

DON'T FORGET TO PRAY AND HAVE A GREAT DAY!

 THINGS TO PRAY FOR TODAY:

Day 24

Today's Reading:
John 3:22–36

He must increase, but I must decrease." What a powerful statement. John had certainly gained a great deal of notoriety and a large following during his preaching in the wilderness. No doubt, some of his followers, motivated by their respect for and loyalty to John, felt threatened by Jesus' presence. But John understood that it wasn't about him. It was about Jesus. John had fulfilled his role in preparing the way for Jesus, and it was now time for him to humbly and submissively give way to the Master. There is a great lesson there for us. So often, we know Jesus and want to have a relationship with Him, but don't want to get out of the way so that He can have control. We are happy to share our lives with Him, but we are not willing to give Him our lives. We would do well to learn from John and follow his example in saying, "He must increase, but I must decrease."

Why is it important that we give our lives to Christ?

DON'T FORGET TO PRAY AND HAVE A GREAT DAY!

⏳ THINGS TO PRAY FOR TODAY:

Day 25

 Today's Reading:
John 4:1-14

There are many lessons that can be learned from this event, but I want to draw your attention to one that we often miss. Verse 4 says, "And He had to pass through Samaria." Normally, we consider that statement nothing more than an insignificant geographic detail, but that is not necessarily the case. Though Samaria was located directly between Judea and Galilee, it was not uncommon for Jews to travel well out of their way to avoid Samaria because of their disdain for the Samaritan people. But Jesus made a point to go through that region, not necessarily because He had to, but because He knew that He could make a difference there. He took the message and offer of living water to a woman and people that most Jews would have considered a lost cause and not worthy of their time or effort. He reached out with God's love, and as a result, many believed in and followed Him. What an example from the Master Teacher!

Who have you not mentioned Christ to because
you considered them a lost cause?

DON'T FORGET TO PRAY AND HAVE A GREAT DAY!

⌛ THINGS TO PRAY FOR TODAY:

Day 26

Today's Reading:
John 4:13–26

G ive me this water, so that I will not be thirsty..." Oh, the thought of never being thirsty again; never having to come to the well to do the difficult work of drawing water again! She wanted the living water that Jesus offered, but she misunderstood. She was thinking physically and missed the spiritual point. The water that Jesus offered (and still offers) had nothing to do with physical things but was the gift of spiritual life. Those who drink from that spiritual fountain that flows from Christ will never want for any spiritual thing again. Forgiveness, redemption, relationship, joy, peace, hope, salvation, eternal life—it is all available to the person who accepts the living water that Jesus offers. What a gift and blessing that water is! "Give me this water..."

What makes the living water that Jesus offers such a special thing?

DON'T FORGET TO PRAY AND HAVE A GREAT DAY!

 THINGS TO PRAY FOR TODAY:

DAY 27

 Today's Reading:
John 4:27–38

"L ift up your eyes, and see that the fields are white for harvest." As Christians, we are all laborers in God's fields. In some lives, we will sow seeds; in others, we will reap the fruit of the seeds sown by someone else. Maybe the important and greatest lesson to learn here is that, in any life that we have contact with, we can influence and affect spiritually. We may not win everyone personally, but we might plant a seed that will later bear fruit that someone else will reap. Or we might reap the fruit of seeds that were planted years before by someone else. We must always be aware of our influence and be ready to work in whatever capacity we are called to fill. What a privilege and responsibility it is to be workers for God!

Who in your life have you or can you influence for God?

DON'T FORGET TO PRAY AND HAVE A GREAT DAY!

 THINGS TO PRAY FOR TODAY:

Day 28

 Today's Reading:
John 4:39-42

She was not exactly the ideal messenger—a woman, married five times, and currently living with someone out of wedlock. There wasn't much about the Samaritan woman that was admirable or even respectable. Yet she had a great story to tell—a Man who knew all about her, though they had never met; One who offered her living water, and who claimed to be the Messiah. She was excited. She couldn't contain herself. And they believed her—not because of her credibility, but because of the Man that she told them about. They came to Him, they heard Him teach, and they believed on Him; all because of one woman who believed in Him and shared Him with others. We are not perfect. We all have our pasts and our shortcomings, our struggles and failures. Yet Jesus has offered us that same living water and the opportunity to be changed forever. And, as with the Samaritan woman, if our lives have been changed by Jesus, shouldn't we tell someone else about Him?

What are some things that keep us from
talking to others about Jesus?

DON'T FORGET TO PRAY AND HAVE A GREAT DAY!

⧗ **THINGS TO PRAY FOR TODAY:**

Day 29

 Today's Reading:
Matthew 4:12–17

Matthew focuses a great deal of his gospel account on Jesus as the fulfillment of the Messianic prophecies. In His life, Jesus was wholly committed to fulfilling God's will. Every day, every act, every word was about doing the will of His Father and fulfilling His purpose. One of the greatest proofs of Jesus' authenticity, especially to Jewish audiences, was His perfect fulfillment of no less than 333 Old Testament prophecies that had been made concerning the coming Messiah. As we live our lives, Jesus is, as always, the perfect example to us. Though our heart's desire may be to be so perfectly committed to God that we completely rid our lives of sin, we are quickly confronted with the reality that we will certainly never reach the level of perfection that Jesus demonstrated. Yet our devotion to living out God's will for our lives needs to be uncompromising and complete. It is a challenge that most of us will struggle to achieve for most of our Christian lives, but the rewards are great!

What are some ways that we can work
to fulfill God's will for our lives?

DON'T FORGET TO PRAY AND HAVE A GREAT DAY!

 THINGS TO PRAY FOR TODAY:

Day 30

Today's Reading:
Mark 1:14–20

C an you imagine walking away from everything that you know as "normal" in your life—your job, your family, your home? When Jesus asked these fishermen to follow Him and become fishers of men, He was asking them to do just that—to leave everything behind and become his full-time followers, students, and apostles. He didn't promise them riches or fame or a life of ease; He offered them something even better. He offered them the unparalleled opportunity to learn from the Master Teacher, to be first-hand witnesses to His power, wisdom and compassion, and to be daily companions of the Son of God. And He gave them the opportunity to live out a greater purpose in their lives—to bring the saving message of Christ to the world and to become fishers of men. In a sense, Christ still calls us to walk away from this world as we know it and follow Him. And while the cost of following Him might be high, the rewards and blessings of making that commitment are still beyond compare.

Is there anything that you have sacrificed in order to follow Christ?

DON'T FORGET TO PRAY AND HAVE A GREAT DAY!

⏳ **THINGS TO PRAY FOR TODAY:**

Day 31

Today's Reading:
Luke 4:14–22

A s Jesus begins His teaching ministry, He does something that is simultaneously expected and remarkable—He reads from the Word of God. As Jesus reads these words from Isaiah the prophet that pertain to Him, He demonstrates a truth and principle that is still vitally important for us today—that the Word of God continues to be trustworthy, timely, and relevant. Though written hundreds of years before Jesus read them, the Word of God spoken through the prophet proved to be true and accurate. And though we live thousands of years after the penning of the Bible, God's Word is no less true or relevant than it was when it was written. God's wisdom and power continue to shine through His timeless Word, which can still change lives and lead us to salvation. Thank God for the wonderful blessing of His Word!

What do you consider to be the greatest blessing of God's Word?

DON'T FORGET TO PRAY AND HAVE A GREAT DAY!

 THINGS TO PRAY FOR TODAY:

Day 32

Today's Reading:
Luke 4:23–30

J esus' words always seemed to invoke a strong response from His audiences. The truth has a way of doing that. Whether it was to leave everything behind and follow Him or, as in this case, to become violently offended and angry at His teaching, people often responded to Jesus with zeal and conviction. But why? Maybe it is because truth—the kind of truth that Jesus brought—requires it of us. It brings to light our thoughts, our motivations, and even our shortcomings. It then requires us to make a choice and to commit our very lives to that decision. The truth of Christ is life-changing. Many embrace that opportunity, accept the truth, and allow themselves to be transformed into the image of Christ. Others, like those in Nazareth, become adamantly opposed to the truth that challenges the paths they have chosen. May we choose the former and always be open to and accepting of Jesus, the Truth.

How has accepting Christ been life-changing for you?

DON'T FORGET TO PRAY AND HAVE A GREAT DAY!

 THINGS TO PRAY FOR TODAY:

DAY 33

 Today's Reading:
Mark 1:21–28

"The Holy One of God." This was not a title used by a follower of Jesus, one of the apostles, or a prophet of God. It was the name by which an unclean spirit referred to Him. It is ironic that in a world where so many people—religious people, God-fearing people—would deny Jesus and refuse to accept Him, this unclean spirit, possessing an awareness of things beyond this physical world, acknowledges the truth of who Jesus is with a term of respect and honor. While this certainly does not justify the evil spirit, it does illustrate the truth that "even the demons believe—and shudder!" (James 2:19). It also provides us with yet another piece of evidence for the fact that Jesus is indeed "the Holy One of God," a truth that many in the world still need to be convinced of.

Why is it so important that people recognize Jesus as the Son of God?

DON'T FORGET TO PRAY AND HAVE A GREAT DAY!

 THINGS TO PRAY FOR TODAY:

Day 34

Today's Reading:
Mark 1:29–34

How amazing it must have been to witness the healing of those who were sick and suffering as Jesus repeatedly demonstrated His power over the physical world. So often, many would flock to wherever He was to see these amazing miracles performed and, perhaps, to have their own infirmities taken away. It was an infallible proof, not only of Jesus' power, but of His compassion and mercy. But do you realize that we are the recipients of an even greater healing and an even more amazing demonstration of Jesus' power, compassion, and mercy? Jesus came to bring healing to a world that had been ravaged by the disease of sin, and He brought with Him the only cure—His atoning blood. Through the sacrifice of Christ, and only through that sacrifice, we can find cleansing, healing, and salvation. As incredible as the physical healings performed by Jesus were, they cannot compare to the spiritual healing that we have through Christ. "Thanks be to God for His inexpressible gift!" (2 Corinthians 9:15).

Why do you think people today do not flock to Jesus for healing?

DON'T FORGET TO PRAY AND HAVE A GREAT DAY!

⏳ **THINGS TO PRAY FOR TODAY:**

Day 35

 Today's Reading:
Matthew 4:23–25

G ood news! Jesus travelled around the towns of Galilee, preaching the good news of the kingdom of God. For centuries, the Jews had waited on the Messiah to come and for the kingdom of God to be established. Now He was here, and that kingdom was on the verge of appearing. No, it would not be the physical kingdom that many of the Jews longed for and expected. It would, in fact, be a much greater spiritual kingdom whose borders would stretch to the ends of the earth, and that would never be destroyed. It would be a kingdom that would bring salvation to all who entered it through Christ. It was certainly good news—and still is! That kingdom, Christ's church, still exists today, and you and I have the wonderful opportunity to be a part of it, to be redeemed by the blood of Christ, and to share in the wonderful blessings of being children of God. It is indeed good news!

What are some blessings that you have received
from being part of the Lord's kingdom?

DON'T FORGET TO PRAY AND HAVE A GREAT DAY!

⏳ THINGS TO PRAY FOR TODAY:

Day 36

Today's Reading:
Mark 1:35–39

The demands on Jesus' time were rigorous—long days spent teaching and healing, huge crowds following Him wherever He went, traveling from town to town spreading the message of the coming kingdom of God. Rarely was there down time and never a day off. Yet Jesus often sought out places and times of solitude, moments to spend in prayer to His Father. It was important, no, *vital* for Him to do so. He longed for that communion with God and for the renewal of mind and spirit that came from it. That special relationship with God that Jesus enjoyed is one that He also came to make accessible to us. Through Him, we can approach God in prayer as His children. We too can know the renewal and comfort that comes through communion with the Father. We must only learn to seek out those places of solitude and yearn for those quiet times with God.

How has your prayer life impacted your relationship with God?

DON'T FORGET TO PRAY AND HAVE A GREAT DAY!

 THINGS TO PRAY FOR TODAY:

Day 37

 Today's Reading:
Luke 5:1-11

The power of "one more time." That, in a sense, is the lesson that Jesus was teaching the apostles (and us) in this scene. Despite the fact that the apostles had fished all night with no success, Jesus had the power to give them an enormous catch, but it required their willingness to cast their nets one more time. They had to be willing to trust Him enough to make the effort, and they were. How often during their lives, when they were frustrated and discouraged, must they have thought back on this event and tried one more time. As we struggle with life and its challenges, the principle of "one more time" is relevant for us as well. We must learn to trust God and make the effort to overcome temptation, repent of our sins, talk to someone about Christ—one more time. It may be that that time is the time when we find success through Christ.

What have you become discouraged by
in your life that deserves another try?

DON'T FORGET TO PRAY AND HAVE A GREAT DAY!

 THINGS TO PRAY FOR TODAY:

DAY 38

 Today's Reading:
Mark 1:40–45

"If You will…" It wasn't Jesus' ability or power that this leper questioned; it was His willingness. He understood that he had no right to demand, and that it was ultimately Jesus' decision whether to heal Him. His life was in Jesus' hands. We often find ourselves in a similar position—praying to God about some problem or hardship in our lives, understanding that we are subject to His will. We ask, hope, beg, and wonder about God's will for our lives. We know He has the power but hope that He is willing. But just as Jesus was willing to heal the leper, God is willing to help and bless us. His answers to our prayers may not always come in the way that we requested or hoped, but His answers are always perfect and best for us. While we do not always know exactly what God's will is for the different circumstances of our lives, we should never waver in our faith that He is willing!

Why is it important that we submit to God's will as we pray to Him?

DON'T FORGET TO PRAY AND HAVE A GREAT DAY!

 ⏳ **THINGS TO PRAY FOR TODAY:**

DAY 39

 Today's Reading:
Mark 2:1–12

Faith—that is the word used to describe this paralytic man and those who brought him to Jesus. But their faith did not consist only of a belief that Jesus could heal the man. No, it went far beyond that. Consider all the effort that was involved in getting their friend to Jesus. They had to find their way through the crowds to get to the house, get themselves and their paralyzed friend onto the roof, remove a section of the roof, fashion a means of lowering the man into the house, and accomplish the task of placing the man in the presence of Jesus. The proof of their faith was found in the great effort that they put forth in coming to Jesus. In a similar way, Christ can make us whole and cleanse us of our sins, but we must be willing to put forth the effort to come to Him. The effort itself doesn't save us, but it does bring us into the presence of the One that can! May God help us to have a faith that puts forth the effort.

What are the things that we do to come to Jesus?

DON'T FORGET TO PRAY AND HAVE A GREAT DAY!

 THINGS TO PRAY FOR TODAY:

Day 40

 Today's Reading:
Matthew 9:9–13

One of the characteristics of Jesus' ministry that made Him such a polarizing figure with the Jews was the time He spent with the "undesirables." Unlike the religious leaders of the day who simply condemned and avoided them, Jesus spent time with the sinners and tax collectors. He did not do so to condone their behavior or justify their sins, but to let them know that God loved them and call them to repentance, giving them the opportunity for spiritual healing. It is the same message the Word of God continually sends to us today. Whoever you are, whatever your sins might be, there is hope. God loves you and wants to have a relationship with you. If you are willing to repent and come to Him, forgiveness and spiritual healing are available through Christ. What a beautiful message of compassion and hope!

What does the mercy and love of God mean to you?

DON'T FORGET TO PRAY AND HAVE A GREAT DAY!

 THINGS TO PRAY FOR TODAY:

Day 41

 Today's Reading:
Mark 2:18–22

New vs. old—it is a never-ending debate among many. Some hold to the theory that anything new is better, while others contend that the old and familiar is always preferable. The Jews of Jesus' day wanted to force Jesus into the mold of the old law and of the traditions that had become so important to them. What they failed to understand was that Jesus had come to bring the old covenant to a close and establish a new, better covenant with mankind. With Jesus came the dawning of a new day in man's relationship with God, and with that new day came some necessary changes to the way man viewed that relationship. Our relationship with God through Christ is the result of Jesus' redeeming work and the covenant that He established through His death on the cross. That "new" covenant which allows us to be children of God and have eternal salvation continues to be the one that God desires for us and the greatest blessing of our lives.

What blessings do we receive from our covenant with Christ?

DON'T FORGET TO PRAY AND HAVE A GREAT DAY!

 THINGS TO PRAY FOR TODAY:

Day 42

Today's Reading:
Luke 6:1–5

As was often the case, the Pharisees were questioning the authority of Jesus and the conduct of His disciples while, at the same time, trying to assert their own authority. They were not accustomed to being challenged when it came to matters of obedience to the law. Jesus' last statement to them in this passage is very telling: "The Son of Man is lord of the Sabbath." Jesus was, and is, Lord of heaven and earth and of all things pertaining to the kingdom of heaven. He has all authority. Interestingly, people are still trying to assert their own authority and have their own way. But as it was with the Sabbath, so it is with all things concerning the Lord's church today—He is Lord! The church is His to own and to direct. Ours is simply to submit to Him and do His will. May God help us to ever recognize Him as Lord of our lives.

How do we acknowledge Jesus as Lord in our lives?

DON'T FORGET TO PRAY AND HAVE A GREAT DAY!

 THINGS TO PRAY FOR TODAY:

Day 43

 Today's Reading:
Luke 6:6–11

From the very beginning of His ministry, Jesus' mission was to change the way people viewed God and religion. Having a relationship with God was not supposed to be about a mindless, arbitrary, and inflexible adherence to a set of laws and traditions. It was to be about the devotion of one's heart to God and the infusion of godly characteristics and principles into one's life. Jesus' healing of a withered hand on the Sabbath was not really about challenging observance of the Sabbath. It was about challenging the way people viewed God and their fellow man. What Jesus tried to instill in the people of His day is still true for us today. Being God's children and disciples of Christ is still about being wholly devoted to God in heart and committed to godly principles and conduct in life. A life lived in Christ and for God is a life full of love and faithfulness, and it is the best life of all!

How do you think this text relates to our lives today?

DON'T FORGET TO PRAY AND HAVE A GREAT DAY!

 THINGS TO PRAY FOR TODAY:

DAY 44

Today's Reading:
Luke 6:12–16

When I read and consider this list of men that Jesus chose to be His apostles, the thing I find most interesting is who they were (or maybe who they were not). They were not educated, they were not wealthy, they were not well-connected, they were not highly esteemed. They were, well, ordinary—they came from varied backgrounds and professions, they had lives, families, and interests, and maybe most notably, they were not perfect. These men were not "spiritual giants" who never struggled with their faith or made mistakes in judgment. They were men who believed in Jesus, but who often failed to understand His purpose and their place within it. They were sometimes guilty of being impetuous, selfish, or worldly. At times, they lacked faith, courage, and strength. And yet Jesus saw in them the potential to be great leaders in His church. He chose them, patiently trained them, and ultimately used them to do great things. This is an encouragement to me because, if Jesus could use them, then maybe, just maybe, he can use me too. What about you?

How are the apostles an encouragement to you?

DON'T FORGET TO PRAY AND HAVE A GREAT DAY!

⧗ THINGS TO PRAY FOR TODAY:

FIVE MINUTES WITH GOD

DAY 45

 Today's Reading:
Luke 6:17–19

Jesus "healed them all." Such a simple, matter-of-fact statement, yet consider the life-changing effect of those words for those who came into contact with the healing power of the Great Physician. The blind saw, the lame walked, the lepers were made clean, the possessed were freed from unclean spirits. With these healings came normalcy and quality of life. They could once again work, provide for their families, enjoy relationships, and take part in day-to-day activities. Their interaction with Jesus was absolutely life-changing! As amazing and effectual as these miracles must have been, Jesus offers us an even greater healing. If we are willing to bring Him our broken and sin-sick lives, He offers to heal us of the spiritually fatal disease that we all suffer from. With that healing comes renewal—renewal of our spiritual lives, and renewal of our relationship with God, renewal of our hope for eternal salvation. The healing that Jesus offers us is still absolutely life-changing!

How does spiritual healing change our lives?

DON'T FORGET TO PRAY AND HAVE A GREAT DAY!

 THINGS TO PRAY FOR TODAY:

Day 46

Today's Reading:
Matthew 5:1–12

Happiness—the universal desire. Everyone wants to be happy, and most spend a lot of their lives searching for it. Success, money, notoriety, relationships, adventure—on some level, all of these things are sought out by many people for the purpose of finding happiness. But while any of these things can bring some level of happiness or satisfaction to our lives, Jesus tells us that the key to being truly happy (blessed) is not to be found in any physical thing, but rather in filling one's life with the attitudes and characteristics that draw him closer to God and deeper into relationship with Him. These attributes, which we often call the beatitudes, can help to shape our souls and our lives into what God would have us to be, and to point us toward true and lasting happiness. What a priceless treasure of wisdom these teachings of Jesus are!

Which of the beatitudes is most meaningful to you and why?

DON'T FORGET TO PRAY AND HAVE A GREAT DAY!

⧗ **THINGS TO PRAY FOR TODAY:**

Day 47

Today's Reading:
Matthew 5:13–16

A s Christians, we have the wonderful blessing of being children of God and heirs of the kingdom of heaven. In a sense, we have stepped out of the world to live with and for God. But in another sense, we are called to continue to live in the world, not according to the world's thinking, but in a way that makes this world a better place and brings it a little closer to God. As salt, we are called to bring goodness, healing, and preservation to a lost and hurting world through the love that God has shown to us. As lights, we are to bring Christ's light into a dark world and allow our good works to illuminate God to His glory. As the world witnesses our lives, they should catch a glimpse of the love and goodness of God and be drawn to Him through our influence. What a privilege it is to be children and servants of God, and what a great opportunity we have to share God with this world through our lives!

How can you use your Christian life
to make your world a better place?

DON'T FORGET TO PRAY AND HAVE A GREAT DAY!

 THINGS TO PRAY FOR TODAY:

DAY 48

Today's Reading:
Matthew 5:17–20

Jesus came to fulfill the law and the prophets. It is a concept that the Jews of Jesus' day had a very difficult time coming to terms with. They failed to understand that the old law was never intended to be permanent. God designed it to be a temporary law to fulfill a specific purpose—to preserve God's people and prepare the way for the coming of the Messiah when the time was right. Jesus came to fulfill the prophecies and bring to fruition all of the spiritual promises of God. Though you and I never lived under the old law, the fact that Jesus came to fulfill that law is also very meaningful to us. In fulfilling the law and prophets, Jesus also brought to completion God's plan to bring redemption and salvation to everyone, including you and me. We have the great advantage and wonderful blessing of having God's plan for redemption revealed to us through Christ and becoming partakers of the saving grace of God through the precious blood of His Son. Thanks be to God, and to Him be all the glory!

Why is it so important to us that Jesus fulfilled the old law?

DON'T FORGET TO PRAY AND HAVE A GREAT DAY!

⏳ **THINGS TO PRAY FOR TODAY:**

Day 49

**Today's Reading:
Matthew 5:21–22**

The law was simple and clear: "You shall not murder." The Jews of Jesus' day had settled on a strict observance of that law, prohibiting the act of maliciously taking another's life. Jesus, though, teaches them (and us) that there is a higher standard and greater principle to which we are accountable. While the Jews were content simply to stop short of acting on their murderous thoughts or desires, Jesus teaches us not to allow those malicious feelings or thoughts to enter our hearts. Not only does God care about our actions, He also cares about our hearts, thoughts, and motives. The real meaning of Jesus' teaching is that God does not desire simply an obligatory, physical observance of a law; He wants our hearts. In addition to our actions, He wants our thoughts, intentions, and motives to be godly. To put it simply: God wants all of us!

Why does God care about our hearts and motives?

DON'T FORGET TO PRAY AND HAVE A GREAT DAY!

⏳ THINGS TO PRAY FOR TODAY:

DAY 50

Today's Reading:
Matthew 5:23–26

P art of being a faithful child of God is found in taking care of our relationships with others. God desires that we treat others with kindness and compassion and show the same love toward others that God has shown toward us. Admittedly, this is sometimes a challenge as we face our own imperfections and the shortcomings of others. To patiently and lovingly forgive others and to humbly ask forgiveness of our wrongdoings is often a difficult thing to do. But what Jesus wants us to realize is that our relationships with others have an indelible effect, not only on our physical lives, but also on our spiritual well-being and relationship with God. The feelings, thoughts, and motives with which we view our earthly relationships can enhance or hinder our worship, our prayer life, and our faithfulness to God. Thus, Jesus teaches us to take those relationships seriously and to take care of them, understanding that they are related to our all-important relationship with God.

How has your spiritual life been affected
by your earthly relationships?

DON'T FORGET TO PRAY AND HAVE A GREAT DAY!

⧗ THINGS TO PRAY FOR TODAY:

Day 51

 **Today's Reading:**
Matthew 5:27–28

Adultery begins in the heart. The point of this and most of what Jesus says in this part of the Sermon on the Mount is that sin of any kind finds its origins in the heart and mind. Before we do the act, we think the thought and have the desire. The real lesson to be learned from Jesus' teaching here is that, if we desire to keep our lives and bodies pure from sin, we must first harness our eyes, minds, and hearts. The body will not go where the eyes and mind do not lead. We cannot allow our minds and eyes to wander into the territory of sin, and then expect our actions to stay close to God. Having a heart that is pure and fully committed to God is the first and best defense that we have against temptation and sin. May God help us to love Him more and to sin less.

What are some ways that a Christian can help keep his heart pure?

DON'T FORGET TO PRAY AND HAVE A GREAT DAY!

 ⏳ **THINGS TO PRAY FOR TODAY:**

Day 52

 Today's Reading:
Matthew 5:29-30

Is Jesus seriously suggesting that we should resort to mutilating our bodies for the sake of avoiding sin? Not necessarily, but there are two very important principles that Jesus is trying to impress upon us with this harsh imagery. First, He is making the point that there is nothing in this world, even including our own physical lives or bodies, that is more important or that should be valued more than our eternal salvation. Second, He is making the point that if there is something in our lives that is coming between us and our faithfulness to God, that thing should be removed (unplugged, disconnected, gotten rid of, severed) from our lives. The point is that there is nothing, absolutely nothing, that is more important than spending eternity in heaven with God, and our lives should reflect that great truth!

Why is heaven and eternal salvation so important?

DON'T FORGET TO PRAY AND HAVE A GREAT DAY!

⏳ **THINGS TO PRAY FOR TODAY:**

Day 53

 Today's Reading:
Matthew 5:31-32

Covenant. Commitment. These are words that have a great deal of meaning and importance in the mind of God. They are words that are often used in describing our relationship with Him, and they are also words used to describe the relationship that God desires to exist in marriage. When God joins a man and woman in marriage, His intent is for that bond to last a lifetime—through thick and thin, good times and bad, "till death do us part." But marriage in our world today often does not follow God's pattern or will. "Till death do us part" has become "till the relationship is no longer mutually satisfying." But despite our world's attitude toward marriage, God's is still the same. He still desires for marriage to be a lasting covenant in which two people commit to loving and caring for each other for life. What a beautiful plan God has given us!

*Why do you think that commitment
in marriage is so important to God?*

DON'T FORGET TO PRAY AND HAVE A GREAT DAY!

 THINGS TO PRAY FOR TODAY:

DAY 54

Today's Reading:
Matthew 5:33–37

L et what you say be simply 'Yes' or 'No.'" Such a simple concept, but so lacking in our world today. In Jesus' day, the Jews were accustomed to making vows or taking oaths in the name of things closely related to God. But in some cases, they felt no obligation to keep those vows or to be truthful in their oaths. In so doing, they were in essence profaning the name of God. Jesus' solution to this problem was to simply speak truthfully, for if one always tells the truth, there is no need for an oath. In our world today, as children of God, we honor our Father by being people of integrity, character, and honesty. Those around us should know confidently that our word is our bond and that our "yes" means "yes" and our "no" means "no." This is God's desire for us.

How does our honesty (or lack thereof) reflect upon God?

DON'T FORGET TO PRAY AND HAVE A GREAT DAY!

⌛ THINGS TO PRAY FOR TODAY:

Day 55

 Today's Reading:
Matthew 5:38–42

"Turn the other cheek." While it is still a popular cliché in our world today, it is a seldom-seen practice among the majority of people. Far too often, we instead tend to adopt the "eye for an eye" mentality that Jesus condemns. We focus on what we see as "fair," what we deserve, or what our rights are. Have you ever considered what would happen if God approached us with that attitude? What is fair is for us to pay for our own sins. What we deserve is eternal condemnation. God's right was to spare His own perfect Son and allow us to suffer instead. Aren't you glad that God was willing to turn the other cheek—to treat us with mercy and grace, instead of an "eye for an eye" attitude. Though it may be difficult for us to turn the other cheek in our dealings with others, God is not asking us to do anything that He has not already done toward us. As we strive to take on the nature and image of God in our own lives, we are called to rise above the mentality of the world and our own selfish desires and to be people of kindness, mercy, and forgiveness. May God help us to become more like Him in all our ways.

Why do you think God wants us to treat others in the way this passage describes?

DON'T FORGET TO PRAY AND HAVE A GREAT DAY!

 THINGS TO PRAY FOR TODAY:

DAY 56

Today's Reading:
Matthew 5:43–48

S ome people are easy to love—family, friends, those who are kind to us and who we have much in common with. We care about those people. We treat them with kindness and compassion. But what about the others—the ones that we don't know, the ones that think, believe, or live differently than we do, or even the ones that treat us badly or disrespectfully? How are we to feel toward them? How are we to treat them? While the world might tell us that we have no obligation to treat anyone in a better way than they treat us, Jesus teaches us the opposite. What a challenge it is at times to open our hearts to those whose hearts are closed to us. But when we do—when we love those who hate us, when we are kind to those who are unkind to us, when we bless those who curse us—we become a little more like our Father in heaven, and a little closer to becoming what He desires us to be. May God help us to treat others as He would have us to.

Why is it important that we treat people with kindness and love?

DON'T FORGET TO PRAY AND HAVE A GREAT DAY!

 THINGS TO PRAY FOR TODAY:

Day 57

**Today's Reading:
Matthew 6:1-4**

What is your motive? Where is your heart? These are the issues that are really behind much of what Jesus teaches throughout the Sermon on the Mount. Doing good deeds is certainly admirable, and should be something that is important to all of us. But Jesus takes the doing of good deeds one step further by asking the question, "Why are you doing them?" He says, if you do them only for the sake of being recognized and praised by men, then your reward is only that recognition, and there is no further reward from God. In every aspect of our lives, God cares about our hearts. He wants us to live right and do good, but the "why" is also vitally important. We should do good deeds because we love God and love others, because we desire to serve God and point others to Him. The recognition and reward that we seek is one that comes from God, and that is greater than any reward this world has to offer.

Why do you think our hearts are so important to God?

DON'T FORGET TO PRAY AND HAVE A GREAT DAY!

 THINGS TO PRAY FOR TODAY:

Day 58

Today's Reading:
Matthew 6:5-8

Prayer—a special time of communion between Creator and creation, Father and child, God and worshipper. Prayer is a time of communication, praise, and relationship. It is a time to express to God our thanksgiving and love and to lay our troubles, cares, and petitions at His feet. It is a time to be strengthened, uplifted, and encouraged. Most of all, prayer is a time to draw near to God, to be reminded of His greatness and His love, and to be comforted by the closeness of God's heart to our own. Prayer is special and sacred. What prayer is not is a time to flaunt our religion and spirituality. It is not a time to seek praise and accolades from men. It is not a time to fill the air with words that have no meaning. Jesus says that, before we utter the first word of prayer, God knows—He knows our needs and concerns; He knows our hearts and motives. Prayer is one of our greatest blessings and a privilege that should never be taken for granted or abused. So pray—pray sincerely, pray humbly, and pray with love and thanksgiving in your heart!

Why is it important that we pray if God already knows our needs?

DON'T FORGET TO PRAY AND HAVE A GREAT DAY!

⌛ **THINGS TO PRAY FOR TODAY:**

Day 59

 Today's Reading:
Matthew 6:9-13

The model prayer. In his gospel, Luke records that this prayer is in response to a disciple's request, "Lord, teach us to pray" (Luke 11:1). Jesus had a way of praying that was different, more personal, more meaningful than people of His day were accustomed to. He had an intimate relationship with His Father, and that relationship was reflected in His prayers. His disciples wanted to be able to pray that way. They wanted to know God as Jesus knew Him, to approach God with the same intimacy and confidence that Jesus had as He prayed. So as He always did, Jesus taught them. He taught them, and us, how to talk to God, how to go before Him with our praise and our petitions, our needs and cares, how to put our lives into His hands and know that He will care for us. This beautiful little prayer teaches us so much, not only about prayer, but about our relationship with God. What a great lesson from the Master Teacher!

What effect does prayer have on your daily life?

DON'T FORGET TO PRAY AND HAVE A GREAT DAY!

 **THINGS TO PRAY FOR TODAY:**

DAY 60

Today's Reading:
Matthew 6:14-15

D o you desire and appreciate forgiveness? Sure you do. We all do. When we make mistakes, we want to know that those around us will be compassionate towards us and willing to forgive our shortcomings. And then there is God. Where would we be without God's forgiveness? We need it, cherish it, and are thankful for it. But there are times when we are much less willing to forgive someone who has wronged us than we are to accept forgiveness for our own wrongdoings. We were hurt, defamed, taken advantage of, lied to. Why should we forgive someone who was so unloving towards us? But Jesus teaches the simple truth that, if we desire to have the forgiveness God offers to us for the wrongs that we have committed against Him, then we must learn to be forgiving to others for their wrongs against us. A simple concept, but often a challenge to apply. May God help us to be more forgiving towards others, and may He continue to be merciful and forgiving towards us!

Why do you think that it is so important
to God that we forgive others?

DON'T FORGET TO PRAY AND HAVE A GREAT DAY!

⏳ **THINGS TO PRAY FOR TODAY:**

DAY 61

Today's Reading:
Matthew 6:16–18

W hy? It is not a question that we consider often enough when it comes to our spiritual lives and service to God. Why do we worship? Why do we give our time and effort to serving God and others? Why do we strive to be lights in a dark world? Many times, we fall into the trap of giving our worship and service to God without considering our purpose, or worse yet, with a self-serving and impure motive for our devotion to God. But we learn from this passage, and others in this same extended text, that the "why" is very important to God. While God certainly desires our worship and devotion, He desires those things to come from a pure, sincere heart and motive. To worship or devote ourselves to God for the purpose of being seen or praised by men is unacceptable and ineffective. As we worship and devote ourselves to God, let us do so with a heart filled with love and gratitude, and with a desire to draw ever closer to Him.

Why should we give our worship and devotion to God?

DON'T FORGET TO PRAY AND HAVE A GREAT DAY!

⏳ **THINGS TO PRAY FOR TODAY:**

D<small>AY</small> 62

Today's Reading:
Matthew 6:19–21

"I f I only had more—more money in the bank, a bigger house, a nicer car, a more impressive investment portfolio. If I only had more, then I would be happy! I would have nothing to worry about." This mindset dominates our culture, and it pushes us to chase the almighty dollar and lay up treasures on earth. But Jesus reveals a simple truth that often eludes our thinking: nothing physical lasts forever. That bank account, house, car, investment portfolio—it is all temporary. It is all subject to destruction, theft, or loss, and even if we can avoid these disasters, those things will only be ours for as long as our physical lives last. But Jesus reminds us that there is a treasure we can lay up for ourselves that will never be destroyed. It is not a physical treasure, but a much grander, spiritual one. It is the greatest of all treasures, laid up in heaven for those who devote their lives to God. As Jesus teaches, the greatest investment we can make is the laying up of spiritual treasure that will pay eternal dividends.

How do we lay up treasure in heaven?

DON'T FORGET TO PRAY AND HAVE A GREAT DAY!

⧗ THINGS TO PRAY FOR TODAY:

DAY 63

Today's Reading:
Matthew 6:22–23

These verses are found sandwiched between teachings on laying up treasure in heaven instead of on earth (vv. 19-21) and the impossibility of serving both God and riches (v. 24). It stands to reason, then, that this passage also pertains to having a proper attitude toward worldly things. In ancient thought, having a "healthy (good) eye" was indicative of being generous, while having a "bad eye" was used to describe those who were greedy or stingy. Therefore, as Jesus describes, one who has a good eye is one who sees his worldly things as a tool to be used to help others and to bring glory to God. This good eye fills the whole body with light, which represents goodness, truth, and godliness. In contrast, the person with the bad eye is one who puts his love and faith in those earthly things and is thus filled with a great darkness that cannot abide in the presence of God. May God help us all to have a healthy eye.

Why do you think our attitude toward worldly things has such a great effect on our lives?

DON'T FORGET TO PRAY AND HAVE A GREAT DAY!

 **THINGS TO PRAY FOR TODAY:**

DAY 64

Today's Reading:
Matthew 6:24

Money—riches, wealth, physical things. It is one of the most popular gods of our time. So many covet it, pursue it, devote themselves to it, and make it the most important thing in their lives. And yes, they serve it. The god of riches entices us, it makes vain promises, and it leads us down a road that can only end in destruction. But by far the most devastating consequence of serving the god of riches is that it takes the place of our service to God and robs us of our relationship with Him. We must choose whether we will serve the god of riches—a god that is enticing, but offers no real joy, lasting peace, or eternal hope, or the God of the universe, who offers His love, mercy, and grace, and who is the source of a joy, peace, and hope that can only be found in Him. The choice is ours, but... "You cannot serve God and money."

Why do you think so many people choose the world over God?

DON'T FORGET TO PRAY AND HAVE A GREAT DAY!

⧗ THINGS TO PRAY FOR TODAY:

Day 65

 Today's Reading:
Matthew 6:25–34

D o you ever worry? Most likely, the answer to this question is "yes." Most of us worry from time to time. After all, there is plenty in our world to worry about—financial struggles, health issues, family problems, crime, violence, terrorism, declining morals... You get the idea. As Jesus says in this passage, "Sufficient for the day is its own trouble." In other words, each day has enough problems of its own. So what is the cure for worry? Jesus teaches us that the way to overcome worry is to be more spiritually minded, to "seek first the kingdom of God and His righteousness." By focusing more on God and our relationship with Him, we are constantly reminded that this world and all of its problems are temporary, and that our greater needs, the spiritual ones, are all met perfectly through Christ, so that we want for nothing. The more we learn to trust and depend on God, the more our worry is replaced with peace and confidence. What a wonderful blessing from God!

Why do you think that we struggle to let go of our worries?

DON'T FORGET TO PRAY AND HAVE A GREAT DAY!

 THINGS TO PRAY FOR TODAY:

Day 66

Today's Reading:
Matthew 7:1–6

I love the imagery of this passage. Can you picture it? You have a speck of dust in your eye and are struggling to find relief, when someone walks up to you: "Let me help you with that." As you look up, you find the person standing before you with a 2x4 protruding from their own eye. Jesus uses this exaggerated language to demonstrate a simple principle: before you begin to judge and "fix" other people, make sure you have examined yourself. Jesus is not teaching that we should not be concerned for others, or that we should not try to help those who are obviously involved in behavior that is destructive to their spiritual lives. He is simply stating that we must not fall into the trap of hypocrisy by ignoring our own shortcomings while haughtily pointing out the errors of others. We must learn the lesson of humility and understand that it is only by the grace of God that any of us have the opportunity to be freed from the shackles of sin. Let us approach God, others, and even our own lives with that spirit of humility, and let us examine our hearts and lives to be sure that we are in a faithful relationship with God.

How can we help others to overcome sin
without unrighteously judging others?

DON'T FORGET TO PRAY AND HAVE A GREAT DAY!

⏳ **THINGS TO PRAY FOR TODAY:**

Day 67

 **Today's Reading:**
Matthew 7:7–12

W e often mistake this passage as being about us—us getting what we want or need; us pursuing or asking of God the things that are needed in our lives; us being satisfied with provision from above. But in reality, this passage is not about us as much as it is about God. It is a wonderfully comforting and encouraging passage that teaches us that God is a God who loves us and wants to bless us. He yearns to meet our needs, answer our prayers, and care for us as a loving Father. He is the giver of all good things and, in His omniscience, knows exactly what we need. By His good pleasure, He meets our needs perfectly and blesses us beyond measure, constantly considering our spiritual well-being, even while caring for our physical needs. So "ask, and it will be given to you; seek, and you will find; knock, and it will be opened to you," because God, our Father, loves us and is our great provider.

Why do you think God wants to give us good things?

DON'T FORGET TO PRAY AND HAVE A GREAT DAY!

 THINGS TO PRAY FOR TODAY:

Day 68

 Today's Reading:
Matthew 7:13-14

Two gates, two ways, two destinations. This passage is a metaphor for life—everyone's life. We all have to make a choice: which gate to enter, which way to travel, which destination will be ours. Every person, every life, will travel down one path or the other, and so we must all choose. But how do we make the choice? What makes the difference? As we consider Jesus' words here, the primary differentiating factor between the two ways is not found in the journey—a wide or narrow gate, an easy or hard way—but rather in the results of the journey. Any journey is defined by its destination, and in this case, there could not be two destinations that are more diametrically opposed to one another. As we choose our path through life and consider the desires of our hearts with regard to that journey and its outcome, we would surely choose "life" over "destruction." With that in mind, let us choose the narrow gate and the hard way, understanding that the outcome of that journey is the destination that we desire—eternal life.

Why do you think that "few" will find
the narrow gate that leads to life?

DON'T FORGET TO PRAY AND HAVE A GREAT DAY!

 THINGS TO PRAY FOR TODAY:

DAY 69

Today's Reading:
Matthew 7:15-20

Have you ever played a role, maybe in a school musical, community theatre, or youth group skit? Playing a role often involves dressing up in costume, taking on the persona of your character, and pretending to be someone or something other than yourself. It is fun and harmless in a theatrical setting, but can be anything but harmless in real life. This activity of playing a part is the picture from which we get the word "hypocrite," and it is the activity that Jesus describes and condemns in this passage. What appears to be harmless, good, and even helpful, Jesus says, is actually evil and destructive. But Jesus tells us that there is a way to see through the mask and identify the real person. "You will recognize them by their fruits." Regardless of the image that someone tries to portray, their life will tell the tale. There are two lessons that we need to keep in mind here: one is to beware of wolves in sheep's clothing. Don't be deceived and led astray by someone's act. The other lesson is that we must always be careful to make sure that our lives reflect who we really are. Be genuine, sincere, and godly. There is no greater way to bring glory to God.

Why do you think some choose to pretend
to be something they are not?

DON'T FORGET TO PRAY AND HAVE A GREAT DAY!

 THINGS TO PRAY FOR TODAY:

DAY 70

Today's Reading:
Matthew 7:21–23

What does it take to enter the kingdom of heaven? It is a question that has been asked many times over the centuries and answered in many different ways. It is an issue that mankind has made complicated and controversial, but Jesus answers the question in a clear, concise, and easy-to-understand way if we will only listen to Him. He tells us that entrance into heaven will not be granted based simply on whether someone is willing to acknowledge, believe in, or call on the name of the Lord. As important as those things are, they are not enough by themselves. Neither will someone be saved by the works they do, even works done in the name of the Lord. Those works, while good and important, can never earn salvation for the one performing them. Jesus says very simply that entrance to the heavenly kingdom will be granted to those who do the will of the Father—those who submit themselves to God, give Him their lives, and live for Him in faith and obedience. Only in this way of life can one truly be cleansed by the blood of Christ and enjoy the gift of salvation. May we all have a heart of submission and a desire to always do the will of our Father.

Why do you think there is so much confusion
on the subject of salvation today?

DON'T FORGET TO PRAY AND HAVE A GREAT DAY!

⌛ THINGS TO PRAY FOR TODAY:

Day 71

 Today's Reading:
Matthew 7:24–27

Does the foundation matter? You better believe it does! A house that is built on a poorly planned or constructed foundation will not be able to survive. A marriage that is not based on a foundation of love, trust, and commitment will not last. And a life built on an unstable foundation will crumble and fall under the stress of life's storms. At the end of all the teaching Jesus does in the Sermon on the Mount, He leaves us with one final admonition: be careful what foundation you are building your life on. The teachings of Jesus, the Word of God, provides a foundation that is firm, stable, and unshakeable. It provides an anchor point for life that allows it to withstand any storm, any hardship, any challenge, any trial. In contrast, any other foundation on which we can build our lives— this world, riches, worldly relationships, achievement—is unstable. Those foundations cannot and will not be able to withstand the storms of life. The lesson is very simple—build your life on the firm and solid foundation of Christ!

How does the Word of God provide a firm foundation for our lives?

DON'T FORGET TO PRAY AND HAVE A GREAT DAY!

 ⏳ **THINGS TO PRAY FOR TODAY:**

DAY 72

Today's Reading:
Matthew 7:28-29

Jesus was different. His teaching was different. He wasn't like the scribes, who were the Jewish lawyers of the day. They had devoted their lives to copying the law, and so they knew what it said. The Jews looked to them as experts and authorities. But Jesus was different. The scribes could tell them what the law said, but Jesus told them what it meant. He spoke with an insight into the mind and will of God that was unknown to the scribes. He taught with authority, the type of authority that could only come from God Himself. Jesus still speaks to us, through the Word, with an authority and insight into God's will that can only come from God. And whether we realize it or not, Jesus' teaching is still astonishing, because of its timeless relevance and perfect accuracy. Astonishing because of its enduring wisdom and life-changing truth. As we open up the Word of God and immerse ourselves into the teachings of Jesus, may God help us to be impressed, astonished, convinced, and changed by what He teaches us.

What impresses you about the teaching of Jesus?

DON'T FORGET TO PRAY AND HAVE A GREAT DAY!

⏳ THINGS TO PRAY FOR TODAY:

Day 73

Today's Reading:
Luke 6:20–23

In Luke's account of what we call the Beatitudes, he focuses on the now vs. later aspect of these teachings of Jesus. While this life might hold hardships, struggles, sorrows, and trials of different kinds in the here and now, Jesus gives us the comfort of knowing that those difficulties will be turned into joy and rejoicing in the hereafter. Maybe Paul states it best when he says, "For I consider that the sufferings of this present time are not worth comparing with the glory that is to be revealed in us," (Romans 8:18). There are definitely times in our lives when we encounter situations and circumstances that are difficult and painful, some almost unbearable. God understands those times and knows our struggles. But He has a plan for us, and those hardships that we are asked to bear in this life will only serve to strengthen us and make the rest and rewards of heaven that much sweeter. So be patient and be strong, for the reward is well worth the struggle.

How have your struggles strengthened you and your faith?

DON'T FORGET TO PRAY AND HAVE A GREAT DAY!

 THINGS TO PRAY FOR TODAY:

Day 74

Today's Reading:
Luke 6:24–26

This reading represents the other side of the coin. If Jesus desired to comfort and reassure those who were suffering in the last passage, He certainly intends to warn and condemn those to whom He is speaking in this passage. Understand that Jesus is not condemning those who are rich, happy, or respected based simply on their station in life. There is nothing intrinsically wrong with any of these situations; in fact, to be joyful or well-spoken of is admirable. Jesus is speaking to and condemning those who have given their love and devotion to their earthly things instead of to God, those who revel in this world and its pleasure with no regard for spiritual things, those who strive for acceptance in the world, sacrificing truth and godliness to find it. The greatest lesson for us to learn here is that there is nothing in this world—not riches, pleasure, or popularity—that offers what a faithful relationship with God offers, and none of those things are worth the price they require.

Why do so many people struggle to choose God over worldly things?

DON'T FORGET TO PRAY AND HAVE A GREAT DAY!

 **THINGS TO PRAY FOR TODAY:**

Day 75

 Today's Reading:
Luke 6:27-36

W e call it the golden rule: "And as you wish that others would do to you, do so to them." It is one of those teachings of Jesus that has found its way into our modern-day vernacular, though it is often not as prevalent in practice as it ought to be in our world today. It is such a simple principle, yet it can shape our behavior toward others and transform our relationships with them. Do you want others to be kind to you? Then be kind. Do you want others to be patient with you and understand that you are not perfect? Then be patient and understanding. Do you want others to forgive you when you fail? Then be forgiving. Imagine a world where every person lived by this simple rule of human interaction. It may be that the world as a whole never comes around to living by this rule, but that should not prevent us from living by it. And it may be that, as we apply this teaching of Jesus to our lives, it causes those around us to decide to live out the golden rule in their lives as well. May God help us treat others as we want to be treated.

Why do you think more people do not apply this rule to their lives?

DON'T FORGET TO PRAY AND HAVE A GREAT DAY!

⧗ **THINGS TO PRAY FOR TODAY:**

Day 76

Today's Reading:
Luke 11:1–4

There are many people who struggle with prayer. How should I pray? What should I pray for? What should my attitude be in prayer? These and many other questions have been asked by sincere children of God who want to deepen and improve their prayer life. The disciples of Jesus had similar desires and questions. They wanted to know how to pray like Jesus prayed, and in this "model prayer," Jesus answered many of their, and our, concerns. In this short and simple prayer, Jesus showed them and us how to pray and what to pray for. How should we pray? Pray to your Father, understanding and appreciating the relationship you have with Him—"Father." Pray with respect, reverence and praise, understanding the majesty, glory, and holiness of God—"Hallowed by Your name." What should we pray for? Pray for the church—"Your kingdom come." Pray for your earthly needs—"Give us each day our daily bread." Pray for your spiritual needs—"Forgive us our sins." Pray for God's protection and deliverance—"And lead us not into temptation." What a beautiful prayer, and what a wonderful model for us.

Why do you think people struggle with knowing how to pray?

DON'T FORGET TO PRAY AND HAVE A GREAT DAY!

 THINGS TO PRAY FOR TODAY:

Day 77

 **Today's Reading:**
Luke 12:22–31

We often think of the creative role of God—the God who spoke the world and everything in it into existence in an amazing display of His transcendent power and wisdom. But God's involvement in this world did not end there. Jesus portrays God as the caregiver of His creation. It is He who feeds the birds of the air and arrays the flowers of the field in colorful glory. He sustains and provides for the world and its inhabitants in a way that is not just sufficient, but abundant and beautiful and perfect. So what is the point of this description of God as care-giver of the world? Have you ever considered that, of all of God's creations, we are the only ones that worry? We—the centerpiece of God's wonderful creation, made in His own image, recipients of His love and greatest gift—have no reason to worry, yet we do. But God is a faithful God. He loves us and will care for us. If we put Him first and trust Him with our lives, He will bless us and provide for us in greater ways than we can imagine. So trust and don't worry!

What are some things we can do to minimize our worry?

DON'T FORGET TO PRAY AND HAVE A GREAT DAY!

 ⏳ **THINGS TO PRAY FOR TODAY:**

DAY 78

Today's Reading:
Luke 12:32–34

"It is your Father's good pleasure to give you the kingdom." Have you ever given thought to that idea? We know that God sent His Son into the world to redeem us from sin. We know that, through Him, He offers us the opportunity to be in relationship with Him. We know that God has promised a home in heaven to those who are saved through Christ. But have you ever considered the idea that doing these things brings pleasure to God? God wants us to be saved. He yearns for it. To take our sins away and to make us His children brings joy to the heart of God. To see people come to Him in faith and obedience makes Him smile. So great is the love of God for us that he delights in being our Father and blessing us with all things, spiritually and physically. What a wonderful thought to know that, not only does God save us, but that it is His pleasure to do so.

Why do you think God finds pleasure in saving us?

DON'T FORGET TO PRAY AND HAVE A GREAT DAY!

 THINGS TO PRAY FOR TODAY:

Day 79

 Today's Reading:
Luke 6:37–38

It was not uncommon in the first-century world that, as one went to the market place to buy a measure of wheat, he would be short-changed by the merchant receiving a lesser amount than the full measure desired and paid for. Jesus uses this well-known occurrence to describe God's generosity toward us and the generosity that we are to have toward others. When God gives a blessing, He gives a "good measure, pressed down, shaken together, and running over." We can envision, in these words, the fair-minded merchant measuring out the portion of grain, pressing and shaking down the contents to make sure that all the air pockets are removed, and every corner and crevice of the vessel is filled, even to the point of overflowing the container. That is the way God gives to us. He gives generously, abundantly, fully. But in return, God asks that we give to Him and to others in the same way, not skimpily or with hesitation, but that we give with a generous and joyful heart. May we always be thankful to God for His generous blessings, and may we strive to be like Him in our own giving.

Why is it important how we give to God?

DON'T FORGET TO PRAY AND HAVE A GREAT DAY!

 THINGS TO PRAY FOR TODAY:

Day 80

Today's Reading:
Luke 6:39–42

"Can a blind man lead a blind man?" From a physical perspective, this is an easy question to answer and almost a comical scenario to consider. How can one lead another if the leader himself cannot see (or does not know) where he is going? But from a spiritual perspective, it is a serious question that affects each of us in some way. As Christians, we are all called to be leaders—lights to the world, leading those around us to better know God and to glorify Him in their own lives. We are to be examples, influences, teachers, and ambassadors for Christ. But how can we lead others if we do not know the way? How can we help the blind to see if we are blind ourselves? This passage encourages us, even commands us, to prepare ourselves to be leaders for Christ—to be knowledgeable of the way in which we are to lead others, to remove the obstacles of clear sight from our own lives, and to have the attitude of love and humility that will allow us to take others by the hand and lead them closer to God.

What are some things that we can do to
prepare ourselves to be leaders for God?

DON'T FORGET TO PRAY AND HAVE A GREAT DAY!

⏳ THINGS TO PRAY FOR TODAY:

Day 81

 Today's Reading:
Luke 6:43-45

Who are you? On the surface, it seems to be a simple question, but the answer is often more complicated and difficult to discover than we think. When we think about who we are, we consider how we want others to see us, and what we want them to think of us. We also think about who we want to be or wish we were. But as we consider our lives and who we really are, we are taught by passages such as this one that the answer is found, not in the opinions of others or even in our own eyes, but deep within our hearts. Our lives are made into what they are by the things we choose to put into our hearts—thoughts, actions, images, attitudes, and feelings. The abundance of those things that we put into our hearts then come out as words, actions, and attitudes of our own. If we fill our hearts with good and godly things, then our lives will reflect godliness. If we fill our hearts with sinful and worldly things, then our lives will become like the world. May God help us to have hearts that are filled with Him!

What are some things we can do to fill our hearts with godly things?

DON'T FORGET TO PRAY AND HAVE A GREAT DAY!

 THINGS TO PRAY FOR TODAY:

DAY 82

Today's Reading:
Luke 6:46–49

T his passage highlights the danger of doing nothing. We typically think of the man who built his house on the sand (better known from Matthew's account) as being one who founded his life on sinful, worldly things, one who had actively rejected God and filled his life with ungodly and wicked pursuits. But this is not the picture that Luke paints in his record of Jesus' teaching. Notice that "the one who hears and does not do them is like a man who built a house on the ground without a foundation..." Many people feel that, by attempting to "ride the fence" and not make a decision one way or the other about Christ, whether to reject Him or accept Him, they are safe on middle ground. But Jesus teaches us that not making a decision is just as destructive to our lives as to actively reject Him. There is only one way to build our lives on a firm foundation—to accept Him and live by His words.

Why is the middle ground of non-committal
not a good foundation for our lives?

DON'T FORGET TO PRAY AND HAVE A GREAT DAY!

⏳ **THINGS TO PRAY FOR TODAY:**

D<small>AY</small> 83

Today's Reading:
Luke 11:5–8

Because of his imprudence…" Some have asked if it is wrong to pray about the same thing repeatedly, to petition God over and over concerning the same situation. "Doesn't it show a lack of faith?" some want to know. This little parable gives the answer to that question. Jesus is teaching a lesson about the persistence in prayer that God desires for us to demonstrate. But don't misunderstand the meaning of this parable. In the story, it appears that the friend, who initially refused the borrower's request, eventually grants the request because of the continual bothering of the borrower. Does that mean that God is, at first, hesitant to answer our prayers, but might be willing to grant our petitions if we pester Him enough? Not at all! God is never bothered by our prayers, nor is He hesitant to answer. The meaning of this teaching is simply that God desires our persistence in prayer. He wants to hear from us over and over again. He wants us to rely upon Him and to pray to Him "without ceasing" (1 Thessalonians 5:17). For it is in prayer that we find the comfort and solace that only God can provide.

Why do you think that God has such a desire for us to pray to Him?

DON'T FORGET TO PRAY AND HAVE A GREAT DAY!

 THINGS TO PRAY FOR TODAY:

Day 84

 Today's Reading:
Luke 11:9–13

God gives, God answers, God opens. As Christians, we don't struggle with this truth, but we do sometimes struggle with what God gives, how God answers, and which door God opens. When we pray, we typically have a very specific idea in mind about what we need and how we desire God to answer. As long as God's answers are in line with our desires, we are satisfied, but what if they are not? What if God's answers to our petitions are much different than we had asked? In those times, we often wonder why God is not blessing us in the way we need. When it comes to understanding our lives, we are much like children. Our children may want to eat candy at every meal and stay up as late as they can each night, but as parents, we know that those choices are not the best for them. So, we give them more nourishing foods and help them get the sleep they need. In much the same way, the things we often think are best or needed are, in reality, not what is in our best interest. Just like we do with our children, God sometimes overrules our requests and desires in order to give us what is more needful and beneficial. He is always a giver of good things. Our part is to take our requests to Him and then trust Him to give us what is best.

How can we learn to see the good in God's answers to our prayers?

DON'T FORGET TO PRAY AND HAVE A GREAT DAY!

⏳ **THINGS TO PRAY FOR TODAY:**

Day 85

 Today's Reading:
Luke 7:1-10

What faith and what a statement of commendation by Jesus! This Gentile man was said to have a faith that surpassed even the faith of any Jew. Rarely did Jesus use such flattering words. What was it that demonstrated this great faith and prompted such a commendation from the Lord? First of all, he believed in Jesus and in His ability to heal his sick, dying servant. But more importantly, he understood that Jesus had authority and power over this illness that was not bound by proximity. With great humility and recognition of his own unworthiness to even be in the presence of Jesus, he acknowledged that, even without seeing the servant, without touching him, without the servant being able to hear Him, Jesus had the power to heal. Despite the distance and seriousness of the illness, the Centurion was confident of Jesus' ability to make his servant whole. Oh, that God would help us to have that kind of faith—a faith that fully trusted in Him to meet our needs and answer our prayers despite our own unworthiness.

What can we do in our lives to strengthen our faith in God?

DON'T FORGET TO PRAY AND HAVE A GREAT DAY!

 THINGS TO PRAY FOR TODAY:

DAY 86

Today's Reading:
Luke 7:11–17

For the woman in this story, the mother of the man who had died, this was not only a sorrowful situation but a desperate one. Being a widow and having only one son who had now died, she was left with no one to care for her. There would be no one to provide for her needs, no one to take her in, no one to care about her at all. She would become a helpless and hopeless victim of her society. But Jesus cared. He recognized her plight, had compassion on her, and provided for her in a way that no one else could. God still has a way of caring for us. He looks down on us in compassion to see our needs, and He meets those needs in ways that no one else can, many times in ways that we do not even recognize. Through His perfect wisdom and wonderful providence, He brings people and opportunities into our lives when we need them most and sees that we are taken care of. What a wonderful, loving, compassionate God we serve!

What are some ways in which God has cared for you?

DON'T FORGET TO PRAY AND HAVE A GREAT DAY!

 THINGS TO PRAY FOR TODAY:

DAY 87

Today's Reading:
John 4:46–53

A nd he himself believed…" He had not seen his son healed. He had no proof, no evidence. He only had the word of Jesus, yet he believed. He met the challenge of believing without seeing with incredible faith, and in so doing, left us a great example. How do we respond when we are challenged to believe without seeing? There are times for all of us when we pour out our hearts to God, pleading with Him for His help, His blessings, His intervention in our lives. We do not typically see immediate results from those prayers but must, as the man in this text, go our way and wait on God. Not knowing when or even how God will answer our prayers, we are called to believe without seeing. What a challenge that is for us. But if we can approach those times with faith, we, like the nobleman, will find that God is faithful, and that He can and will answer our prayers in a way that is good and perfect.

How can we learn to deepen our faith in God's promises?

DON'T FORGET TO PRAY AND HAVE A GREAT DAY!

 THINGS TO PRAY FOR TODAY:

DAY 88

Today's Reading:
Matthew 11:2–6

While there is much to think about in this short text, I want to focus on the final statement Jesus makes: "Blessed is the one who is not offended by Me." The word "offended" is from the same root word from which we get the word "stumbling block." Following Jesus was not, and is not, always easy. It requires commitment and sacrifice. In Jesus' day, many found a stumbling block in the fact that Jesus did not take the form they were expecting or in the difficulty of His teaching. Many rejected Him from the beginning, while others were disciples for a while, only to turn back and follow Him no more. Not much has changed in today's world. Many still reject Him for reasons that are not much different from those of His own time. But it also remains true that "Blessed is the one who is not offended by [Him]." May God help us be committed and faithful followers of Christ!

What are some of the reasons people reject Christ today?

DON'T FORGET TO PRAY AND HAVE A GREAT DAY!

⏳ **THINGS TO PRAY FOR TODAY:**

Day 89

 Today's Reading:
Matthew 11:7–15

W hat a statement of praise and commendation given here to John by Jesus! John was not "a reed shaken by the wind"—he was not one to be blown about by every changing current of social or religious ideology. He was not "a man dressed in soft clothing"—one who was self-indulgent and worldly. John was a man of conviction and courage, one who was sacrificially committed to His God-given purpose. He was a prophet—more than a prophet, he was the forerunner of the Messiah. "Among those born of women," Jesus says, "there has arisen no one greater than John the Baptist." But Jesus doesn't stop there. He goes on to say that "the one who is least in the kingdom of heaven is greater than he." As great as John and his work was, he did not get to see the Lord's kingdom come. He was never a citizen of that kingdom, the church. We, who have the privilege of being washed in the blood of Christ and thereby added to His body, are far more blessed and privileged than even John. What a wonderful blessing it is to be citizens of the kingdom of heaven!

Why is it such a blessing to be part of the Lord's kingdom?

DON'T FORGET TO PRAY AND HAVE A GREAT DAY!

 **THINGS TO PRAY FOR TODAY:**

DAY 90

Today's Reading:
Matthew 11:16–19

Have you ever known someone who was determined to be unsatisfied? That is the way Jesus describes some of His day. They were hard-headed and hard-hearted, obstinate, and close-minded. They rejected John because he separated himself from the world. He dressed differently, spoke differently, acted differently, and even ate differently, and so they accused him of having a demon. Then Jesus came and interacted in people's lives, attended normal activities of life, had relationships with people, and He was also rejected because of the way He lived. Neither of these men fit the Jews' mold or conformed to their way of thinking, so they were refused. They were determined to be unsatisfied. It is still true today that many people are determined to be unsatisfied— unsatisfied with the church, the elders, the preacher, or even with Christ Himself. They are hard-headed and hard-hearted. May God help us avoid that attitude and always be open and accepting of Jesus.

Why do you think some people are so determined to be unsatisfied?

DON'T FORGET TO PRAY AND HAVE A GREAT DAY!

 **THINGS TO PRAY FOR TODAY:**

DAY 91

Today's Reading:
Luke 7:36-50

There are many lessons that come to mind from this reading, but I want to focus on one that we might overlook. This woman who is called a sinner (the label of "sinner" was reserved for the worst offenders of the Jewish law) comes to Jesus weeping. In fact, so copious were her tears that they were sufficient to wash Jesus' feet. The context makes clear that these tears were because of her sins—tears of sorrow, remorse, and repentance. Her heart had been touched by the words or actions of Jesus, and it had been broken by the recognition of her many sins. She came to Jesus in repentance and humility, desiring to give honor to Jesus and receive mercy from Him. It is for this reason that Jesus looks upon her with compassion and forgives her many sins. What a blessing it is to know that, despite our many sins and shortcomings, we have a God and Savior who is willing to show mercy toward us and forgive us. Oh, that we might learn from the example of this sinner who was broken-hearted over her sin and came to Jesus with a repentant heart.

Why should we be broken-hearted over sin?

DON'T FORGET TO PRAY AND HAVE A GREAT DAY!

⏳ THINGS TO PRAY FOR TODAY:

Day 92

Today's Reading:
Matthew 12:22–30

As Jesus so often does, He takes the accusations or criticisms of the Pharisees and turns them into a teaching moment about their (and our) relationship with God. In response to their claims that He was casting out demons by the power of Beelzebul, Jesus points out the absurdity of that idea. Why would Satan cast out Satan? How can one survive if he is against himself? Jesus uses simple logic to defeat their accusations, but then He makes an application of that very principle to Himself. "Whoever is not with Me is against Me..." It is simple, it is logical, yet it is often forgotten or misunderstood in our world. You either stand with Christ or against Him. There is no middle ground. A person cannot be neutral concerning Christ. If we say that we are with Him but live as if He doesn't exist, we are not really with Him but against Him. If we say that we love Him but ignore His teachings and commands, we are not with Him but against Him. May God help us always to be firmly and truly with Christ.

What are some ways that you might improve in being "with" Christ?

DON'T FORGET TO PRAY AND HAVE A GREAT DAY!

⌛ **THINGS TO PRAY FOR TODAY:**

Dᴀʏ 93

Today's Reading:
Matthew 12:31–32

This is a difficult passage for us because it seems to fly in the face of everything we know and want to believe about God and His forgiveness. Is there really a sin that cannot be forgiven? This is, in fact, one of several New Testament passages that speak of an inability to receive forgiveness (Hebrews 6:4-6; 10:26-31; 1 John 5:16-17), but this passage is unique in pinpointing a specific sinful act that is unforgiveable—blasphemy against the Spirit. Why is this sin so severe that it cannot be forgiven? Remember that it is through the Holy Spirit that we have the word of God (see John 16:12-15; 1 Peters 1:12; 2 Peters 1:21). To blaspheme, or speak evil of, and reject the Holy Spirit is to reject our only source of truth leading to faith (Romans 10:17). Without faith, one cannot have forgiveness. The message of this passage (and the entire New Testament) is that if we are unwilling to believe in Jesus Christ and come to Him in faith and obedience, then we cannot have forgiveness and salvation.

Why is faith so vital to receiving forgiveness from God?

DON'T FORGET TO PRAY AND HAVE A GREAT DAY!

⏳ **THINGS TO PRAY FOR TODAY:**

DAY 94

 Today's Reading:
Matthew 12:33–37

These verses are reminiscent of Jesus' words in the Sermon on the Mount, teaching us that we can know a tree by its fruit (Matthew 7:15-20). In this passage, though, He specifically targets the words we speak, emphasizing that we will be accountable for and judged by them. The word "careless" in this text has a different meaning than we would give it today. It means malicious, slanderous, or harmful. He was still speaking to and about the Pharisees that had accused Him of casting out demons by the power of Beelzebul, and He was warning them of the danger of speaking words of slander against the Holy Spirit. But more importantly, He reminds them (and us) that their words, and ours, come from what's in the heart. The real lesson of this text is deeper than just watching our words. It is that we must guard our hearts to protect them from unbelief and unholy influences that would turn us against God and cause us to think and say things that put our souls in peril. May God help us to strive constantly to be "good trees" that bring forth good fruit.

What are some things that we can do
to guard our hearts against sin?

DON'T FORGET TO PRAY AND HAVE A GREAT DAY!

 THINGS TO PRAY FOR TODAY:

Day 95

 Today's Reading:
Matthew 12:38–42

D o we ever seek signs from Jesus? Though ours may not be as outward and obvious, there are times when we might require some "sign" from God in exchange for our faith and obedience. A sick loved one being healed, a financial hardship resolved, a trial in our lives taken away. If God will answer our prayers and provide these blessings for us, then we will be thankful and devoted to Him. But if He fails to deliver the things we ask for, we become angry, bitter, and skeptical of God's worthiness of our faith. When we adopt this attitude, we require a "sign" just as the scribes and Pharisees did. But Jesus' response to them is still true and relevant today. The only sign that will be given—the only one that should be required—is the "sign" of Jesus' death, burial, and resurrection. God sent His Son into the world to take on flesh and give Himself as an atoning sacrifice for all of mankind. Jesus then, after three days in the tomb, overcame death in the resurrection. There is no more proof needed that Jesus is the Christ, and that God cares for us. Thanks be to God!

Why do you think so many people fail
to believe in Jesus as the Christ?

DON'T FORGET TO PRAY AND HAVE A GREAT DAY!

⏳ **THINGS TO PRAY FOR TODAY:**

DAY 96

Today's Reading:
Matthew 12:43–45

Jesus uses this interesting little parable to describe the condition of the Jewish leaders of His day, but it also contains a powerful lesson and warning for us. The unclean spirit represents anything sinful or ungodly that might find its way into our lives. When that unclean spirit goes out (is cast out), meaning we repent of the sinful activity and rid our lives of it, there remains a clean but empty space in our lives. If that space remains vacant, that sin (and others) will find their way back into our lives, causing us to be in a worse condition than before. The danger is not in ridding our lives of sin, for this is what God desires and commands of us. The danger is in failing to replace the sin with good, godly things, filling the void and leaving no room for sin to re-enter. As we strive to live faithful lives, let us be determined not only to defeat sin in our lives, but also to be filled to overflowing with godliness.

What are some godly things we should put into practice?

DON'T FORGET TO PRAY AND HAVE A GREAT DAY!

 THINGS TO PRAY FOR TODAY:

DAY 97

 Today's Reading:
Matthew 12:46–50

O n the surface, it may seem that Jesus was being disrespectful toward His mother and brothers in disregarding their request. Why would He *not* speak to them? Why make the statements He made concerning them? To understand what Jesus does and says here, we must understand that Jesus was always focused on His mission and was always looking for opportunities to teach. This request from his family provided just such an opportunity. Jesus' purpose here was not to disrespect His physical family, but to make the point that there is an even more important spiritual family made up of those who are obedient to God. Jesus wanted His followers, then and now, to understand the importance of being His disciples and of the relationship with God that comes through that discipleship. There is no greater family that we can be a part of than the family of God!

Why is being part of God's spiritual family so important?

DON'T FORGET TO PRAY AND HAVE A GREAT DAY!

 THINGS TO PRAY FOR TODAY:

Day 98

Today's Reading:
Luke 8:1-3

When we think of the followers of Jesus during His earthly ministry, our minds most likely go immediately to the twelve apostles. They are the most present and visible companions of Jesus as we read through the gospels. But it is important to remember that they were not the only faithful followers of the Lord. There were others, many others, who believed in Him and followed Him from place to place because of their devotion to Him. Some of the most faithful and devoted among these followers seem to be the group of women mentioned in this text. They show up from time to time in the gospel accounts, but most notably in the events surrounding the death, burial, and resurrection of Christ. When most of the apostles had abandoned Jesus, these women were at the foot of the cross, grieving for their friend and Lord. Some of them were there when Jesus' body was laid in the tomb, and they returned on the resurrection morning to properly prepare His body for burial. They were among the first to witness the resurrection. These women were faithful, devoted, courageous followers of Christ who serve as wonderful examples for us.

What can we learn from the example of these women?

DON'T FORGET TO PRAY AND HAVE A GREAT DAY!

⏳ **THINGS TO PRAY FOR TODAY:**

Day 99

 Today's Reading:
Matthew 13:1–9

As Jesus looked over this great crowd that had gathered to hear Him teach, He saw their hearts and knew them. They had come to Him from different backgrounds and for different reasons. Jesus told this parable to describe them and the conditions of their hearts. Some had hearts that were hard and impenetrable by the seed of God's word. Others had hearts that were shallow and did not allow the word to take root. Still others had hearts that were filled with cares and desires that choked out the truth of God's word. Then there were the fertile hearts—those that were soft and accepting of God's word; those that offered an environment that nurtured its truths and encouraged growth. It was this heart that Jesus desired His hearers to have, and it is this same heart that God still desires for us today. What kind of heart do you have? May God help us to have a heart that is open and accepting to the truth of God's word.

What are some of the things that cause hearts to be infertile today?

DON'T FORGET TO PRAY AND HAVE A GREAT DAY!

 THINGS TO PRAY FOR TODAY:

DAY 100

Today's Reading:
Matthew 13:18–23

We often call this parable, "The Parable of the Seeds," or "The Parable of the Soils," but Jesus calls it "The Parable of the Sower." Without the sower, there is no seed sown, and thus no opportunity for it to take root and grow. The sower's task was not to dig a hole and carefully plant a seed just right; it was to walk along through the field and scatter the seeds in abundance wherever they might fall. The more seeds he scattered, the more likelihood of a harvest. The "seed" is the word of God, and we are called to be the sowers. Our purpose and God-given task is to sow the seed of God's word into the hearts of men. It is not our place to judge the fertility of the soil and discriminately plant seeds only in the best of soils, but rather simply to sow. Some soils (hearts) will receive the seed and allow it to take root and grow; others will reject or resist the seed, and it will ultimately fail. Still, God wants us to sow. Sow in hard ground, sow in rocky ground, sow in ground overgrown with weeds, and sow in good ground. If we will sow, then God will bring the increase (1 Corinthians 3:6)!

What are some ways we can be sowers of the word of God?

DON'T FORGET TO PRAY AND HAVE A GREAT DAY!

⏳ THINGS TO PRAY FOR TODAY:

Day 101

 Today's Reading:
Matthew 13:10–17

Whenever Jesus spoke, his audience was made up of many types of hearers, including those who were faithful followers and sincere listeners, and those who had already rejected Him but sought some basis for accusing Him of wrongdoing. Jesus' use of parables was for the purpose of differentiating between these two groups. Those who were insincere and simply looking to trap Him by His words would only hear an earthly story and miss the spiritual meaning. However, those who sincerely desired to learn from Him and were listening with "spiritual" ears would gain knowledge about and insight into the kingdom of God. It occurs to me that the word of God is much the same for us today. Those who view it skeptically and look into it only to discredit it will surely miss out on the wonderful blessings gained through knowing God and His will for us. But conversely, the diligent and sincere student of God's Word who seeks to be taught and strengthened by its precepts will be blessed beyond measure by the timeless truths of that holy book. May we all approach God's word with willing and open hearts!

What are some of the blessings of studying God's word?

DON'T FORGET TO PRAY AND HAVE A GREAT DAY!

 THINGS TO PRAY FOR TODAY:

Day 102

 Today's Reading:
Matthew 13:24–30

While this parable is really about the eventual separation of the good from the bad (we'll think about that tomorrow), there is another truth that I want to think about now. In the story, the tares exist because they are sown by an enemy. The good seed represents godly and faithful lives produced by the seed of God's word (as we saw in the Parable of the Sower). But there are also bad seeds—seeds of unbelief, worldliness, greed, hatred, and sinfulness that are sown among the good. These seeds produce ungodly and sinful lives. The enemy is Satan. He is constantly trying to contaminate people's minds, hearts, and lives with his bad seed. His hope is that, as those bad seeds spring up in the lives of many, they will destroy the fruit of the good seed and cause all to be lost. What we must remember is that God's enemy is our enemy as well. Satan's desire is to take us away from God and destroy us. We must be diligent and purposeful in our efforts to fend off the attacks of Satan and nourish the good seed of God's word so that we may continue to grow in faith and knowledge and bear the good fruit that God intends.

What are some things that we can do to
protect ourselves against Satan's bad seeds?

DON'T FORGET TO PRAY AND HAVE A GREAT DAY!

⏳ **THINGS TO PRAY FOR TODAY:**

Day 103

Today's Reading:
Matthew 13:36–43

Good and bad existing together. It is difficult, frustrating, and often discouraging for those who are struggling to be faithful children of God. It certainly doesn't seem to be a situation that would exist by God's will, yet it does. While it is not God's will that any be disobedient to Him and be lost eternally, He has chosen to allow His faithful children to coexist with those who choose to reject Him and live in disobedience. But this parable teaches us that that coexistence will not last forever. At "the end of the age," Jesus says He will send out His angels to harvest the good seed and destroy the bad. The two will be eternally separated as wheat is separated from the poisonous tares. Knowing that the day of harvest is coming, there are two goals that should be of highest priority in our lives: 1) to be faithful to God so that we might be numbered among the righteous who "will shine like the sun in the kingdom of their Father," and 2) to do all that we can to help those around us to come to know, love, and obey God as we do. In view of judgment and eternity, nothing is more important than these.

What can we do to help prepare ourselves for the day of judgment?

DON'T FORGET TO PRAY AND HAVE A GREAT DAY!

⏳ **THINGS TO PRAY FOR TODAY:**

DAY 104

Today's Reading:
Mark 4:21–25

There are several phrases within this passage that remind us of statements made by Jesus in the Sermon on the Mount (Matthew 5-7). In this passage, however, all of those statements are made in reference to Jesus' teaching. Though Jesus was teaching many things by parables, He here indicates that the whole truth of God would soon come to light. That being the case, it was imperative that His followers listen and pay careful attention to the things Jesus taught. That truth has since been revealed to us in the written Word which God has delivered to us through His Spirit and has preserved for all generations by His power and providence. In our day and time, the teachings of Jesus are just as timely and relevant as they ever were, and they are just as vital to our spiritual lives as they were to those who stood in His physical presence. The admonition that Jesus gives to his hearers extends to us as well: "If anyone has ears to hear, let him hear."

Why is it so important that we heed the teachings of Jesus?

DON'T FORGET TO PRAY AND HAVE A GREAT DAY!

⏳ **THINGS TO PRAY FOR TODAY:**

Day 105

Today's Reading:
Mark 4:26–29

This kingdom parable is short and simple and has a very straightforward point. In gardening, your chore is to plant and harvest. Everything that happens between those two tasks is largely out of your control. Sure, you might pull some weeds, give some water, or apply some other type of maintenance from time to time. But the actual processes of growth and production of fruit are things that we cannot control or even fully understand. Jesus says that this is also true of the kingdom of God. Our duty is to plant the seed. How that seed (the word of God) germinates, sprouts, grows, and produces fruit in the life of a person is not within our ability to control or understand. Ours is simply to sow the seed and then do what we can to water and nurture it, understanding that it is God who will bring about the increase (1 Corinthians 3:6).

Why do you think God gives us the responsibility of sowing the seed?

DON'T FORGET TO PRAY AND HAVE A GREAT DAY!

 THINGS TO PRAY FOR TODAY:

DAY 106

Today's Reading:
Matthew 13:31–32

Of all the herbs common to first-century Palestine, the mustard seed was the smallest. But along the banks of the Sea of Galilee, the plant that came from that tiny seed could grow to be ten to fifteen feet tall, with branches rigid enough for birds to nest in. Jesus uses this image, so well-known to His listeners, to describe the kingdom of heaven. That kingdom, He says, though it will begin very small, will grow to be very large and expansive. Just as Jesus prophesied, His church started very small with just a few individuals. But as the word of God was planted in the hearts of men, the church grew and expanded quickly so that, before the end of the first century, it had spread all over the world (Acts 17:6; Colossians 1:5-6). Through the centuries, the Lord's church has continued to exist, often enduring persecution from without and apostasy from within, yet continually working to serve God faithfully and to plant the seed of the Word of God into the hearts of men. The church, the body and bride of Christ, purchased and paid for with His blood, was and continues to be the glorious kingdom of heaven and a wonderful blessing to all who enter it through Christ.

Why is it important to God that the church continue to grow?

DON'T FORGET TO PRAY AND HAVE A GREAT DAY!

 **THINGS TO PRAY FOR TODAY:**

DAY 107

 Today's Reading:
Matthew 13:33

This short little parable, like the last, is intended to foretell the growth and influence of the church in the world. Leaven, the object that is used here, is often used in the Bible to represent evil influences and the negative effect that those influences can have on God's people. Here, however, Jesus uses leaven to represent the good influence of the church. Leaven is the substance used to cause bread to rise. It works on the inside, causing the dough to increase and expand, often to several times its original size. In the same way, Jesus says, as the Word of God is spread through the church, the hearts and lives of people are changed, and the church will grow and expand. The question for us is, are we continuing to be like leaven in the world? Are we striving to change those around us through the Word of God lived out in our lives and thus enlarging the kingdom of heaven? If not, why not?

What are some things that we can do
to help enlarge the kingdom of heaven?

DON'T FORGET TO PRAY AND HAVE A GREAT DAY!

 THINGS TO PRAY FOR TODAY:

Day 108

Today's Reading:
Matthew 13:44–46

All that they had—that is the price that they were willing to pay. Their homes, land, animals, business, possessions—everything. Why? Why were they willing to forfeit everything they owned, everything they had worked so hard to acquire, everything that brought comfort and security to their lives? The answer is that both of these men had found the one item that was worth more to them than all that they owned. It was, to them, a priceless treasure that was worth any sacrifice and any price that had to be paid. These two parables relate to us the great and matchless value of the Lord's kingdom. Do we really consider the kingdom of heaven to be a priceless treasure? Are we willing to forfeit all that we have to be part of it? The fact of the matter is that there is nothing that can compare to what God offers us in that kingdom, and nothing that we should not be willing to give in exchange for it.

What is it that makes the kingdom of heaven so priceless?

DON'T FORGET TO PRAY AND HAVE A GREAT DAY!

⧗ **THINGS TO PRAY FOR TODAY:**

Day 109

Today's Reading:
Matthew 13:47–52

This kingdom parable is about the coming judgment. It paints a picture of the separation of the righteous from the wicked on that day and brings to mind a picture of God that many people struggle with. It is easy for us to read and think about the love and mercy of God, but the righteousness and justness of God, those characteristics that render God incapable of ignoring sin and that demand a just consequence of sin, are harder to bear. We often see these two sides of God as being polar opposites and opposed to one another. However, we must understand that the righteousness and mercy of God are inseparably linked together. The righteousness that demanded a price to be paid for sin is the same righteousness that would not allow us to die in sin without hope. And so, in His righteousness and mercy, God sent His Son to pay the price for sin on behalf of mankind, giving everyone the opportunity to avoid condemnation and to be numbered with the saved. When that great gathering day comes, and the angels are sent to divide the good from the wicked, God's desire is that there be no wicked found. He has made that end possible through Christ but, ultimately, the choice is ours.

What is our responsibility in being prepared for that day?

DON'T FORGET TO PRAY AND HAVE A GREAT DAY!

 THINGS TO PRAY FOR TODAY:

DAY 110

Today's Reading:
Mark 4:33–34

Over the past several days, we have read and thought about many parables of Jesus. During this period of Jesus' ministry, according to this text, He taught exclusively through these "earthly stories with heavenly meanings." As the Master Teacher, Jesus understood perfectly the hearts of His hearers and knew exactly what they needed to hear and how best to present it. He used these everyday scenes and images to convey spiritual lessons that were difficult to understand otherwise. He also used parables to hide these teachings from His hard-hearted enemies who were constantly looking for a reason to accuse Him of wrongdoing. Jesus' parables continue to be a valuable source of learning for us today. The vivid pictures that Jesus paints with His words still help us understand His teachings and timeless truths. What a blessing it is to be able to sit at the feet of the Master Teacher and to learn from Him.

Why do you think parables were (and still are)
such an effective way of teaching?

DON'T FORGET TO PRAY AND HAVE A GREAT DAY!

 THINGS TO PRAY FOR TODAY:

Day 111

 **Today's Reading:**
Matthew 8:23–27

There are several clues in the telling of this event that indicate to us that Jesus' disciples did not yet fully understand who He was or the extent of His power. In Mark's account (which we will read tomorrow), they ask Jesus, "Do you not care that we are perishing?" Then there is their pondering: "What sort of man is this, that even the winds and the sea obey Him?" Clearly, they were still struggling to understand this Man and His purpose. But despite that lack of clarity, when they were in trouble and feared for their lives, it was Jesus that they came to for help. "Save us, Lord; we are perishing." They may not have understood exactly how, but they knew that He could save them. And He still can! Many people in the world fail to come to Jesus because they do not fully understand. Maybe they don't understand how His dying can save them, or how their baptism can wash away sins. Maybe they don't fully comprehend the concept of eternity or heaven and hell. There may always be things that are beyond our ability to clearly understand, but that does not detract from Jesus' power to save. We must learn to trust what we do not see and depend on what we cannot fully grasp. That is faith!

What are some things that we can do to help strengthen our faith?

DON'T FORGET TO PRAY AND HAVE A GREAT DAY!

 THINGS TO PRAY FOR TODAY:

Day 112

Today's Reading:
Mark 4:35–41

Peace! Be still!" These are the words that Jesus used to rebuke the storm and calm the seas, but they could just as easily have been said to the disciples. As this storm raged, the winds violently tossed the boat about in the sea. The boat was "being swamped by the waves" (Matthew's words) so that it was filling with water. But the sea was not the only thing that was unsettled that night. The disciples were frightened, panicked, and desperate. As the waves of the sea filled the boat, waves of fear filled their hearts. *How could Jesus be sleeping while we are dying? Does He not care?* Jesus' words to them are very telling: "Why are you so afraid? Have you still no faith?" The disciples still had much to learn. There were going to be many volatile and unsettling times in their lives of discipleship. They needed to learn the meaning of the words that Jesus spoke to the storm. They needed to learn to trust and to have an inner peace, knowing that they were safe in the hands of the Master. We need to learn that lesson as well. When we face the storms of life, we need to be stilled and calmed as we hear Jesus say to us, "Peace! Be still!"

Why is faith so important during difficult times in our lives?

DON'T FORGET TO PRAY AND HAVE A GREAT DAY!

 THINGS TO PRAY FOR TODAY:

DAY 113

 Today's Reading:
Luke 8:26-39

The one element of this story that stands out the most in my mind is the reaction and attitude of the demons toward Jesus. These demons, who called themselves "Legion" because they were many (we don't know how many, but Mark's account tells us that there were about 2,000 swine that the demons were allowed to enter into), recognized Jesus and acknowledged Him as "Son of the Most High God." Not only did they identify Him, but they acknowledged His power and submitted to His authority. Notice that they "begged" Him not to command them to go into the abyss (referring to the place of imprisonment for evil spirits) and asked permission to enter into the swine instead. In a world where those who flaunted the position of being God's chosen people would refuse and reject Jesus as the Son of God and Messiah, these demonic spirits acknowledged and submitted to Him. There is certainly a lesson there for us and our world today. Jesus is the Christ. He has been given the name that is above all names (Philippians 2:9) and He has all authority (Matthew 28:18). We must learn to submit to Him and allow Him to be the Lord of our lives.

Why do you think so many have such a difficult
time acknowledging and submitting to Christ?

DON'T FORGET TO PRAY AND HAVE A GREAT DAY!

⧗ THINGS TO PRAY FOR TODAY:

Day 114

Today's Reading:
Mark 5:21–24, 35–43

We often think of the Jewish leaders of Jesus' day as being an unbelieving lot who, as a whole, rejected Jesus and ultimately were responsible for His death. But this Jewish ruler had great faith in Jesus—so much so that he was willing to leave the side of his dying daughter to find Jesus and plead for Him to come and heal her. But even his faith had its limit. While he wholeheartedly believed in Jesus' power to heal, he could not bring himself to believe that anyone, even Jesus, could raise his child from the dead. As Jesus was delayed by the crowds, and one came from Jairus' house to report that the girl had died, all hope seemed lost. Their feelings of hopelessness were summed up in the question asked of Jairus: "Why bother the Teacher any further?" But Jesus quickly reassures them. This was not to be a day of mourning, but of celebration. Jairus' daughter would live. Even the chains of death had no power over Jesus. His command for her to "arise" was promptly obeyed, and she lived, causing her parents to be "overcome with amazement" and rightly so, for our God is an amazing God!

What lesson(s) can we learn from this great miracle of Jesus?

DON'T FORGET TO PRAY AND HAVE A GREAT DAY!

 THINGS TO PRAY FOR TODAY:

DAY 115

 Today's Reading:
Mark 5:25–34

Faith is one of the great cornerstones of our salvation; without it, we cannot be pleasing to God (Hebrews 11:6). While the gospels give us a clear picture of the rejection and ridicule Jesus faced at the hands of His enemies, they also show us many great examples of faith. Miraculous healings were no more common in the days of Jesus than they are in our day. The woman at the center of this story had suffered from a condition for many years and had exhausted all medical options available to her. She was, for all practical purposes, incurable. But she had faith! So much faith, in fact, that she believed just touching the hem of Jesus' garment would provide the healing she so desperately needed. She wasn't looking for some great display of Jesus' power, no impressive speech, no awe-inspiring demonstration—just the simple touch of her hand to the cloth of His garment. She believed that would be enough, and she was right! She was healed through Jesus' power, but He reveals that it was, in fact, her faith that had made her well. What a great and powerful example of faith!

How can we demonstrate our faith in Jesus today?

DON'T FORGET TO PRAY AND HAVE A GREAT DAY!

 THINGS TO PRAY FOR TODAY:

Day 116

 Today's Reading:
Matthew 9:27–34

It is no wonder that people constantly came to Jesus, pleading with Him to heal them of their afflictions. The blind, the mute, the lame, the demon-possessed—they all needed healing that had never been available to them before and was not available through any other source. Jesus alone offered them hope. Why wouldn't they come to Him? Any of us would most likely have done the same, right? Well, have you considered that we all suffer from a terrible and fatal disease? It is an epidemic that afflicts all of mankind, and there is no treatment or cure other than that offered by Jesus. The disease is sin, and Jesus is our only hope. He still offers healing, the type of healing that we desperately need but cannot find anywhere else. The question is: do we desire the healing that He offers, and are we willing to come to Him to find it?

Why do you think so many do not come to Jesus for spiritual healing?

DON'T FORGET TO PRAY AND HAVE A GREAT DAY!

⏳ **THINGS TO PRAY FOR TODAY:**

DAY 117

 Today's Reading:
Mark 6:1-6

Jesus' time in Nazareth was difficult and disappointing. He came to them as the Master Teacher, but they only saw the one who had grown up in Nazareth—the son, the brother, the carpenter. They discounted His authority and wisdom and questioned His power. Such was their unbelief that, people had flocked to Jesus in other places to have their sick healed, in Nazareth, even His restorative powers were not accepted, and He had little opportunity to display His mighty works. What can we learn from this event in the life of Jesus? While there are several valuable lessons to be learned here, maybe the greatest is the one revealed in the last statement: "And He went about among the villages teaching." Jesus was refused by His own city, the people who had known Him the longest, but He kept teaching. He faced their ridicule, skepticism, and rejection, but He kept teaching. Many times in our lives, we will be rejected, turned down, maybe even scoffed at for our attempts to share Jesus with friends, family, coworkers, and others. Many will not accept us or our message, but we must remember that not even Jesus was successful all the time, so keep teaching!

How should we deal with people who reject
or ridicule us for trying to share our faith?

DON'T FORGET TO PRAY AND HAVE A GREAT DAY!

⏳ **THINGS TO PRAY FOR TODAY:**

DAY 118

Today's Reading:
John 5:1–15

It has been said that, "Jesus never left anyone where they were." The meaning of this short little statement is that, such was Jesus' compassion, wisdom, power, and influence, that anyone who encountered Him was changed by Him in some way. In this text, we meet a man who had suffered from an infirmity (probably some form of paralysis or lameness) for 38 years. Jesus' healing of this man certainly changed his physical life, but that is not the change I want to focus on. One of the unique things about this healing is that it was not prompted or made possible by the faith of the healed. This man did not even know Jesus' name and was looking for some magical cure from the pool for his healing. Nothing is said about faith, but Jesus healed him. But how did this interaction with Jesus change the faithless man? Notice Jesus' statement to him: "See, you have been made well. Sin no more, lest a worse thing come upon you." While Jesus often healed because of an existing faith, in this case, it seems that He healed in order to produce faith. He expected a change to take place in the spiritual life of this man to whom He granted physical healing. As always, Jesus was focused on the all-important spiritual life. What a great lesson for us!

How have you been changed by Jesus?

DON'T FORGET TO PRAY AND HAVE A GREAT DAY!

 THINGS TO PRAY FOR TODAY:

Day 119

 Today's Reading:
John 5:16–23

John began his gospel with the declaration that, "In the beginning was the Word, and the Word was with God, and the Word was God." In this passage, Jesus confirms and expounds upon that statement of unity and oneness between the Father and the Son. Jesus came into the world to show us God. Every word, action, and attitude demonstrated by Jesus was a perfect reflection of the heart, mind, and will of God. The Father and the Son were (and are) one in mind and in motive. Nothing that Jesus did during His life and ministry was done independently of God. What does all of this mean for us? It means that, as we read and study about the life of Jesus, we are learning about God. He has shown Himself to us through His Son. As Paul would later write: "He was manifested in the flesh" (1 Tim. 3:16). God has given us the wonderful blessing of seeing and knowing Him through the life of Jesus, so that we might draw nearer to Him in love and faith. What a great God we serve, and what a wonderful Savior!

What are some things we learn about
God through the life of Jesus?

DON'T FORGET TO PRAY AND HAVE A GREAT DAY!

 THINGS TO PRAY FOR TODAY:

DAY 120

Today's Reading:
John 5:24–30

One of the things that often drew people to Jesus in large crowds was His ability to heal the sick and even raise the dead. His power over physical life was remarkable, and many came to Him seeking the restoration of health for themselves or their loved ones. But the physical lives of people were never Jesus' primary concern. Beyond the power to restore physical life and health, Jesus held the power of eternal life. For those who would hear His word and believe in Him, He had been granted by the Father the authority to give eternal life. But this text also reveals that Jesus has been given authority to execute judgment upon all who are in the grave, both the good (obedient) and the evil (disobedient). To the good, he would grant the resurrection of life, and to the evil, the resurrection of judgment. This text serves both to comfort the faithful and to warn the unfaithful. That day of resurrection and judgment is surely coming. Are we ready to stand before Christ the judge?

How and by what standard will we be judged by Christ?

DON'T FORGET TO PRAY AND HAVE A GREAT DAY!

⏳ **THINGS TO PRAY FOR TODAY:**

DAY 121

 Today's Reading:
John 5:31–40

How many witnesses does it take to confirm something as true? Typically, one eyewitness is enough, but in Jesus' case, there were multiple witnesses. Jesus says that among His witnesses were John, the great works that He had done, God the Father, and the Scriptures (i.e. Old Testament prophecies). Surely these witnesses would be sufficient to establish His identity, but many still refused to believe. Though they were waiting and looking for the coming Messiah, they were not willing to accept Jesus as the One sent by God to redeem them. Today, we have the mystery of Christ revealed to us through God's word. The Bible is filled with witnesses to Jesus' identity and purpose—prophecies and fulfillments, Jesus' own words and actions, other inspired writers. But many still refuse to believe. Even in the face of all the evidence and proof of God's love and Jesus' saving work, many continue to look for salvation in other things, or fail to consider the need for salvation at all. May God help us all to see our need for Jesus and be willing to accept His gift of salvation.

Why do you think so many still refuse to believe in Jesus?

DON'T FORGET TO PRAY AND HAVE A GREAT DAY!

 ⏳ **THINGS TO PRAY FOR TODAY:**

Day 122

Today's Reading:
John 5:41-47

Among the great leaders of their history, Moses occupied a special place in the minds and hearts of the Jews. As the law-giver of Israel, he was revered because of his special relationship with God and special role in receiving the law. They gave their honor and undying allegiance to him. But Jesus reminds them that Moses spoke of Him, and if they believed Moses, they should believe in Him. He rebuked them for receiving Moses, a man, but rejecting the Son of God. You know, it occurs to me that many are still guilty at times of receiving and honoring men—preachers, authors, influential speakers, celebrities—while rejecting Christ. We will listen to and follow their teachings and ideas, but turn a blind eye to the pure and simple truths of God's word. In so doing, we in essence give honor to men but reject the Son of God, and demonstrate, like those of Jesus' day did, that we "do not have the love of God" in us. May we honor Christ above all else and follow His teachings above those of any man.

How can we show honor for Jesus today?

DON'T FORGET TO PRAY AND HAVE A GREAT DAY!

⧗ **THINGS TO PRAY FOR TODAY:**

DAY 123

 Today's Reading:
Matthew 9:35–38

We often see Jesus teaching and healing, but if we are not careful, we can forget why He spent so much time doing those things. He did not teach just to change people, and He did not heal just to demonstrate the great power of God. Jesus' ministry was defined by compassion. As He looked out over the crowds that constantly gathered around Him, He saw people who were lost and in need of someone to help them. He looked on them with care and concern and desired to meet their needs, to provide for them, protect them, and lead them as a shepherd does his sheep. Ultimately, He desired to lead them to God and salvation. That compassion, so evident in Jesus' life and ministry, is still extended to us today. As our Savior and Lord, Jesus still looks upon us with care and concern. He continues to love us and desires to provide for, protect, and lead us. Oh, that we would accept His loving care and allow Him to be a shepherd to our souls.

Why is the compassion of Christ so important in our lives?

DON'T FORGET TO PRAY AND HAVE A GREAT DAY!

⧖ THINGS TO PRAY FOR TODAY:

Day 124

**Today's Reading:
Matthew 10:1–15**

In this text, which is often refered to as the "limited commission," Jesus is giving His apostles instructions on where and how to go out preaching. Much of what Jesus says to them can be summed up in two principles:

1. *Put your trust in God.* They were not to take provisions for their travels but were to trust in God to provide for them through the hospitality and generosity of good and godly people along the way. It was important that they learn, not to trust in worldly things, but in God Almighty to be their provider.

2. *Be uncompromising.* As they went out, they were to teach the simple truth, "The kingdom of heaven is at hand." In their teaching and their lives, they were not to bend to the will of the people, but to remain firm in their commitment to God and to His word. They were also not to do anything to compromise their influence or integrity, thus compromising their mission.

Though our mission might be somewhat different today, these principles continue to serve us well as we seek to spread the gospel and bring others to Christ.

How can we apply these principles to our lives today?

DON'T FORGET TO PRAY AND HAVE A GREAT DAY!

 THINGS TO PRAY FOR TODAY:

Day 125

Today's Reading:
Matthew 10:16–26

J esus never promised His apostles, nor does He promise us, that being a disciple of His would be a life of ease. In this prophetic warning, He tells them that they would face rejection, trials, and persecution from the Jews, the Gentiles, and even from their own families. They would be called on to endure much hardship and suffering because of His name, the name that they wore and proclaimed. In facing that persecution, He says, they would be following in His steps, enduring the same hardships that He had endured. Though we are blessed to live in a land of religious freedom, a life lived in the name of Christ is still not without its hardships. We may face the occasional mocking, malicious comment, or false accusation. We may be called upon to stand boldly for Christ in the face of opposition. But none of the hardships that this life holds can compare to the glory of the prize that awaits the faithful. As Jesus promised, "the one who endures to the end will be saved."

What are some specific things that
Christians might have to endure today?

DON'T FORGET TO PRAY AND HAVE A GREAT DAY!

⏳ **THINGS TO PRAY FOR TODAY:**

DAY 126

 Today's Reading:
Matthew 10:27–31

In yesterday's reading, we saw the hardships that often accompany a life of devotion to Christ. In today's text, Jesus follows those warnings with an assurance of God's care and concern. While man might can harm or even kill the body, there is nothing that man can do to destroy the soul. Therefore, the reverence and devotion that we feel toward God should far outweigh the fear we have toward man. God cares—so much so, Jesus says, that the very hairs of our heads are numbered. He knows everything about us, both the significant and insignificant. He is aware of every joy and every sorrow, every victory and every defeat, every accomplishment and every hardship. We are valuable to God, and as we face the difficulties of life and are called to endure suffering for His name's sake, He knows, and He cares. He is watching over us, ready to strengthen, help, and bless us according to His perfect will. What a comforting thought, and what an awesome God!

How has God demonstrated His love for you in your life?

DON'T FORGET TO PRAY AND HAVE A GREAT DAY!

⏳ **THINGS TO PRAY FOR TODAY:**

Day 127

Today's Reading:
Matthew 10:32–33

When we think of confessing Christ, we typically think of the quick and easy step that usually immediately precedes baptism. Following the example of the Eunuch in Acts 8, we, standing before our friends and family, confidently state: "I believe that Jesus Christ is the Son of God" (Acts 8:37). But as Christians, we must understand that confession is not reserved for that singular time in our lives. We must be willing to confess Christ at any time and under any circumstances. The annals of church history are filled with stories of valiant Christians who were ordered to denounce their faith in Christ or die an unspeakable death. Under those unimaginable circumstances, they courageously confessed their belief and faith in Christ even to death. We may never face those kinds of situations, but in the course of our own lives, we must always be ready and willing to wear the name of Christ proudly. When we face ridicule or mocking, we must confess Him. When we face being ostracized, we must confess Him. When we face the loss of friends or opportunities, we must confess Him. May God give us the courage and strength, both through our words and lives, to confess Christ!

Why is it so important that we are willing to confess Christ?

DON'T FORGET TO PRAY AND HAVE A GREAT DAY!

 THINGS TO PRAY FOR TODAY:

DAY 128

Today's Reading:
Matthew 10:34-39

In human thinking, there is no relationship more precious or protected than the relationships of family. The bonds among husbands and wives, parents and children, and siblings are typically tighter and stronger than any other relationships we have. For that reason, this statement by Jesus seems difficult, harsh, and unloving. Isn't He contradicting His usual advocacy of the family? Is He asserting that those relationships aren't as important as we think they are? Not at all! On the contrary, He is using those very relationships because of their great importance. He is using them to make a strong and unmistakable statement about the commitment that is required in following Him. Our commitment to Christ must be our greatest priority—more important than our family or our marriage; more important, in fact, than any earthly relationship or priority of our lives. To be a faithful disciple of Christ requires our ALL! This is not to say, of course, that we should not love or be committed to our family or other earthly relationships. In fact, if Christ is first and our commitment to Him is lived out each day, we will be better spouses, parents, children, and friends. Thus is the nature of following God and submitting to His perfect will.

Why does Jesus demand to be the greatest priority in our lives?

DON'T FORGET TO PRAY AND HAVE A GREAT DAY!

⏳ **THINGS TO PRAY FOR TODAY:**

Day 129

Today's Reading:
Matthew 10:40–42

The thing that strikes me about this short passage is the attachment and closeness Jesus feels between Himself and His disciples. He is not a Lord who is detached from those who serve Him. He cares for us, is watching over us, and is well aware of our labors and of the response of others to our work. In our lives as Christians, we are not just servants, but ambassadors and representatives. As we work and serve in the name of Christ, we represent His hands and feet and light. Therefore, Jesus says, if anyone receives us, they receive Him. And conversely, if anyone rejects us, they reject Him. Those who do good to us have a reward from our Lord. This passage reminds us of the great responsibility that we have been given to be ambassadors for Christ in the world, but it also reminds us that, as we go into the world to serve Him, we are not alone. The Lord is always with us.

Why does Jesus demand to be the greatest priority in our lives?

DON'T FORGET TO PRAY AND HAVE A GREAT DAY!

 **THINGS TO PRAY FOR TODAY:**

Day 130

Today's Reading:
Mark 6:14–29

As this passage recounts the events that led to the death of John the baptizer, it serves as a sobering reminder of the devastating effects that sin can have in the lives of people. John, a man who was obviously respected and even liked by Herod (v. 20), was imprisoned because he condemned the sin of adultery that Herod and Herodias were involved in. Then, because of the feelings stirred up in Herod by the lascivious acts performed by Herodias' daughter as she danced before the king and his guests, John was beheaded. Sin, and his attempts to hide it, justify it, and avoid its consequences, had caused Herod to murder a man he knew to be a just and holy man. It continues to be true today that sin, if left unchecked, can cast us into a downward spiral of actions and attitudes, leading us deeper and deeper into depravity and further and further away from God. May God help us to avoid the pitfalls of sin and be constantly renewed in our commitment to God.

Why do you think sin has such an ability to lead us into more sin?

DON'T FORGET TO PRAY AND HAVE A GREAT DAY!

 THINGS TO PRAY FOR TODAY:

Day 131

Today's Reading:
Matthew 14:13–21

"You give them something to eat." It was an impossible command. How could Jesus expect His apostles to feed thousands of hungry people? They had made no preparations and had no resources. They themselves were tired, hungry, and frustrated. What was the meaning of such an unreasonable request? What did Jesus hope to accomplish by putting His apostles in such a difficult position? The answer is simple. In His work to train the apostles to be the leaders and servants He needed them to be, there were two very important lessons they needed to learn. The first was that they needed to take advantage of opportunities to serve. The love of God could not be demonstrated by sending people away to fend for themselves. The apostles needed to develop hearts of service. Second, they needed to understand that the things that were impossible for them were altogether possible for Christ. There is no way they could feed this crowd, but with a very modest amount of food, Jesus fed them with ease. Likewise, we're called to shine and serve for God, and in so doing, these same lessons are vital for us to learn as well. May God help us to be the servants and leaders He would have us to be.

What lessons can we learn from Jesus' feeding of the five thousand?

DON'T FORGET TO PRAY AND HAVE A GREAT DAY!

⏳ **THINGS TO PRAY FOR TODAY:**

DAY 132

Today's Reading:
John 6:1–15

We have already thought about Matthew's telling of this event. We have considered the impossible command of Jesus and the doubt and frustration of the apostles. But in the midst of their skepticism, John reveals a shining example of faith in the response of Andrew. The only available food on that day was found in the possession of a young boy who was brought to Jesus by Andrew. He wasn't completely confident that Jesus could feed the masses with these morsels. There was no grand pronouncement made by Andrew of Jesus' power and miraculous ability. Instead, there was a simple query: "What are these among so many?" He wondered, questioned, maybe even doubted, but he brought the lad to Jesus anyway. His faith may have only been that of a mustard seed, but nevertheless, he acted on that faith and, in so doing, provided a means by which Jesus' command could be obeyed and His will be done. What a wonderful example Andrew is to us. We may look at our abilities, resources, or opportunities and ask, "What are these among so many?" But we must never forget that God can use what we bring Him, in faith, to do His will.

What can you bring to God that He
might use to accomplish His will?

DON'T FORGET TO PRAY AND HAVE A GREAT DAY!

 THINGS TO PRAY FOR TODAY:

DAY 133

**Today's Reading:
Matthew 14:22–33**

P eter did the impossible! Can you imagine the feeling of stepping out of the boat and resting your foot on the unsteady surface of the wind-tossed sea? Just to take that step required an incredible amount of courage and faith. But Peter's faith was no match for the boisterous wind. As the winds howled and the waves crashed, Peter lost his focus on Jesus and, with it, his faith. Just as his faith had allowed him to stand upon the water, his fear caused him to sink into it. In one final, desperate plea, Peter calls out to the Lord for salvation. As we consider this amazing event, there are so many parallels to our own lives for us to learn from. As we face the many storms of life—hardships, trials, sorrows—we are called to step away from the comfort of the familiar and trust God with our lives. But just like Peter, we can often find ourselves distracted by the chaos around us, losing our focus and faith, and sinking into despair and hopelessness. May God help us to be strong in our faith and, like Peter, to look to Him for help in our times of greatest struggle.

How can our faith in God help us as we face the storms of life?

DON'T FORGET TO PRAY AND HAVE A GREAT DAY!

⧗ THINGS TO PRAY FOR TODAY:

Day 134

 Today's Reading:
Mark 6:53–56

This is a scene that we see repeated time and again during the ministry of Jesus—people from surrounding villages and towns flocking to Him wherever He is to have their sick and afflicted healed. It was a daily occurrence in the life of Jesus. As we have discussed before, Jesus possessed an ability and offered an opportunity that was not available anywhere or through anyone else. Through His healing power, He gave people the ability to return to a normal and productive way of life, to reenter their world in a way they never thought possible. Is there any wonder why so many came to Him, looking for healing? Did you know that Jesus still offers healing? The healing He offers us is far more effective, permanent, and important than the physical healing that He offered during His earthly ministry. Jesus, today, offers us spiritual healing. He offers to make our souls whole and pure and ready for salvation. The question is, why do people not flock to Jesus today for that healing just as people did in this passage? May God help us recognize the importance of spiritual healing and the desire to be made whole by Christ.

Why do you think so many people do not see the importance or need for spiritual healing?

DON'T FORGET TO PRAY AND HAVE A GREAT DAY!

⏳ **THINGS TO PRAY FOR TODAY:**

Day 135

 Today's Reading:
John 6:22–29

Here, Jesus speaks to one of the great challenges He faced in trying to reach the people of His day. Like many people today, they were more interested in the physical things than the spiritual. They followed Him because He fed them or because He healed them. They wanted the physical benefits of being a follower of Jesus. He quickly chastises them for that attitude and instructs them to seek (or desire) the spiritual food that leads to eternal life. Many in our world are no different. They are interested in what physical benefits might be available as a follower of Christ. Will He heal me or my loved one? Will He take my debt away or bless me financially? Will he protect me from the hardships and difficulties of life? But Jesus' message is still true and relevant today. There is no doubt that God blesses us with many physical things, but it's the spiritual blessings, not the physical, that are the most important. It is those spiritual things that we ought to seek as our priority, because it is those things that can and will affect our eternity.

How can we seek spiritual things?

DON'T FORGET TO PRAY AND HAVE A GREAT DAY!

 THINGS TO PRAY FOR TODAY:

Day 136

Today's Reading:
John 6:30–40

I t must have been frustrating for Jesus to deal constantly with people who, despite the many miraculous works they had witnessed by His hand, continued to doubt and demand more proof. This particular audience had witnessed many sick and infirmed receive health and strength by Jesus' power. They had eaten a meal that He had provided by miraculous means. There was plenty of proof, yet their curiosity and fascination with the spectacular had motivated them to ask for still another sign. Jesus responds to them by simply saying that He is the one they should be seeking and, though they had seen Him, they still did not believe. What they needed—what we all need—is not to be found in signs and wonders but in Jesus Himself, the bread of life. It is in Him and Him alone that eternal life can be found, and it is He alone that should be the focus of our search.

What are some things that people search for today instead of Jesus?

DON'T FORGET TO PRAY AND HAVE A GREAT DAY!

 THINGS TO PRAY FOR TODAY:

DAY 137

 Today's Reading:
John 6:41–51

Much of John 6 deals with the attitude of unbelief expressed by the Jews of Jesus' day. Despite His many acts of power and His teaching of the truth of God, His audiences in large part were unwilling to see Him as anything but a man, a son, and a teacher. But Jesus wanted them to see so much more. He wanted them to see Him as the bread of life, as the giver of eternal life, as the Son of the Father. But even beyond these things, Jesus desired that, as they witnessed Him and heard His teachings, they would see God. He desired that they know God and His love for them through His words and actions. He desired that they see in Him the way to God and to an everlasting abode with God. Jesus still allows and encourages us to see God. Even as we take this journey together through the life of Christ this year, we have the opportunity to peer through the window of Jesus and see the Father—His righteousness and holiness, His love and mercy, His care and concern. While Jesus' life was ultimately about His atoning death, it was also about giving us a picture of God and allowing us to know Him through His Son. What a wonderful opportunity!

What are some things that we can know about God through Jesus?

DON'T FORGET TO PRAY AND HAVE A GREAT DAY!

 THINGS TO PRAY FOR TODAY:

DAY 138

Today's Reading:
John 6:52–59

As we read these verses, our minds most likely go immediately to the Lord's Supper, the communion that we share with Christ each Lord's day as we remember His death through the memorial feast that He instituted (e.g. Matthew 26:26-29). While there may be an application of these verses to the Lord's Supper, it is not that memorial that Christ is referring to in these statements. To "eat" His flesh and "drink" His blood is symbolic language that represents the "taking in" of Christ. To take Him in means to make Him a part of your life and inner-most being, to make His life one with your own. There is also an allusion here to His death on the cross and our willingness to take up our own cross and follow after Him. The lesson is this: if we want to have eternal life, we must accept the crucified Christ, give our lives to Him, and become obedient to His will and teaching. As Paul would later state: "I have been crucified with Christ; it is no longer I who live, but Christ who lives in me…" (Galatians 2:20).

In view of all that the New Testament teaches,
how does one become obedient to Christ?

DON'T FORGET TO PRAY AND HAVE A GREAT DAY!

⏳ **THINGS TO PRAY FOR TODAY:**

DAY 139

Today's Reading:
John 6:60-71

I n today's thought, I want to focus on the words of Peter in response to Jesus' question, "Do you want to go away as well?" Peter quickly responds, "Lord, to whom shall we go? You have the words of eternal life..." At this point in his relationship with Jesus, Peter did not fully understand Jesus' mission or his place in it, but there was one thing that he understood very clearly: there was no one else on earth—no Jewish leader, no teacher, no prophet—who could offer him what Jesus could: eternal life. Though the way might be rough at times, though Jesus' teachings might sometimes be difficult to understand or swallow, Peter was committed to following Him. There was nowhere else and with no one else that he wanted to be. There are still many people who walk away from Jesus because He asks more of them than they are willing to give. If only we too could be convinced that there is nowhere else to go and no one else to go to who can offer what Jesus Christ offers: eternal life.

What are some of the reasons people leave Christ today?

DON'T FORGET TO PRAY AND HAVE A GREAT DAY!

 THINGS TO PRAY FOR TODAY:

Day 140

Today's Reading:
Mark 7:1-13

As creatures of habit, we like traditions. They are comfortable, familiar, and easy. They have a way of imbedding themselves in our thinking and practice and quickly become an indelible part of who we are and what we believe. In that mindset, "the way it's always been" becomes the standard by which our decisions are made, and the line between tradition and doctrine is easily blurred. If we are not careful, those traditions come to identify us and become more precious and binding than even the doctrinal teachings of God's word. This is the very sin the Jewish leaders were guilty of, and Jesus gives them, and us, a grave warning about the danger of this mentality. The truth of the matter is that there is nothing wrong with traditions. They provide roots for us and give us a pattern of order to follow, but traditions must never be more important to us than are the teachings of God's word. They must never interfere with our carrying out of God's will, and they must never form a basis for making doctrinal decisions. May God's word always be our first and only guide and creed.

Why do you think traditions so easily become so important to us?

DON'T FORGET TO PRAY AND HAVE A GREAT DAY!

⏳ **THINGS TO PRAY FOR TODAY:**

DAY 141

Today's Reading:
Mark 7:14-23

Most of us pay some attention to what we eat. Maybe you are on a special diet because of a health issue. Maybe you are trying to lose weight or just be healthier. Maybe there are certain foods or ingredients that you are allergic to and, therefore, must avoid. Regardless of the reason or motivation, many of us pay attention to the foods we eat and consequences of eating certain things. If you understand that concept, then you understand what Jesus is teaching in this passage. In contrasting the physical with the spiritual, He is saying that, in reality, the food that you eat does not defile you (i.e. make you spiritually unclean or impure). It is what you put into your heart and mind—the images, thoughts, attitudes and influences—that can defile you. Who you are and what comes from you in your life is a product of what you put into your heart. Therefore, we need to be very diligent, much more so than with our food, to guard our hearts against those things that would defile us.

What are some of the things that we need
to beware of allowing into our hearts?

DON'T FORGET TO PRAY AND HAVE A GREAT DAY!

 THINGS TO PRAY FOR TODAY:

Day 142

 Today's Reading:
Matthew 15:21–28

The words and attitude of Jesus in this encounter seem to be harsh and unloving, but we must remember that, as we have stated before, Jesus always had a purpose for everything He said and did. It is often revealed in the gospels that Jesus knew the hearts of those whom He encountered, and there is no reason to believe He did not know the heart of this woman. His words and actions toward her were intended to develop and deepen the faith that He knew already existed in her heart. She came to Him in humility and reverence, acknowledging Him as Lord and as the Messiah of Israel. She did not presume to stand in the place of the Jews, but rather trusted in the compassion of the Lord. Jesus commends her great faith—one of only two such commendations of faith given by our Lord in the gospels (both to Gentiles)—and He grants her request and heals her daughter. There may be times in our lives when our faith is challenged, when God doesn't seem to be listening or responding, but those are times when our faith can be developed and deepened if we will continue to trust in the Lord as did this woman.

What should we do when our faith is tested?

DON'T FORGET TO PRAY AND HAVE A GREAT DAY!

 THINGS TO PRAY FOR TODAY:

Day 143

 Today's Reading:
Mark 7:31–37

As we read through the gospel accounts of Jesus' life, we see many examples of Jesus healing those who were sick and afflicted with different infirmities (and remember that we are given only a small sampling of the many healings Jesus performed). While amazing and miraculous, these healings can become somewhat commonplace to us as we consider the ministry of Jesus. "Oh, it's another healing" may become our attitude. But it occurs to me that the people of Jesus' day never lost their fascination with Jesus' power to heal. Wherever He went, people came to Him in droves to be healed or to witness healings. Then, even when commanded to not tell anyone about the healing, they could not keep the amazing news to themselves. The excitement over being healed was more than they could contain. I think that there is a spiritual parallel here for us. The spiritual healing Jesus offers us is something that oftentimes becomes commonplace in our thinking. We don't rejoice in it or tell others about it as we should. May God help us to regain the excitement of having our souls healed and lives renewed by the saving power of Christ.

What are some things that can help us be
more excited about our spiritual healing?

DON'T FORGET TO PRAY AND HAVE A GREAT DAY!

 THINGS TO PRAY FOR TODAY:

Day 144

Today's Reading:
Matthew 15:29-31

M any commentators believe that this is the same occasion as yesterday's reading. While Mark, writing to a Gentile audience, chooses to focus on one particular example of Jesus' healing power (and that toward a Gentile), Matthew gives us the bigger picture of the many who came to Jesus for healing on that occasion and received it. As we have stated before, Jesus always had a purpose. Every word, every action, every teaching was carefully crafted to bring about God's will and to fulfill His earthly purpose. So if not simply to restore health and life, what was His purpose in healing so many? I believe that this text states that purpose: "And they glorified the God of Israel." Beyond His ultimate mission of becoming the perfect sacrifice for our sins, Jesus came to this world to bring glory to God, and that He did. Every word and action pointed to and illuminated God. He caused people to think about and see God in a different way than they had before. He renewed their faith and zeal. He gave them hope. And He calls us to do the same in our lives—to glorify God as we point people to Him. "Let your light shine before others, so that they may see your good works and give glory to your Father who is in heaven" (Matthew 5:16).

How can we glorify God in our lives?

DON'T FORGET TO PRAY AND HAVE A GREAT DAY!

 **THINGS TO PRAY FOR TODAY:**

Day 145

Today's Reading:
Matthew 15:32–39

More than enough. It is interesting to me that in both this event and in the telling of the feeding of the 5,000 (Matthew 14), the gospel writers make a point to tell us that several baskets of leftovers were collected. Why? Why is it important that there was food left over? Is it not spectacular enough that Jesus fed thousands with a very small quantity of food? While I don't pretend to understand exactly why God chose to include this detail in the telling of these events, there is one thought that comes to my mind. Jesus certainly could have turned the small amount of food into just enough so that everyone was filled and satisfied without one morsel remaining, but He didn't. He created an abundance of food, more than enough, maybe to make the point that He is not only able to meet our needs but that He can bless us with abundantly more than our needs require. If Jesus can feed thousands with a few loaves and fishes and have baskets of leftovers to spare, surely there can be no limit to the blessings that He can provide in our lives (see Ephesians 3:20-21).

How has God blessed your life abundantly?

DON'T FORGET TO PRAY AND HAVE A GREAT DAY!

⏳ THINGS TO PRAY FOR TODAY:

Day 146

 Today's Reading:
Matthew 16:1–4

T he ironic thing about the request of the Pharisees and Sadducees in this passage is that Jesus' ministry had been full of signs (we have read about many of them lately). On a daily basis, Jesus displayed power over the elements, the human body, and even life itself in ways that were not possible by human means. He had proven, over and over, that He was the Holy One of God. The problem was that these Jewish leaders simply refused to see the signs. They refused to allow themselves to believe that Jesus was who He claimed to be. They wanted something greater, something unmistakable. They wanted Jesus to bow to their will and provide a sign that was grand enough to be worthy of their belief. But Jesus refused. He refused to offer them any sign other than the sign of Jonah, that He would spend three days in the earth as Jonah did in the belly of the great fish, and then be raised to life once more. May God help us to "see the signs" and believe in the Lord Jesus with all of our hearts, giving our lives fully to Him.

What "signs" do you see in the life of Christ that help you believe?

DON'T FORGET TO PRAY AND HAVE A GREAT DAY!

 ⏳ **THINGS TO PRAY FOR TODAY:**

Day 147

Today's Reading:
Matthew 16:5–12

Confusing the spiritual with the physical. It was a common problem with the apostles. Like us, they tended to let the physical world they lived in dominate their thinking and focus. They struggled to properly understand Jesus and His teaching because of this worldly-mindedness. When Jesus spoke of the leaven of the Pharisees and Sadducees, their minds immediately went to physical bread for that was the physical understanding of leaven and its use. By bringing up the feeding of the 5,000 and 4,000, Jesus reminds them of His ability to meet their need for bread with abundance, thus negating any cause for concern over those things. The leaven that He was warning them about was spiritual in nature. It was the ungodly influence of the Jewish leaders who had turned the law of Moses into something to be used for their own purposes and gain. Today, our concern is not with the Pharisees or Sadducees, but with any number of people who would, in the name of religion, twist and corrupt the word of God into something that will only lead us away from Him. Like the apostles, we must beware of their leaven (influence) and its potentially devastating effect on our lives.

What can we do to protect ourselves from negative influences?

DON'T FORGET TO PRAY AND HAVE A GREAT DAY!

 THINGS TO PRAY FOR TODAY:

DAY 148

Today's Reading:
Mark 8:22–26

T his is a curious miracle in that the blind man was not totally healed by Jesus' initial action. The obvious question is: Why? The answer to this query is not given in the text, but it has been suggested by many that Jesus healed this man in stages in order to demonstrate His full power over the healing, to heal partially or completely. Jesus was fully in control of what He did and of what the results were going to be. It has also been suggested that He may have healed this man in this way in order to build his faith—partially at first to strengthen the blind man's faith in Jesus' power, then fully to validate and further build his faith. Whatever Jesus' purpose might have been, one thing is for sure: as always, Jesus showed compassion and demonstrated great power in helping this blind man to see clearly. He always knows exactly what we need and how best to provide for us—not only to meet our physical needs, but to strengthen and build us up spiritually. What an awesome Savior!

What encouragement do you receive from this passage?

DON'T FORGET TO PRAY AND HAVE A GREAT DAY!

⏳ **THINGS TO PRAY FOR TODAY:**

Day 149

 Today's Reading:
Matthew 16:13–20

This passage marks a turning point in Jesus' ministry and in His relationship with the apostles. It also reveals to us the vital importance of our belief in and confession of Jesus Christ. "Who do people say that the Son of Man is?" It was a simple question that led to a great confession of faith. After giving several different ideas that men had about who Jesus was, Peter says with confidence, "You are the Christ, the Son of the living God." It is that great truth confessed by Peter that Jesus says would be the foundation of His church. It is that same confession of faith that each believer is asked to make before becoming a child of God. There is power in that confession. If one does not believe in Jesus as the Son of God, then he will not take advantage of the saving power of Jesus' shed blood, and therefore cannot have the forgiveness and salvation that He offers. If one is not willing to make that confession of faith in Christ, then he, as we have read recently, will be denied by Christ before the Father. Oh, that we all might be fully convinced of Christ and have the courage to confess Him before men.

Why is our willingness to confess Christ so important?

DON'T FORGET TO PRAY AND HAVE A GREAT DAY!

 THINGS TO PRAY FOR TODAY:

Day 150

 **Today's Reading:
Matthew 16:21-28**

Jesus' words in vv. 24-26 are challenging. Discipleship is not easy, and it is not cheap. It requires conviction, sacrifice, and commitment. In order to be a true disciple of Jesus, we must be willing to put Him first, walk away from the world, and devote ourselves to Him completely. That does not mean, however, that we do not continue to live in the world or be a part of it. Therein lies the difficulty. Discipleship demands that, even while living in this world, we die to ourselves and allow Christ to direct our lives. Conforming to His will must affect every aspect of life, from work to family, to social activities, to relationships. Why would or should we make that kind of commitment? Because there is nothing that this world holds that is more valuable, precious, or permanent than our eternal souls. It is that truth that prompts Jesus' powerful questions: "For what will it profit a man if he gains the whole world and forfeits his soul? Or what shall a man give in return for his soul?" The blessing and reward of giving our lives to Christ is the wonderful relationship that we enjoy with God and the blessed assurance of knowing that our soul is eternally safe in His hands.

Why does discipleship require such strong commitment?

DON'T FORGET TO PRAY AND HAVE A GREAT DAY!

⏳ **THINGS TO PRAY FOR TODAY:**

Day 151

 Today's Reading:
Matthew 17:1–13

L isten to Him!" This command of God concerning His Son was brief but full of meaning and power. As Jesus stood, transfigured before them, talking with Moses, the giver of the law, and Elijah, the greatest of the prophets, Peter, James, and John must have been overwhelmed with awe at the great site before them. Their response, worded by Peter, was the suggestion that they build three tabernacles, giving equal honor and allegiance to each. God's response was that Jesus was His Son and worthy of their undivided devotion. To the Jews (which the apostles were), there was no one greater than Moses, the friend of God and great lawgiver. Among the prophets, no one was exalted in their minds as was Elijah. But God makes it abundantly clear to them that His Son was greater than either Moses or Elijah. No longer was Moses' law to be their guide. No longer were the prophets to be their basis of belief. They now had the Son of God Himself, and it was He that they were to hear and follow. The same is true for us today. There is no teaching, no creed, and no philosophy that is to come before, or even stand on common ground with, the teachings of Christ.

Why is it important that we place Christ above all other teachers?

DON'T FORGET TO PRAY AND HAVE A GREAT DAY!

 **THINGS TO PRAY FOR TODAY:**

Day 152

Today's Reading:
Mark 9:14–29

Though there are many lessons to be learned from this text, I would like to focus on one statement made by the father of the possessed boy. "I believe; help my unbelief!" What a beautiful statement both of faith and of his struggle with faith. He believed. He had brought his son to Jesus for healing. He had trusted in Jesus' power over the demon that was afflicting his child. But he struggled. He struggled to believe that his son could really be freed from the evil spirit's grasp and made whole. He struggled to trust that the nightmare that his family had been living could really come to an end. He had faith, but he needed for that faith to be strengthened. The thing that impresses me most about this man is the brutal honesty with which he responds to Jesus. How many of us can relate to this man and his struggles? We trust God. We know that He hears our prayers and answers according to His will. We know that He knows exactly what we need and when we need it. We know that He loves us and is caring for us. Yet we worry, we question, we struggle. Lord, we believe. Help our unbelief!

What can we do to help overcome our struggles with faith?

DON'T FORGET TO PRAY AND HAVE A GREAT DAY!

⏳ **THINGS TO PRAY FOR TODAY:**

Day 153

 Today's Reading:
Mark 9:30–32

We are reminded in this passage of the ultimate purpose of Jesus' life in this world. While He came to show us God, to do good, and to leave an example that we might follow, He came ultimately to offer Himself as an atoning sacrifice on the cross. Even while in the midst of the demands of His daily ministry, His eventual death and resurrection was never far from His mind. As that time grew ever closer, Jesus began to try to prepare His apostles for it. On this occasion, He avoids the crowds in order to spend some private time with those closest to Him in order to teach them about His coming sacrifice. He wants them to understand. He wants them to be prepared. He wants them to find comfort in the fact that His death, while harsh and brutal, would not be final. Unfortunately, the apostles were not yet ready to understand, and Jesus would have to continue to patiently prepare them for His coming death.

*Why do you think the apostles did not
understand what Jesus was telling them?*

DON'T FORGET TO PRAY AND HAVE A GREAT DAY!

⏳ THINGS TO PRAY FOR TODAY:

DAY 154

Today's Reading:
Matthew 17:24–27

Jesus, here, teaches us a valuable lesson concerning our relationships and influence on others. As the Son of God, He was not obligated to pay the temple tax. He had every right to refuse. But lest He cause offense to the Jewish leaders, He paid the tax with the coin that was miraculously placed in the mouth of the fish that He instructed Peter to go catch. So often, we are prone to passionately defend our rights and do so regardless of the effect that our stance might have on others. When we adopt this mindset, our "rights" become more important than someone else's well-being, and possibly their soul. Certainly, there are times when our faithfulness to God depends on our standing up for what is right and putting God's will above all else. But there are many times when proper discretion would urge us to put aside our rights, such as Jesus did, in order to avoid the negative influence of offense. As Paul would later write: "'All things are lawful,' but not all things are helpful; 'all things are lawful,' but not all things build up" (1 Corinthians 10:23).

Why should we be concerned about
offending others with our "rights"?

DON'T FORGET TO PRAY AND HAVE A GREAT DAY!

 THINGS TO PRAY FOR TODAY:

DAY 155

 Today's Reading:
Matthew 18:1-6

C hildren are special, not only in our eyes, but also in the eyes of God. They possess traits that God desires for all of us to have in our lives. Their innocence, honesty, forgiving nature, and joy are all characteristics that we should aspire to. But there is one child-like quality that stands above the others. Jesus says, "Whoever humbles himself like this child is the greatest in the kingdom of heaven." As humans, we come into this world in humility. We have nothing of our own and can do nothing for ourselves. Children readily accept that dependence on their parents, and in their relationships with others, they are willing to share, serve, and quickly forgive. Oh, that we could become more like little children, recognizing and accepting our dependence upon our heavenly Father and being willing to share with and serve those around us. Only in this humility can we hope to find greatness in the kingdom of heaven.

Why is humility such an important trait of the Christian life?

DON'T FORGET TO PRAY AND HAVE A GREAT DAY!

 THINGS TO PRAY FOR TODAY:

Day 156

Today's Reading:
Mark 9:33–37

T his passage is parallel to yesterday's reading, but Mark gives us a little more background information. The apostles' query recorded in Matthew 18:1, "Who is the greatest in the kingdom of heaven?" was motivated by their debate on which of them would be the greatest, and by the implied desire of each of them to be in that position. The desire to be great is a common one among people. We like the idea of being prominent, sought after, influential, and admired. It is a goal that many spend their lives chasing after. But Jesus teaches the vital lesson that, with God, greatness means service. One who is great is not served by others, but is himself a servant. Contrary to the thinking of the world, the person who would be great in the eyes of God must clothe himself with humility and put others before himself. In this way, we become more like God and His Son and fulfill His will in our lives, thus becoming great in His kingdom. May God help us all to be great by being servants.

Why is God so concerned with our being servants?

DON'T FORGET TO PRAY AND HAVE A GREAT DAY!

 THINGS TO PRAY FOR TODAY:

Day 157

Today's Reading:
Matthew 18:7-9

Jesus, in this passage, drives home a point that is largely lost in our world—the horrible nature and danger of sin. In our world, the concept of sin has been minimized or illegitimized to the point that we are often no longer to call any action sin, regardless of how reprehensible it is. Permissiveness and tolerance have replaced righteousness and faithfulness. But Jesus' words are still as true now as when He spoke them. He came to rescue us from sin, but it continues to threaten us. Sin is dangerous, destructive, and deadly. It is pervasive and if allowed, will invade our lives and take us away from God. Therefore, Jesus says, we must constantly be on guard against falling into sin and against leading others into its path. Avoid it all cost, Jesus says, for the price of sin is far too high.

Why do you think that the world
doesn't see the horrible nature of sin?

DON'T FORGET TO PRAY AND HAVE A GREAT DAY!

 THINGS TO PRAY FOR TODAY:

Day 158

 Today's Reading:
Mark 9:38-41

There is a good bit of curiosity attached to this passage. Who was this man of whom John spoke, and how could he cast out demons? While we do not know the answer to these questions, there are some things that we can assume. He was a follower of Christ. "He was not following us" does not mean that he was not a disciple of Christ, but that he did not accompany the apostles in their daily following of Christ. This man obviously believed in and followed Christ; otherwise, he would have no ability to cast out demons miraculously. It has been suggested that John reacted as he did largely out of a sense of jealousy, thinking that no one but those closest to Jesus should be able to do such things. This passage comes right on the heels of the teaching of Jesus that those who wanted to be great should be servants. There is no room in the service of Jesus for jealousy, envy, or prideful arrogance. We all have a place within the body of Christ and are called to use our gifts to His glory. All who are faithful to Christ are on the same side—a sentiment worded by Jesus like this: "For the one who is not against us is for us."

Why do you think we sometimes become envious of others?

DON'T FORGET TO PRAY AND HAVE A GREAT DAY!

 THINGS TO PRAY FOR TODAY:

Day 159

 Today's Reading:
Mark 9:49-50

These verses are difficult and have perplexed many interpreters throughout the centuries. Therefore, any attempt to apply them is speculation to some degree. That being said, it seems to me, given the context of the statements, that Jesus is here giving the reason for such a strong stance against sin in vv. 42-48. Every life, He says, will be seasoned (salted) with fire. The fire that He refers to, I believe, are the temptations and trials of life that God allows for the purpose of purifying and preserving our souls. While we may not enjoy those challenges in life, Jesus says that "salt is good." But if the salt has lost its potency (i.e. its ability to purify and preserve), then it is useless. If the temptations and trials that are intended to season our lives and prepare us for eternity are met with weakness and yielding, then they have not accomplished God's intended purpose, but have left us in sin and without hope. So accept the "fires" that you encounter in life with courage and strength, for God is using them to prepare you for much greater things in this life and in eternity!

How should we react when faced with a "fire" of life?

DON'T FORGET TO PRAY AND HAVE A GREAT DAY!

 ⏳ **THINGS TO PRAY FOR TODAY:**

Day 160

Today's Reading:
John 7:1–9

Jesus' time had not yet come. He had made the decision to stay in Galilee and not go to Judea because of the determination of the Jews to kill Him. It was not that He was afraid to die, for that was His ultimate purpose. Rather, He did not want the hostility of the Jews to hinder His mission. Prudence demanded that Jesus proceed carefully. On that backdrop, Jesus' earthly brothers make a rare appearance in the gospel account. They are not yet believers in Christ and come to Him, tempting and taunting Him to go to Jerusalem for the Feast of Tabernacles. Their challenge to Him is essentially this: "If you are who you claim to be and desire for people to follow you, then go where the people are. You cannot gain followers by hiding." It occurs to me that people still try to tempt and taunt Christ into giving in to their demands, wanting some show of proof before giving themselves to Him. But just as Jesus was on this occasion, He continues to be constant and uncompromising with us. He gave His all for us and has made clear what He expects if we are to follow after Him. May we be willing to believe in Him and submit to His will for our lives.

Why do you think that Jesus' brothers had
such a difficult time believing in Him?

DON'T FORGET TO PRAY AND HAVE A GREAT DAY!

⏳ **THINGS TO PRAY FOR TODAY:**

Day 161

 Today's Reading:
John 7:10–18

Despite the hostility of the Jews and the prudence of Jesus in traveling to Judea, He does go to Jerusalem for the feast—not in the caravan with his brothers, but privately in His own time and way. While in Jerusalem, He enters the temple and begins to teach, causing many to marvel at His knowledge and skill in discussing the Scriptures despite His lack of formal training. His message is a simple one: if anyone has a sincere heart in wanting to do what is right, he will know whether Jesus' teaching is from God or from His own authority. The prophets had pointed to this time and to the coming Messiah. Their words were being fulfilled before the hearers' very eyes in the life and message of Jesus. His desire was not to bring glory to Himself, but rather to God who had sent Him. The same is still true today. Anyone who has a sincere heart in wanting to do what is right can open up the pages of Scripture and find the truth. It is not hard to believe for those who are honestly seeking. May we all be honest and sincere seekers of Truth.

*Why do you think sincerity is an important
quality in accepting the truth?*

DON'T FORGET TO PRAY AND HAVE A GREAT DAY!

 THINGS TO PRAY FOR TODAY:

Day 162

 Today's Reading:
John 7:19-24

As Jesus continues His teaching to the crowd in Jerusalem, He points to the event that was the "final straw" in precipitating the determination of the Jewish leaders to destroy Him—the healing of a lame man on the Sabbath (John 5:1-9). The Jews had manipulated the Law of Moses for their own purposes and had forgotten its true meaning. While they were willing to set aside the Sabbath day restrictions on work for the purpose of keeping the law regarding circumcision, they were unwilling to allow mercy to be shown and a man's body to be healed on that day of rest. It was a hypocritical stance, and one that was unpleasing to God. As we seek to apply the law of Christ to our own lives and teaching, we must beware of the lessons learned from the Pharisees, lest we adopt a similar attitude of staunchly holding to one command while neglecting others. May God help us to approach His Word with a desire to apply and keep it in a way that is pleasing to Him.

Why do you think the Pharisees were unwilling
to allow Jesus' healing on the Sabbath?

DON'T FORGET TO PRAY AND HAVE A GREAT DAY!

⧗ **THINGS TO PRAY FOR TODAY:**

DAY 163

 Today's Reading:
John 7:25–31

This scene—Jesus teaching in the temple during the feast—had created a very volatile situation. There were many different attitudes and mindsets present that day. There were those who questioned the authority and motives of the Jewish leadership: "Why do they not do something? Do they know that He is really the Christ?" There were also those who could not be convinced that Jesus was the Christ: "When the Christ comes, no one will know where He is from." There were those who believed on Him because of the signs (miracles) that He had performed. And then there were the Jewish leaders, whose anger reached a boiling point as they tried to lay hands on Him and take Him—no doubt, to kill Him. But despite all the confusion, all the questions, all the varying opinions and ideas, notice that God's will and purpose still reigned supreme. Why did no one lay a hand on Him? "Because His hour had not yet come." God's plan was for Jesus to die at the appointed time and in the appointed way. This was not it. It continues to be true today that, despite varying attitudes and mindsets regarding Christ, the plan and purpose of God will reign supreme.

Looking forward, what is God's plan and purpose?

DON'T FORGET TO PRAY AND HAVE A GREAT DAY!

 THINGS TO PRAY FOR TODAY:

DAY 164

Today's Reading:
John 7:32–36

It was often the case that Jesus' teachings were confused and misunderstood by those who heard Him because they tried to attach physical understandings to spiritual statements. In this case, it was the Pharisees who were guilty of this mistake. Jesus is referring to His ascension back to the Father that would take place after His death and resurrection. However, the Pharisees, believing Him to be speaking of a physical place where He could not be found, questioned where He might go. In our world today, we see this same confusion and misunderstanding taking place regarding Jesus and His teaching. Many fail to understand the importance or relevance of many New Testament teachings because they are viewing those teachings through physical eyes, instead of spiritual. Through those physical eyes, we might consider Christ's commands to be nonsensical or irrelevant to our lives, but we must understand that God's desire and plan for us is eternal salvation. His commands, while affecting every aspect of our physical lives, are in reality spiritual commands because they have a spiritual purpose. Only through spiritual eyes can we truly understand God's plan and purpose.

How do we learn to look at the Bible through spiritual eyes?

DON'T FORGET TO PRAY AND HAVE A GREAT DAY!

 THINGS TO PRAY FOR TODAY:

Day 165

 Today's Reading:
John 7:37–39

We are not left to wonder about the meaning of Jesus' words in this short passage, as the inspired writer reveals their meaning to us. This "living water" that Jesus promises to those who believe in Him is the Holy Spirit that would be given after Jesus was glorified (i.e. resurrected and ascended back to the Father). That prophetic statement was fulfilled beginning in Acts 2 when the Spirit came upon the Apostles, leading them into all truth and giving them miraculous abilities to spread that message to the world. Many first-century Christians were also granted a miraculous measure of the Spirit's power to ensure a proper instruction and understanding of God's will. But all of that was working toward an even greater gift of the Spirit—one that would be available to all of mankind and would be able to lead any open and receptive heart to salvation in Christ. That gift, of course, is God's holy Word, given by the inspiration of the Spirit, and through its teachings, we have access to all of God's blessings. What a wonderful gift!

Why is God's Word so valuable to us today?

DON'T FORGET TO PRAY AND HAVE A GREAT DAY!

 THINGS TO PRAY FOR TODAY:

Day 166

 Today's Reading:
John 7:40–44

Confusion. It is an unexpected reaction to Jesus. It wasn't that they were confused about His teaching, but rather what His teaching said about who He was. Some were convinced by the authority and wisdom of His teaching that He was the Christ, the promised One of the Old Testament. Others, who knew the prophecies but did not know Jesus, objected because they did not believe Him to be a fulfillment of those prophecies. Ironically, they were correct in stating what the prophets had foretold, but they were wrong in assuming that Jesus was from Galilee. He had been born in Bethlehem, and He was from the lineage of David, just as the prophets had promised. In fact, of more than 300 Old Testament prophecies concerning the coming Messiah, Jesus would fulfill every single one. He was a perfect match for the picture of the Messiah that the prophets painted throughout the Old Testament Scriptures. So convincing was this evidence that, throughout the New Testament, the apostles and other writers continually point to those fulfilled prophecies as proof of the legitimacy of Christ. Jesus is the Christ and, about that, there should be no doubt or confusion.

How do the Old Testament prophecies prove that Jesus is the Christ?

DON'T FORGET TO PRAY AND HAVE A GREAT DAY!

 ⏳ **THINGS TO PRAY FOR TODAY:**

DAY 167

Today's Reading:
John 7:45–52

Nicodemus is an interesting character and a case-study in the development of faith. We first meet him in John 3 where he comes to Jesus by night. He believed that Jesus was special and from God but was struggling to understand exactly who He was. He came by night, presumably, for fear that his fellow Pharisees would discover his fondness for and growing faith in Jesus. In this text, we see Nicodemus challenging his own brethren over their treatment of Jesus. While defending Jesus to some extent, he is very careful to appear to be neutral and simply trying to uphold the law. While still not fully given to Christ, he is convinced enough to withstand his peers on Jesus' behalf. We will see Nicodemus one more time in John's gospel accounts—with Joseph of Arimathea, preparing the crucified and lifeless body of Jesus for burial. Though their actions were taken at night, they were sure to be found out. Nicodemus' faith had grown to a point that it could no longer be withheld. He was a disciple of Christ, and he was willing to risk his position and possibly his life to serve his Lord.

What lessons can we learn from the example of Nicodemus?

DON'T FORGET TO PRAY AND HAVE A GREAT DAY!

 THINGS TO PRAY FOR TODAY:

DAY 168

 Today's Reading:
John 8:2-11

T his story is a familiar example of Jesus' compassion and mercy, but it is also a great example of His wisdom in dealing with the schemes of the Jewish leaders. They had brought this woman to Him as a trap, that they might have a reason to accuse Him of some wrongdoing. Though there is little doubt that she was guilty of the sin of adultery, she was but a pawn in their game—bait by which they hoped to snag the Master Teacher. But Jesus easily saw through their façade. As they were ready to put her to death for her sins, He reminds them of their own transgressions which place each of them in violation of the law just as she was. They have no choice but to walk away, convicted by their own sins. But what of the woman? Did Jesus excuse her sinfulness? Did He ignore her wrongdoing? Not at all! His simple statement to her, "Go and sin no more," was both a condemnation of her actions and a demonstration of God's mercy toward sinners. He gave her another chance, just as God does with us each time we fail to be obedient to Him. Thanks be to God for His loving mercy toward us!

What practical lessons can we learn from this event in Jesus' life?

DON'T FORGET TO PRAY AND HAVE A GREAT DAY!

 ⌛ **THINGS TO PRAY FOR TODAY:**

Day 169

 Today's Reading:
John 8:12–20

You know neither Me nor My Father." Think for a moment about the severity of that accusation. He is speaking to the Pharisees, the religious leaders of the day. They were revered and looked up to by the Jewish people as the most righteous among them. They held themselves up as the most spiritual representatives of the Jewish faith. But Jesus accuses them of not even knowing God. They had become so steeped in their own traditions and self-righteousness that they had forgotten who God was. They had no real understanding of Him. God had been replaced in their minds and lives by a set of stringent rules and traditions that reigned supreme. The law had become more precious to them than the God who had given it to them. Even when Jesus came, showing them God in the flesh, they did not recognize Him and rejected Him as God's promised Messiah. Like so many of these texts, this one reminds us of the danger of losing sight of God in our lives. As we daily examine the life of Jesus, let us see God and know Him more and more each day.

What are some things that we can learn about God through Jesus?

DON'T FORGET TO PRAY AND HAVE A GREAT DAY!

 THINGS TO PRAY FOR TODAY:

Day 170

Today's Reading:
John 8:21–30

M uch of this extended passage is concerned with those who did not believe in Jesus, and who were looking to accuse, condemn and destroy Him. But in this passage, there is one short statement that reminds us of the other side of that coin. "As He was saying these things, many believed in Him." Despite those influential leaders who were set against Jesus, there were a great many people who believed in Him. They had seen His compassionate power. They had heard His authoritative teaching. They had witnessed His flawless character. They were convinced that He was who He claimed to be, the Son of God. In spite of the naysayers and unbelievers, they sincerely and fervently believed in Jesus Christ. What is the lesson for us? In a world that is still full of naysayers and unbelievers, the truth of Jesus Christ is still changing lives. There continue to be people who can and will believe in Him and have their lives changed through Him. Jesus Christ *is* the Son of God, and He is still changing lives!

How does Jesus change the lives of those who believe in Him?

DON'T FORGET TO PRAY AND HAVE A GREAT DAY!

⏳ **THINGS TO PRAY FOR TODAY:**

DAY 171

 Today's Reading:
John 8:31–36

Freedom. As Americans, freedom is paramount. We are well aware of the great price that has been paid, and continues to be paid, to gain and maintain it. We cannot fathom life without the freedom to believe and live as we desire. In reality, freedom is a concept that is vital to all of mankind. No one wants to be enslaved, whether to a tyrannical government, a debilitating disease, or some other controlling influence. However, what the majority of the world does not understand is that all of mankind has been conquered and is controlled by sin. None are immune. We are all slaves of sin. But Jesus offers freedom; a greater freedom than any person, government, or philosophy can offer. He offers to set us free from sin, to deliver us from the grasp of Satan and save us from certain death. Jesus says that, if you want to be free from sin and its devastating consequences, the truth can set you free. What is that truth? It is the good news of Jesus Christ.

How does the truth set us free from sin?

DON'T FORGET TO PRAY AND HAVE A GREAT DAY!

⏳ **THINGS TO PRAY FOR TODAY:**

DAY 172

Today's Reading:
John 8:37–47

Can you imagine how offensive Jesus' statements must have been to this Jewish audience? They took great pride in being from Abraham's seed and God's chosen people. They reveled in this relationship with God that was theirs alone. But Jesus makes the assertion that they are not truly children of God, but rather children of the devil. This identity had nothing to do with their lineage or heritage, and everything to do with their hearts and actions. They refused to hear and accept the truth brought to them from the Father by Jesus. They refused to believe on Him who had been promised and prophesied about for centuries and who now stood before them. They were filled with envy and hatred toward Him, propagated lies about Him, and harbored thoughts of murder in their hearts. It was these attitudes and actions that Jesus used to identify them and condemn them as children of the devil. The obvious application for us is found in the question, "Who is our father?" Are we children of God, made such by our faith and obedience to the truth of His word? Or are we children of the devil, following after his ways of ungodliness and sin? We each have the choice. May we choose God!

What is involved in being a child of God?

DON'T FORGET TO PRAY AND HAVE A GREAT DAY!

⏳ **THINGS TO PRAY FOR TODAY:**

Day 173

 Today's Reading:
John 8:48–59

B efore Abraham was, I AM." It is the climactic point in this discussion with the Jews and the most forthright statement that Jesus makes concerning His deity. Throughout this conversation, Jesus had tried unsuccessfully to convince the Jews that He was sent from the Father and that His relationship with the Father was special and unique. Their hearts were too hard, and their minds were too closed. As they continued to question and accuse Him, Jesus finally makes a statement that cannot be misunderstood. Notice that He doesn't say, "I was," but rather "I AM" after the fashion of the name that God told Moses to use in identifying Him to the Israelites (Exodus 3:14). It was a term that denoted every perfect quality of God, including His eternal and transcendent existence. It was reserved only for God. In applying that term to Himself, Jesus had unequivocally claimed to be deity, and that claim was one that the Jewish leaders could not accept. They had the accusation they had been looking for—blasphemy. The battle lines were drawn, and the stage was set...

Why do you think the Jews could not accept that Jesus was deity?

DON'T FORGET TO PRAY AND HAVE A GREAT DAY!

THINGS TO PRAY FOR TODAY:

Day 174

 Today's Reading:
John 9:1–12

It was commonly believed in that day and time that suffering, such as this man's blindness, was the result and consequence of sin. The disciples were thus perplexed about this man's condition because he had been blind from birth. How could sin have caused his blindness, unless of course it was his parents' sin that had been visited upon him. In answering their query, Jesus teaches them, and us, a very important lesson. While it is true that suffering, hardship, and adversity originally entered this world because of sin (Genesis 3), we must understand that our suffering is not always due to our sins. While there are times when one's sinful choices will bring about negative consequences, there are also many times (e.g. natural disasters, disease, accidents) when our suffering is simply a natural function of our physical world and has no connection whatsoever to our sins. But another important lesson to remember is that, as with this man, our suffering offers opportunities for us to be strengthened and for God to be glorified. Even in our suffering, God is in charge and is worthy of our faith and praise!

How have you grown from your own sufferings?

DON'T FORGET TO PRAY AND HAVE A GREAT DAY!

⏳ THINGS TO PRAY FOR TODAY:

DAY 175

 Today's Reading:
John 9:13–23

I t is amazing to see the hard-hearted refusal of the Pharisees to weigh the evidence and recognize the power and authority of Jesus. They question the healed man, doubted his truthfulness, and even brought his parents before them to testify. But in spite of the overwhelming proof demonstrated by this man's healing, they still refused to believe. Why? What was it that stood in the way of them believing in Jesus and giving themselves to Him? The gospel accounts spell out clearly the issues that prevented the Pharisees from believing—jealousy, pride, envy, and a dogged determination to maintain their positions of authority within the Jewish system. Their desire for prominence and achievement had taken precedence over the plan of God. Sadly, there are many who fall into that same trap today—those who do not obey the teachings of Christ in the New Testament because they refuse to give up their own desires. May we never have that mindset, but rather submit to the will of God as revealed in His holy Word.

Why do you think the Pharisees had
such a hard time accepting Christ?

DON'T FORGET TO PRAY AND HAVE A GREAT DAY!

 THINGS TO PRAY FOR TODAY:

DAY 176

Today's Reading:
John 9:24-34

I f this Man were not from God, He could do nothing." This great expression of truth is not made by the educated, trained, revered leaders of the Jews. It is made by an uneducated, untrained man who, until very recently, had been blind. He was not a theologian, scribe, or prophet. He was simply a man who had experienced the power of God and who recognized that the man through whom that power had been displayed was obviously a Man sent from God. It was a simple conclusion of logic. This was constantly the case with Jesus. His works continually gave testimony to His identity. How could He be anything but One sent from God, considering the great works of power that He displayed? So telling was the testimony and conclusion of the healed man that the Pharisees could do nothing but dismiss him, having him cast out. They had made up their minds about Jesus and no amount of evidence, no matter how convincing, would change them. They had once and for all rejected Jesus as the Christ.

How did Jesus' works prove His identity?

DON'T FORGET TO PRAY AND HAVE A GREAT DAY!

⏳ THINGS TO PRAY FOR TODAY:

DAY 177

 Today's Reading:
John 9:35–41

T he blind receive their sight, and the seeing are made blind. This man, born blind, was made to see by the power of Christ. For the first time in his life, he could see— the vibrant colors of the world around him, the beauty of nature, the faces of his loved ones. His life was changed, made immensely better by a compassionate Lord that he did not yet know. But the other side of this story is not so happy. When presented with this healing—irrefutable proof of Jesus' power and authority—the Pharisees, blinded by their own disbelief and hatred for Jesus, refused to see. They doubted, they questioned, they accused, but they would not allow themselves to believe. Their failure to recognize the Messiah, despite the many proofs of Jesus' identity, is a sad testament to their hard-heartedness and blindness. Represented in this contrast of lives is all of mankind. We all will fall into one of these two categories. We will either be healed by the power of Christ and made spiritually whole, or we will refuse Him and be made blind to His power, authority, and Lordship. The choice is ours.

How do we make this great choice concerning Christ?

DON'T FORGET TO PRAY AND HAVE A GREAT DAY!

⏳ **THINGS TO PRAY FOR TODAY:**

DAY 178

Today's Reading:
John 10:1-6

T he thing that is most striking to me about this passage is the familiarity and relationship that Jesus speaks of between Himself and His followers. The sheep, He says, will hear and recognize the shepherd's voice and follow Him. They know the shepherd. They trust Him. They follow Him, knowing that he has their best interest in mind. Likewise, the shepherd knows the sheep. He calls them by name, indicating that there is an individual knowledge of each sheep. He cares for them, provides for them, and protects them. What a beautiful picture of Christ's care for those who are His. While we are certainly aware of the atoning death of Christ, we often overlook the deep level of daily care and concern that He has for each one who wears His name. He is our shepherd, knowing us individually and perfectly, and desiring to lead us to places of unmatched spiritual blessings. What is our responsibility? To follow Him! To listen to His voice, submit to His leadership, and trust Him to lead us in the way that we should go. If we will be faithful sheep, then we will reap the benefits of a caring relationship with the great Shepherd!

What is involved in being faithful sheep of Christ?

DON'T FORGET TO PRAY AND HAVE A GREAT DAY!

⌛ THINGS TO PRAY FOR TODAY:

Day 179

 Today's Reading:
John 10:7–10

I n this "I am" statement, Jesus describes Himself as the door of the sheep. He is the means of entrance to the Father. As He will later say, "No one comes to the Father except through Me" (John 14:6). He contrasts Himself to those who've come before Him, calling them thieves and robbers. Some have thought Him to be referring to "false messiahs," those who have come before Him claiming to be the promised savior. Others have understood Him to be referring to many of the Jewish leaders of the day who, while playing the part of religious leader, had pursued only their own interests. Whoever they may have been, these "thieves and robbers" had only sought to lead people away from God and rob them of their salvation. But Jesus came to give life. He came to open the door to God and salvation for any who would enter it. And 2,000 years later, He continues to be that open door. He is still the only way to God and to heaven, and He still stands waiting to lead His sheep into eternity.

Why is Jesus the only way to God?

DON'T FORGET TO PRAY AND HAVE A GREAT DAY!

⏳ **THINGS TO PRAY FOR TODAY:**

Day 180

Today's Reading:
John 10:11–16

What is the difference between an owner and a hired hand? An unconscientious hired hand only cares about getting the job done and receiving his pay. The owner, on the other hand, cares about that which he owns. He is invested. He is interested in the well-being of his property and is willing to go the extra mile to make sure that it is protected and cared for. Jesus uses this analogy to help us understand His relationship with His sheep. He is not a hireling—one who has no real concern for the well-being of the sheep and is unwilling to sacrifice for them. Rather, as the owner of the sheep, He knows them by name, cares for them, and has indeed given His life for them. It is sad that so many people in the world see Christ as an unsympathetic, impersonal, heavy-handed Lord who makes unreasonable demands of His followers and has little or no personal interest in their salvation. He is, in fact, the good shepherd. His love and concern for us, His sheep, is great and overwhelming. What a privilege it is to be able to give our lives to a Lord who has already given Himself for us!

Why do you think Jesus cares so much for us?

DON'T FORGET TO PRAY AND HAVE A GREAT DAY!

 THINGS TO PRAY FOR TODAY:

Day 181

 Today's Reading:
John 10:17–21

J esus' statements in this passage are vitally important. He came to be the atoning sacrifice for our sins, but if his life is taken from Him against His will, it cannot be considered a sacrifice. It was in that voluntary shedding of His blood that He became the perfect Lamb of God offered for the sins of the world. If He was to be the fulfillment of the Old Testament prophecies, if He was to exhibit the authority of God as His Son, if He was to be the atoning sacrifice that He was purposed to be, it was crucial that He lay down His own life, and that it not be forcefully taken from Him. While the gospel accounts of the crucifixion seem to show a picture of the Jewish leaders and Romans both taking part in forcefully and wrongfully taking Jesus' life from Him, it is important to remember that He was never an unwilling party in those proceedings. He had the ability to change the course of those events at any time (Matthew 26:53), but chose to go to the cross for us. His death was truly a sacrifice!

Why was it so important that Jesus' death be voluntary?

DON'T FORGET TO PRAY AND HAVE A GREAT DAY!

 THINGS TO PRAY FOR TODAY:

Day 182

 Today's Reading:
Luke 9:51–56

H is face was set toward Jerusalem." Don't underestimate the meaning and importance of this statement. For some time, Jesus had focused His ministry on the area of Galilee and had avoided Jerusalem, but the time was drawing near for God's plan of redemption to be accomplished. The purpose of Jesus going to Jerusalem was to die, to become the lamb of God and offer Himself as a perfect, spotless sacrifice for the sins of the world. It would be, from a physical standpoint, the most difficult, agonizing, and torturous event of His life. But spiritually speaking, it would be the most powerful and effectual act ever witnessed. Despite the great physical suffering that Jesus knew was before Him, the spiritual benefit was worth the sacrifice, and so He set His face toward Jerusalem. He resolved to go there and would not be turned aside. He was determined to see God's plan carried out, even through His own sacrifice. His commitment to His Father's will was absolute, and His love for us was overwhelming. What a great testament to the greatness of Jesus' love and sacrifice.

Why might this journey to Jerusalem have been difficult for Jesus?

DON'T FORGET TO PRAY AND HAVE A GREAT DAY!

⏳ **THINGS TO PRAY FOR TODAY:**

Day 183

Today's Reading:
Luke 9:57–62

Wherever Jesus went, He attracted great crowds and much attention. He displayed power and authority in an unprecedented way. For some, therefore, the idea of following Christ must have seemed a glamorous position of prominence and renown. For others, following Christ was viewed as a hindrance to their daily lives and routines, and something that could easily be put off. In this passage, Jesus warns against both of these attitudes and stresses the importance, commitment, and urgency of following Him. A life of following Christ is truly a life full of blessings and joy. It is the best and most abundant life imaginable. While following Christ should never be viewed as a burden, it is a life that requires a great deal of commitment. As followers of Christ, we must be willing to put Him above all else, be faithful to Him in any circumstance, and allow Him to rule our lives daily. It is indeed the best of all lives, for those who are willing to make the commitment!

Why does following Christ require such commitment?

DON'T FORGET TO PRAY AND HAVE A GREAT DAY!

 THINGS TO PRAY FOR TODAY:

Day 184

Today's Reading:
Matthew 11:20-24

While we do not know a great deal about Jesus' activities in these towns, especially Chorazin and Bethsaida, there are two things that we can know for sure from this text: 1) Jesus had performed many great works in those places as a testament to His identity and power, and 2) Despite those works, these cities had remained hard-hearted and unrepentant, rejecting Jesus as the Son of God. The cities mentioned in comparison to those that Jesus had spent time in were among the most wicked and reviled of the Old Testament—cities filled with idol worship, immorality and ungodliness. But Jesus makes the cutting remark that, if those cities had been witness to His mighty works, they would have repented. These cities in which Jesus did much of His ministering work had been blessed with a great advantage and opportunity. They had been eyewitnesses to the power of God and had heard first-hand the truth from the Master Teacher. They were without excuse for not receiving Him and following Him. Much the same can be said of us. Christ has been revealed to us through God's holy Word in such a way that we are also without excuse if we fail to come to Him!

Why do you think so many refuse to believe in Jesus?

DON'T FORGET TO PRAY AND HAVE A GREAT DAY!

⏳ **THINGS TO PRAY FOR TODAY:**

Day 185

Today's Reading:
Matthew 11:28–30

Who a beautiful invitation! To those who are burdened, weary, and straining under the weight of their load, Jesus offers rest—relief from the hopelessness and despair of sin, rescue from the fear and dread of judgment, respite from the labors and struggles of life. He offers to help, comfort, strengthen, and bless us in ways that only He can. But there is a provision involved in that invitation. Our part is to take on His yoke, to allow Him to guide and direct our lives according to His will, to submit ourselves to His control. What He is truly asking is that we exchange one yoke for another. The one is the yoke placed on us by the world and Satan, a yoke that is heavy and burdensome, bound to us by sin. It is difficult, tiresome to bear, and ultimately destructive. But the yoke that Jesus offers in exchange is a yoke that is bound with love. It is light and easy. It always has our best interest in mind and ultimately leads to eternal life. What an amazing opportunity we have been given to escape the burdensome yoke of sin and find rest in the caring yoke of Christ!

Why is it important that we put on the yoke of Christ?

DON'T FORGET TO PRAY AND HAVE A GREAT DAY!

 THINGS TO PRAY FOR TODAY:

Day 186

Today's Reading:
Luke 10:1–12

There are many aspects of this event that are important and teach us valuable lessons about our own discipleship. But I want to focus on just one in this thought. Why did Jesus place such rigid restrictions on those He was sending out regarding the things they would carry with them, and how they would approach and interact with people along the way? While many suggestions might be offered, I believe Jesus was essentially trying to accomplish two things: 1) He wanted them to learn a dependence upon God instead of trusting in things. To approach this mission without "necessities" would have been a daunting task, but would teach them the great lesson that, as they put their trust in God, He would provide all that they needed. 2) He wanted them to avoid the distractions that often come with worldly desires and activities. Their purpose was singular: to go out as laborers in the field to prepare the way for Jesus and to bring in a good harvest for the Lord. Jesus wanted them to be totally focused on that purpose. These same lessons are very relevant for us today. As Christians, we are laborers for the Lord. May God help us work diligently for His harvest.

What are some of the things that often distract us from our mission?

DON'T FORGET TO PRAY AND HAVE A GREAT DAY!

⏳ THINGS TO PRAY FOR TODAY:

DAY 187

 Today's Reading:
Luke 10:17–20

Obviously, the seventy had followed Jesus' instructions, and their faith and faithfulness had been rewarded by their great success, demonstrated even in the ability to cast out demons. This power over demons seen in Jesus' disciples was a sign of the coming downfall of Satan that Jesus would accomplish through His death and resurrection. But Jesus' accompanies this rejoicing over their success with a warning. "Do not rejoice in this...but rather rejoice because your names are written in heaven." As with all of us, there was the propensity with these disciples to rejoice in this authority over demons to the point that they would become haughty and arrogant, giving themselves the credit and praise for their abilities, and forgetting the true purpose of their work. Jesus reminds them that they must remain focused on the great blessing of salvation as their source of rejoicing, and in that recognition, be ever committed to sharing that message of salvation with others. What a great lesson for us to remember today!

What kinds of things can cause us to
lose our focus on salvation today?

DON'T FORGET TO PRAY AND HAVE A GREAT DAY!

 ⏳ THINGS TO PRAY FOR TODAY:

DAY 188

 Today's Reading:
Luke 10:21–24

I n this text, we get a rare glimpse into the prayer life of Jesus. This prayer of praise and rejoicing is offered in response to the news of the works performed by the seventy. The redemptive plan of God, long veiled in mystery, was being revealed in a powerful way through the life of Jesus and His followers. Jesus, seemingly overwhelmed by the joy of these great events, pauses to thank and glorify God for His gracious works. He then turns to His disciples to share His joy with them and to remind them of how blessed they are to be in a position to witness these things taking place. For centuries, godly men—kings and prophets, great and small—had hoped for, wondered about, anticipated, and waited for the plan of God to be revealed. Now that plan was being revealed in a powerful way before the disciples' very eyes. Did they know or could they comprehend how blessed they were to be in the presence of the Son of God and to witness God's plan coming to fruition? While you and I weren't there to witness Him in the flesh, we are also very blessed to have that same plan of redemption revealed to us in His word and to be the benefactors of God's love and mercy. Let us rejoice with Christ for the wonderful blessing of salvation through Him!

What kinds of things can cause us to
lose our focus on salvation today?

DON'T FORGET TO PRAY AND HAVE A GREAT DAY!

⏳ **THINGS TO PRAY FOR TODAY:**

Day 189

Today's Reading:
Luke 10:25–27

What does it mean to be a neighbor? In this parable, Jesus illustrates what it means to "love your neighbor as yourself." While the priest and Levite provide disappointing examples of apathy and disregard, the Samaritan gives us a wonderful example of an act of neighborly love. His act of care and concern for the injured stranger was compassionate, selfless, and sacrificial. Though, as a Samaritan, he would have no doubt been looked down on and despised by the injured Jewish man, he disregarded his own convenience and safety to help one who was in need and, in so doing, demonstrated what it means to "love your neighbor as yourself." To love our neighbors as ourselves is still a vital concept in living a life that is pleasing to God. I am reminded of the familiar words of Jesus in another passage: "So whatever you wish that others would do to you, do also to them, for this is the Law and the Prophets" (Matthew 7:12). May we all strive to be a good neighbor to those around us, knowing that it is God's will for our lives, and that we may someday need a neighbor ourselves.

What are some ways we can be a neighbor to those around us?

DON'T FORGET TO PRAY AND HAVE A GREAT DAY!

⌛ THINGS TO PRAY FOR TODAY:

Day 190

 Today's Reading:
Luke 10:38-42

M artha was distracted with much serving." Jesus was a very special guest. Martha was concerned with making sure that everything was just right, that her guests, and especially Jesus, had everything they needed. Meanwhile, her sister, Mary, simply sat at the feet of Jesus, basking in His presence, soaking up every word that He spoke. When Martha asks Jesus to rebuke her sister for not helping serve, Jesus responds with a gentle rebuke for Martha instead: "Martha, Martha, you are anxious and troubled about many things." It is not that Martha was doing anything that was overtly wrong. Her desire and efforts to serve Jesus were commendable, but she had become distracted by those efforts and was missing out on more important things. How often do we make the same mistake? Do we ever find ourselves so busy with all that we have to do, including many good and commendable things, that we forget to stop and just spend time with the Lord through prayer or Bible study? As Jesus says, "One thing is necessary," meaning that there is one thing that is more important than anything else—our relationship with Christ. May we never neglect that most important thing!

What are some things that we can be distracted by today?

DON'T FORGET TO PRAY AND HAVE A GREAT DAY!

⏳ THINGS TO PRAY FOR TODAY:

DAY 191

**Today's Reading:
Luke 11:37–44**

Jesus uses harsh language in this passage to condemn the Pharisees for their hypocritical attitudes and actions. To the casual observer, the Pharisees were the model of faithfulness and religious service. They were held up by the Jews as the most righteous among them. But Jesus saw through the outward appearance and into their hearts. Though their outward appearance and conduct may have seemed to be righteous, their hearts were unclean and their motives impure. Their lives were full of pretense and appearances, but empty in sincere and selfless devotion to God. Their desire was not to please God, but rather to receive the recognition, praise, and adoration of men. Their negative example and Jesus' condemnation of them reaches through the centuries to instruct us. Hypocrisy is still a problem and is still condemned by God. One's acts of worship and service, no matter how impressive and commendable, are meaningless if not from a sincere and genuine heart that loves God and desires to do His will. God is pleased with our righteous actions only if they are motivated by a holy and pure heart.

*Why do you think God cares so much
about the attitude of our hearts?*

DON'T FORGET TO PRAY AND HAVE A GREAT DAY!

 THINGS TO PRAY FOR TODAY:

Day 192

Today's Reading:
Luke 11:45–54

In yesterday's reading, Jesus condemns the Pharisees for their hypocrisy. In these verses, the lawyers come to the defense of their friends and cohorts and in so doing, bring Jesus' harsh condemnations upon them too. The "lawyers" were often Pharisees themselves and are also often the same ones referred to as "scribes." They were experts in the Law of Moses and were the self-appointed interpreters, teachers, and judges of the law and of the people. They knew the Old Testament Scriptures better than anyone else, so it was especially cutting for Jesus to accuse them of taking away the key of knowledge. They had manipulated and, in some cases, hidden completely God's law from the people. In so doing, they had hindered them from a proper understanding. It occurs to me that far too many in our world today are guilty of the same wrongdoing. They ignore, hide, alter, or manipulate God's Word in order to be accepted, successful, or justified. The result is that those who look to them for guidance and teaching are led astray and hindered from a proper understanding of God's Word. May God help us to be a people of His Word and to seek constantly to know and embrace its truths.

How can we avoid being led astray by one not teaching the truth?

DON'T FORGET TO PRAY AND HAVE A GREAT DAY!

⏳ **THINGS TO PRAY FOR TODAY:**

Day 193

Today's Reading:
Luke 12:1–3

Hypocrisy—the word points to the image of an actor playing a role. The Pharisees, Jesus warns His disciples, were guilty of this sin—pretending to be righteous, spiritual, and godly when in reality they were worldly and sinful. But this passage is not merely another condemnation of the Pharisees. It is a warning to His disciples against being drawn into their sinful nature and becoming like them. He refers to the "leaven" of their hypocrisy, giving the idea that it has the ability to spread and affect those around them. Jesus then gives an assurance that we would do well to heed today— "Nothing is covered up that will not be revealed, or hidden that will not be known." Eventually, the masks of hypocrisy will be removed, and everyone will be known as they truly are. We cannot hide from God. He knows our hearts, minds, and motives and will one day cause the hidden things to be revealed. What is the lesson in this truth? Simply put, it is this: Be genuine and sincere in our faith and lives, and we have nothing to fear.

Why is hypocrisy such a dangerous attitude to have?

DON'T FORGET TO PRAY AND HAVE A GREAT DAY!

 THINGS TO PRAY FOR TODAY:

Day 194

 Today's Reading:
Luke 12:4–7

E ven the hairs of your head are all numbered." Think about that for a second. For every one of us, the number of hairs on our heads is constantly changing. We are always losing and re-growing hair so that the number of them is never the same. But God has them all numbered. What an amazing statement of God's care and concern for His children. It is difficult to imagine that God—the Creator and Sustainer of the universe; the omnipotent, omniscient, omnipresent, glorious ruler of all that is—would be so concerned with us. But that is exactly the picture that is painted of God in this text. He is a God who is carefully attentive to each one of us. He knows every detail of our lives: every thought, feeling, fear, pain, joy, and sorrow. There is not a moment of our lives that escapes His watchful eye, and not a single need that goes unnoticed. Therefore, Jesus says, there is no need to fear. Our lives and souls are safely guarded in the hands of the Almighty God, who will care for us as His dear children. Whatever may come upon us in this life, we can be comforted in the knowledge that God knows, and He cares.

Think of an example of how God has cared for you.

DON'T FORGET TO PRAY AND HAVE A GREAT DAY!

 ⏳ **THINGS TO PRAY FOR TODAY:**

DAY 195

 Today's Reading:
Luke 12:8–12

As comforting as it is to think about standing before God and have Jesus affirm that you are His before the angels of God, can there be any more terrifying thought than to be standing in that same situation and have Him utter the words, "I don't know him"? If you have ever been guilty of thinking that confessing Christ wasn't a big deal, then this passage certainly ought to change your mind. To be willing to confess our belief in Christ and our relationship with Him is vital to our faithfulness and salvation. Sometimes that confession is made amidst the comfort and encouragement of a loving and supportive Christian family and is an easy step to take. At other times, we may find ourselves in a much more hostile environment of skeptics, naysayers, and unbelievers who would scoff at our belief and chosen way of life. But regardless of the circumstances, we are called to confess our faith in Jesus Christ as the Son of God and Savior of the world. May God help us to have the strength and courage to confess Christ whenever and wherever we are given the opportunity to do so.

Why is it sometimes difficult to confess Christ?

DON'T FORGET TO PRAY AND HAVE A GREAT DAY!

 THINGS TO PRAY FOR TODAY:

Day 196

Today's Reading:
Luke 12:13-21

"One's life does not consist in the abundance of his possessions." It is one of the great truths of God's Word that has been lost to our world today. In all of our striving after the things that this world deems as valuable, we have too often come to trust in those possessions as all that we need. It is this danger that Jesus warns against with the telling of the Parable of the Rich Fool. On the surface, this man had done nothing dishonest or unlawful. He had gained his wealth honestly; he had not robbed or cheated anyone. He had not damaged the property or belongings of anyone else. He had simply stored up the fruits of his labors and was preparing himself for the life of leisure that those things would provide. But the Lord calls him a fool because he had foolishly believed that material things were all that he needed and had made no provision for his soul. The clear and unavoidable truth for this man, and for all of us, is that our physical lives will someday end, and we will enter eternity. At that point, our physical wealth will be meaningless, and all that will matter is our relationship with God. Are you prepared?

What can we do to prepare for eternity?

DON'T FORGET TO PRAY AND HAVE A GREAT DAY!

⏳ **THINGS TO PRAY FOR TODAY:**

DAY 197

Today's Reading:
Luke 12:35-41

B e ready! That is the message of Jesus' words in this passage. To "let your waist be girded and your lamps burning" is simply another way of saying, "Be dressed and ready to go." Jesus is speaking here of that day and time when He will return to claim those who are His and to judge the world in righteousness. That day is surely coming, but the time of it is unknown. Jesus says that it will come as a thief in the night. It can be easy, even as faithful Christians, to get caught up in the daily routines of life and forget that we are constantly moving ever closer to eternity, without the promise of even another day. To remain watchful and prepared for Christ's return is a great challenge for us, but to be found unprepared would certainly be the greatest disappointment imaginable. Therefore, Jesus often gives these powerful exhortations to be prepared for His return. Are you ready?

Why is it so important that we be constantly prepared?

DON'T FORGET TO PRAY AND HAVE A GREAT DAY!

 THINGS TO PRAY FOR TODAY:

DAY 198

Today's Reading:
Luke 12:42–48

In this thought, I want to focus on the concept of stewardship. A steward is one who is placed in charge of certain things in his master's absence and given responsibility to do with those things as the master would do. Jesus tells this parable to illustrate the importance of being a faithful steward until He returns, and it is a principle that applies to each of us. The truth of the matter is that all that we have—our abilities, possessions, opportunities, and very lives—are not our own, but in reality are great blessings and gifts from God. Likewise, our families and the church are also things that God has placed in our care. All of these things have been given to us to use according to the Master's will and to use for His good purposes. Upon His return, Jesus says, those things that we have been given by the Master will be brought into account. Those who have used them faithfully according to God's will will be greatly rewarded, while those who have squandered or neglected their gifts will be punished. May God help us all to be faithful stewards!

What are some of the gifts that God has given you to use?

DON'T FORGET TO PRAY AND HAVE A GREAT DAY!

⧗ THINGS TO PRAY FOR TODAY:

DAY 199

Today's Reading:
Luke 12:49–53

Jesus has just been warning about the coming judgment and His disciples' need to be prepared for that day. He now turns His attention to His work and the effect that that work will have on the world. The fire that Jesus refers to is most likely the "fire" of purification. Through His atoning death and victorious resurrection, He will bring cleansing and purification to those who accept Him and are washed in His blood. As Jesus continues His earthly ministry, His sacrificial death, the "baptism" that He refers to, is always on His mind. While He is distressed by the suffering that lies ahead, He is anxious for the purification that it will bring to be accomplished. But as Jesus mentions, His atoning work of reconciliation with God will also bring division. There will be those who desire to be saved and are willing to accept Him, but there will also be those who, with hardened hearts, will resist and ultimately reject Him and His invitation. These two groups will naturally be opposed to one another causing division, even among kinsmen. May God help us to be among those who are willing to be purified by the blood of His precious Son.

Why do you think that there is so much division regarding Christ?

DON'T FORGET TO PRAY AND HAVE A GREAT DAY!

 THINGS TO PRAY FOR TODAY:

DAY 200

Today's Reading:
Luke 12:54–56

These remarks of Jesus are intended for those who had questioned, doubted, and rejected Him and His teaching. These skeptics were very observant and intuitive when it came to the weather. They could read the skies and the conditions and accurately predict the coming weather. But when presented with abundant evidence of the divine nature of Jesus, they failed to see. They had witnessed the amazing miracles, had heard His authoritative teaching, had seen His compassion and mercy, and had been reminded of the many prophecies that He had fulfilled. But they had failed to interpret the signs and recognize Him as the promised Messiah. In much the same way, in our world today, despite the overwhelming evidence and proof of God, Jesus, and the Bible, there are so many who continue to deny and reject them as true. How sad it is that so many are missing out on knowing God and enjoying a relationship with Him through His Son.

What are some things that are helpful
in providing evidence for Christ?

DON'T FORGET TO PRAY AND HAVE A GREAT DAY!

 THINGS TO PRAY FOR TODAY:

DAY 201

Today's Reading:
Luke 12:57–59

Jesus' teaching in these verses has a very practical application for everyday life: when dealing with a complaint or disagreement between would-be adversaries, it is better to solve it and reconcile before taking it through an official proceeding before a judge. Doing so can eliminate much of the animosity, trouble, and penalty that a legal course can create. However, Jesus has a deeper and greater meaning to His teaching than earthly quarrels and judges. He is speaking to those who have rejected Him, and who stand in opposition to God's law and authority through their hypocrisy. Because of their sins, they have an appointment with the great and mighty Judge of the world. Jesus advises them that it is in their best interest to be reconciled to God before that appointment, since it will otherwise surely end in their eternal punishment. When it comes to our appointment with God (and we all have one), we can either stand before Him as a guilty sinner before a righteous Judge, or as a forgiven child before a merciful Father. Just as with those of Jesus' day, the choice is ours.

What is involved in being reconciled to God?

DON'T FORGET TO PRAY AND HAVE A GREAT DAY!

 THINGS TO PRAY FOR TODAY:

DAY 202

Today's Reading:
Luke 13:1–5

The common belief of the day was that human suffering was the direct result of sin. Those who stood listening to Jesus' teaching and accusations, in an attempt to divert attention from themselves and their sins, brought up these Galileans who had been slain by Pilate's soldiers. In this day and time, Jewish uprisings and rebellions were common, especially around feast days. Though we do not know the precise time of this event, those mentioned were probably Galileans who had risen up against Roman soldiers and were killed in the fray, their blood being mingled with the blood of the sacrifices being offered at the time. Jesus' answer is simple and straightforward. These who suffered and died in either example given in this text were no more guilty of sin than Jesus' hearers (or than any of mankind for that matter). Every accountable person is touched by sin, and the penalty for that sin is far worse than any physical suffering or death. The solution to that problem, Jesus says, is repentance—a turning away from sin and to God. If one is willing to walk away from sin and become obedient and submissive to God, he will not perish spiritually. What a hopeful promise!

How does repentance save us from perishing?

DON'T FORGET TO PRAY AND HAVE A GREAT DAY!

⏳ THINGS TO PRAY FOR TODAY:

Day 203

 Today's Reading:
Luke 13:6-9

In this extended passage, Jesus has condemned the impenitence of the Jewish nation and has called them to change their minds and hearts and return to God. With this parable, Jesus warns them that the forbearance and patience of God has its limits and will soon come to an end. His longsuffering has been bountiful toward them, but the time of His judgment is coming. In the parable, the keeper of the vineyard likely represents Jesus, Who has come to give personal attention to the fig tree, representing the Jewish nation, to prune and feed, to nurture and fertilize, in hopes that the tree will be revived and begin to bear good fruit. If it does not, then it will be cut down and destroyed. While this parable speaks directly to the Jewish nation of Jesus' day, it certainly has an application for all of us. Anyone who finds himself away from God and not serving Him faithfully is in the perilous position of the fruitless fig tree. Thus far, God has been patient with us, but a time of judgment is coming. With that in mind, we must heed the warning of Jesus and be sure that we are faithfully bearing fruit for the master.

What does it mean to bear fruit for God?

DON'T FORGET TO PRAY AND HAVE A GREAT DAY!

 THINGS TO PRAY FOR TODAY:

DAY 204

 Today's Reading:
Luke 13:10-17

This text is primarily about the controversy of Jesus healing on the Sabbath, but I would like to think about a different aspect of this story for a moment. Put yourself in the shoes of the woman whom Jesus heals. For eighteen years, she had been afflicted with this "disabling spirit." She was bent over, unable to straighten her body. Her condition was probably painful and no doubt debilitating. But despite her physical condition, she had come to the synagogue on the Sabbath for worship. She obviously had a love for God that was greater than her pain. What a marvelous example of devotion to God she presents to us. She had not come to the synagogue looking for healing and did not ask Jesus for His help. Yet Jesus, in His compassion and love, saw her and healed her. She had come to give God her worship and instead received God's healing touch. Just imagine the relief and joy that she must have felt, knowing that her life had been changed by this brief encounter with the Great Physician.

What lessons can we learn from this text?

DON'T FORGET TO PRAY AND HAVE A GREAT DAY!

⧖ THINGS TO PRAY FOR TODAY:

Day 205

Today's Reading:
Luke 13:22–30

L ord, will those who are saved be few?" This question was asked of Jesus, most likely to test his allegiance to the Jewish nation. The "few" referred to is probably a reference to the Jews among the heathen nations of the world. In other words, "Are the Jews the only ones who will be saved?" Jesus' response represents one of the most direct and straight-forward condemnations of the Jewish leaders recorded in the gospels. Salvation is not guaranteed based on one's nationality or lineage but rather the path that one travels through life. The gate is narrow, and many will not find it. Many who feel deserving of salvation will be shut out and rejected. But those of any nation and background who find that narrow gate and walk with God through this life will have the blessed privilege of sitting down in the kingdom of heaven. What a wonderful and hopeful thought it is to consider that God has provided a way by which we can spend eternity with Him. May we strive to enter through that narrow gate!

What is the narrow gate Jesus refers to?

DON'T FORGET TO PRAY AND HAVE A GREAT DAY!

 THINGS TO PRAY FOR TODAY:

DAY 206

Today's Reading:
Luke 13:31–33

These Pharisees come to Jesus, not as friends warning Him of danger, but as cunning foes, bringing a message from Herod, trying to coax Jesus to Jerusalem where He would be in more danger from the Jewish leaders. But Jesus would not be taken in by their trickery. He was unafraid of the Jewish leaders or of Herod and was wholly devoted to the plan and purpose for which He had come. The "days" in this passage are not to be understood literally, but rather symbolically, representing a short period of time. Jesus was to continue His work of teaching and ministry for a while longer, and then He would go to Jerusalem to fulfill the purpose for which He came to the earth. He reveals to them that He will go to Jerusalem to die, but that He would go in His own time and by His own will. Despite the fact that the Jews had a burning desire to see Jesus destroyed, this text reiterates the point that Jesus died voluntarily according to God's will and plan. When the time was right, He would willingly lay down His life and become the sacrificial Lamb of God.

Why do you think the Jewish leaders
were so determined to destroy Jesus?

DON'T FORGET TO PRAY AND HAVE A GREAT DAY!

 THINGS TO PRAY FOR TODAY:

DAY 207

Today's Reading:
Luke 13:34–35

In my opinion, this is one of the saddest and most beautiful utterances made by Jesus during His earthly tenure. Typically, as He deals with the Jews and their hard-heartedness, there is a tone of exasperation, frustration, and even anger at their refusal to see what is right in front of them and repent. But in this passage, you catch a glimpse of the sadness and broken-heartedness that God feels over the refusal of His people to accept His loving care. His desire is to care for them, protect them, provide for them, and be a Father to them, but in the words of Jesus, they "were not willing." What a sad testament to the Jewish nation and their attitude toward the God who had done so much for them over the centuries. As with all of the biblical text, there is a lesson for us in these words of Jesus. God desires to care for us in the same way that He did for His people under the old covenant. He wants to protect, provide for, and care for us. But we must be willing! God will not force His love or care upon us. But if we will accept Him and faithfully submit ourselves to Him, God will be a loving Father to us. What a wonderful opportunity and blessing!

What is involved in accepting a relationship with God?

DON'T FORGET TO PRAY AND HAVE A GREAT DAY!

 THINGS TO PRAY FOR TODAY:

Day 208

Today's Reading:
Luke 14:1-6

I n this text, Jesus turns the tables on the Jewish leaders. As we have seen before and even recently, the Jewish leaders often condemned Jesus for His miraculous works performed on the Sabbath, taking one of God's laws and twisting it to be used for their own purposes. Typically, you see Jesus healing someone and then being accused of wrongdoing by the rulers. On this occasion, Jesus asks for their judgment on the matter before performing the miracle. If they condemn the healing, they must then justify their own Sabbath activities. If they permit the healing, then they are condoning Jesus' actions. They respond to Jesus in the only way that their hard hearts will allow them to—with silence. After performing the healing, Jesus reminds them that any one of them would quickly and without hesitation rescue an animal that was in a perilous situation, even on the Sabbath. Jesus had once again silenced His adversaries and brought to light their hypocrisy.

What lessons can we learn from this text?

DON'T FORGET TO PRAY AND HAVE A GREAT DAY!

⏳ **THINGS TO PRAY FOR TODAY:**

DAY 209

Today's Reading:
Luke 14:7–11

O ne of the sinful attitudes of the Pharisees and Jewish leaders of Jesus' day was their desire for prominence and praise. They coveted the places of honor and assumed those positions at every opportunity. On this occasion, at a Sabbath dinner hosted by a ruler of the Pharisees, Jesus witnessed this very attitude being demonstrated and told this parable to condemn their haughtiness and teach a valuable lesson about humility. Instead of assuming the highest position and running the risk of being asked to move to a lower place, Jesus says, assume a low position so that you might be asked to move to a higher one. Humility continues to be a much-needed and vital attitude of those who would be faithful servants of God. We cannot and will not be what God would have us to be if we are not willing to humble ourselves and take on the lowly role of servant. But as Jesus and the New Testament often teach, those who humble themselves will someday be exalted by God. May God help us to be humble servants of Him.

What does it mean to be a humble servant of God?

DON'T FORGET TO PRAY AND HAVE A GREAT DAY!

 THINGS TO PRAY FOR TODAY:

DAY 210

Today's Reading:
Luke 14:12–14

In yesterday's reading, Jesus was speaking to those who were attending a feast. In today's text, He turns his attention to the host of the feast. In essence, His teaching is that one should not invite those who would not truly benefit from the feast, and who could and would invite him to a feast of their own in return. Instead, we should invite those who were in need—the poor, the infirmed, the needy—those who could truly benefit from our kindness and generosity and who could not repay the favor. Jesus is certainly not teaching that we should never spend time with friends or show kindness to loved ones, but that we should also be mindful of those who are in need. So often, we spend all of our time and effort on those we know and love, while neglecting those who have no one to care for them or help them. The larger principle here is that we should do good for the sake of doing good. Give to those who cannot give in return. Give your attention, time, and care to those who are needy, Jesus says, and your reward will be from God.

Why is it important that we show
kindness to those who are in need?

DON'T FORGET TO PRAY AND HAVE A GREAT DAY!

⏳ THINGS TO PRAY FOR TODAY:

DAY 211

 Today's Reading:
Luke 14:15–24

The occasion of this text is still the Sabbath day feast prepared by the ruler of the Pharisees that Jesus attended as an invited guest. We do not know who made the statement to Jesus, or exactly what they meant by it. However, in response to that statement, Jesus tells another parable. Those who were invited to the feast but made excuses not to attend probably represent the Jews, God's chosen people under the old covenant, and those to whom Jesus was sent. Because of their refusal, the invitation is extended to all people of any background and walk of life. This parable is certainly applicable to our world today. God's invitation to a place at His table in heaven has been issued. Unfortunately, many are too preoccupied with the affairs of this world and life to accept it. Much like those in the parable, they are consumed with worldly ventures and have no interest in spiritual things. Sadly, Jesus teaches that they will miss out on the wonderful things that God has prepared in heaven. But the invitation continues to be open to anyone who is willing to accept it and come to God in faith and obedience. Will you be there?

What is involved in accepting God's invitation?

DON'T FORGET TO PRAY AND HAVE A GREAT DAY!

 THINGS TO PRAY FOR TODAY:

Day 212

Today's Reading:
Luke 14:25-33

This text expounds on what is involved in accepting the invitation that Jesus spoke of in the previous reading. In His day, as in ours, there were many who were enamored with His teaching and the prospect of being His disciple and who quickly commit to following Him. But Jesus says it is not an invitation that can be accepted without thought and true commitment. Following after Jesus requires that He be first and the greatest priority of our lives. The word "hate" in v. 26 is a harsh word and is not intended to be taken literally, but the concept behind the word is important and not always easy for people to accept. Jesus says that, in order to be His disciples, we must be willing to put Him before even our closest and most precious relationships, and in fact before our own lives. It is a firm and unwavering commitment that discipleship requires. Thus, Jesus says that we should "count the cost" before accepting that invitation to follow after Him. Are we willing to pay the price? To see our commitment through to the end? To make whatever choices and sacrifices that it requires? The price of discipleship is high, but the rewards are well worth the effort!

Why is it so important that we put Christ first?

DON'T FORGET TO PRAY AND HAVE A GREAT DAY!

⏳ THINGS TO PRAY FOR TODAY:

Day 213

Today's Reading:
Matthew 18:10–14

The Parable of the Lost Sheep will be discussed tomorrow, so today's thought will focus on the meaning of v. 10. Jesus had earlier used a nearby child as an object lesson, and here refers back to that child as a representative of the lowliest of people in society. In their culture, children had no rights, no property of their own, and very little regard among people. Jesus uses this child to make the point that every person, regardless of their position in society, was important to God. The phrase "their angels always see the face of My Father" has caused much discussion and confusion, and has even led to the idea of each person having a "guardian angel." This is not Jesus' intended meaning, but using vivid imagery, He is making the point that God is interested and concerned about every person. No person or situation escapes the eye of God. No one is unimportant or unworthy of His attention. For that reason, Jesus says, we should not despise or look down on anyone. Instead, we should strive to look at others with the love and compassion that God has for them.

What are some ways that we can share
God's compassion with the world?

DON'T FORGET TO PRAY AND HAVE A GREAT DAY!

⏳ **THINGS TO PRAY FOR TODAY:**

Day 214

Today's Reading:
Luke 15:1-7

Ninety-nine percent. In most areas of life, that number is acceptable and even exemplary. A score of 99 on a test is excellent. In basketball, a 99% shooting average is amazing. A batter who hits .990 would be the greatest ever. But when it comes to souls, God is not satisfied with ninety-nine percent. Every soul matters. Each one is important. That is the point of Jesus' parable concerning the lost sheep. But in making that point, he also teaches us that we should be just as concerned for that one soul. Which one of you, Jesus asks, would not go out looking for your lost sheep and then rejoice and celebrate when you found it? Implied is the idea that anyone who has a flock of sheep would go looking for one that was missing. Should we not be just as concerned for an eternal soul as we are for an animal? God cares about lost souls. Even one sinner that repents and returns to God causes much joy in heaven. As God's children and servants, we should also be concerned for lost souls and work to help them find their way back to God.

What can we do to help the lost to find their way back?

DON'T FORGET TO PRAY AND HAVE A GREAT DAY!

⧗ **THINGS TO PRAY FOR TODAY:**

Day 215

 Today's Reading:
Luke 15:8–10

T his short parable is very similar in theme and application to the previous one. In this story, Jesus uses a lost coin as the object lesson. What if you lost a $100 dollar bill? You know that it is in your house somewhere, but you can't find it? Do you just say, "Oh well," and forget about it? Most of us would turn the house upside down. We would look in every drawer, under every piece of furniture, and in every corner of the house until we found the money. That is exactly the picture Jesus paints in this parable. What person, He asks, if they lose a silver coin, doesn't search for it tirelessly until they find it? Again, that coin represents a lost soul that God desperately cares about and desires to be saved. And again, as God's servants and ambassadors (2 Corinthians 5:20), we should be just as concerned for that soul as we are for that $100 bill we lost. We should work and pray and never give up on trying to "find" that lost soul. May God help us to be more like Him!

Why does one soul matter so much to God?

DON'T FORGET TO PRAY AND HAVE A GREAT DAY!

 THINGS TO PRAY FOR TODAY:

Day 216

Today's Reading:
Luke 15:11–32

This story is one of the most well-known parables of Jesus. It is rich and full of meaning. Each character in the story—the father, the younger son, and the older son—have valuable lessons to teach us. We don't have time in this thought to explore all the characters and all the lessons, so I want to focus on only one: the father. The loving, patient, forgiving father in the story represents our heavenly Father. Jesus paints for us a picture of a God who never gives up, who is constantly watching and waiting for His lost children to return, and who joyfully forgives us and takes us back when we do. While He certainly does not condone the sinful paths that we might choose from time to time, He never stops loving us. If I as a sinner "come to myself" and am willing to go to Him in humility and with a repentant heart, He is there to wrap His arms of love around me and restore me to my place as His child. What a beautiful picture of the mercy and love of God, and what a powerful message that needs to be heard by our world today.

This thought focused on the father, but
what lessons do you see in the two sons?

DON'T FORGET TO PRAY AND HAVE A GREAT DAY!

⧗ THINGS TO PRAY FOR TODAY:

Day 217

 Today's Reading:
Luke 16:1–13

This parable of Jesus is one of the most difficult to understand. This is partially true because He uses a dishonest and unworthy steward to illustrate a principle applicable to His disciples. Notice that the steward is not commended for his dishonesty (he is still dismissed for being dishonest), but rather for being prudent and shrewd. He was able to use the physical things at his disposal to provide a comfortable living for himself. In His interpretation of the story, Jesus makes the point that those of the world are often wiser in their earthly dealings than those who belong to God. The underlying point of this parable is pretty simple. Jesus is attempting to teach us about the importance of being good stewards of our earthly things. Just as the steward used his master's things to provide security for himself, we are to use the things God has blessed us with in such a way that we are storing up riches in heaven. Certainly, we are not to do that through dishonesty and treachery, but rather through prudence and wisdom. May God help us to be good stewards for Him!

What does it mean to be a steward of God?

DON'T FORGET TO PRAY AND HAVE A GREAT DAY!

 THINGS TO PRAY FOR TODAY:

DAY 218

Today's Reading:
Luke 16:14–18

The Pharisees, like so many in our world today, had succumbed to the temptation of falling in love with this world's things. They were enamored with money, notoriety, and honor from men. But Jesus reminds them, and us, "What is exalted among men is an abomination in the sight of God." All of the worldly things that so many spend so much time and effort pursuing are unpleasing to God, not because they are necessarily evil in and of themselves, but because they threaten to occupy our hearts, minds, and lives and take us away from God. As we strive after riches, success, notoriety, and other worldly achievements, those things have the potential to take the place of God in our lives and effectively become gods to us. For that reason, Jesus often teaches that we must not give ourselves to worldly things but rather devote our hearts and lives to God above all else.

Why is it so important for us to God first in our lives?

DON'T FORGET TO PRAY AND HAVE A GREAT DAY!

⏳ **THINGS TO PRAY FOR TODAY:**

DAY 219

Today's Reading:
Luke 16:19–31

Whappens when we die? It is a question that so many ask and want to understand. In this text, Jesus gives us a rare glimpse into those things that lay beyond this life and world. In this story, we see the wealthy man who lived extravagantly on earth, but had not prepared himself for eternity. His riches and notoriety were of no benefit to him as he lifted up his eyes in torment. We also see the story of Lazarus, a man who had nothing in this life, but who had stored up an eternal treasure in heaven. Jesus paints a beautiful picture of Lazarus' soul being lovingly carried by angels into Abraham's bosom to be comforted and cared for. This story also depicts the vast separation between those two places and the impossibility of changing one's fate once that time has come. There is no comfort and no hope in Hades, and there is nothing that troubles in paradise. As we read these words of Jesus and consider our own lives and fate, we must ask ourselves one very important question: which story will be ours?

What element of this story stands out to you the most and why?

DON'T FORGET TO PRAY AND HAVE A GREAT DAY!

 THINGS TO PRAY FOR TODAY:

DAY 220

Today's Reading:
Matthew 18:15–20

Conflicts among men are inevitable. Differences in personalities, ideas, and opinions will often lead to disagreements, misunderstandings, and even strife. We are often guilty of hurting or wronging others by our words or actions. But the bigger problem often comes as we try to deal with those situations when we have either hurt or have been hurt by someone. We become defensive, make excuses, hold grudges, or try to get even, and only exasperate the problem by these actions. But God has not left us without counsel and guidance on this issue. He has given us a pattern by which we can and should deal with those who have done harm to us and wrong toward us. As we consider the steps God instructs us to take in dealing with those difficult situations, I want to remind us all of the motivation behind those actions. As we go to our brother, as we try to help him see his wrongdoing, even as we separate ourselves from him when necessary, we must remember that our motivation is or should always be love! Our desire should always be to restore the relationship and help him restore his relationship with God. No other motivation is acceptable to God!

Why do we so often not follow these
instructions in dealing with conflict?

DON'T FORGET TO PRAY AND HAVE A GREAT DAY!

⏳ **THINGS TO PRAY FOR TODAY:**

Day 221

 Today's Reading:
Matthew 18:21–35

Forgiveness. It is something that we all want and need, but something that we often struggle to give others. In this text, Peter asks a question that we might all wonder about sometimes. How often should I forgive a person who continues to do wrong toward me? Peter's offer of seven times was a very generous one (the Jewish rule of thumb for the day was three times). However, Jesus' instructions concerning our forgiveness of others were much broader, and much more challenging. "Seventy-seven times" was not meant to pinpoint a specific number of times that we are required to forgive, but rather to teach a principle—forgive as often as is needed. Jesus gives this command based on the nature of God's forgiveness toward us as demonstrated by Jesus' parable. Whatever wrong someone might have committed against us, and however often that wrong might have been committed, it cannot compare to the number of times that we have sinned against God. Yet God's forgiveness is abundant and constantly available. If God is willing to forgive us so often, we ought to extend that forgiveness to others. May God help us to forgive our brother!

Why is it so important that we forgive others?

DON'T FORGET TO PRAY AND HAVE A GREAT DAY!

 THINGS TO PRAY FOR TODAY:

DAY 222

Today's Reading:
Luke 17:1–4

G od cares deeply for His children. Like an earthly father with his children, God is very protective of and caring toward those who are His. In this world of temptation and sin, God understands it is inevitable that his children will face offense and wrongdoing, but He does not look favorably upon those who are the source of that offense. There are two principles related to this characteristic of God that we need to understand. First, we must be very careful to avoid causing offense to those who are children of God. Through our words or example, we must strive to bring others closer to God, not lead them away. Second, when one causes offense to us, we must be ready and willing to love that person and treat them in such a way that they might recognize their wrong and repent. Then we must be willing to forgive them. It should be our earnest desire that no person face the wrath of God, but that all become His faithful children.

What are some ways that we might
work to bring others closer to God?

DON'T FORGET TO PRAY AND HAVE A GREAT DAY!

⏳ **THINGS TO PRAY FOR TODAY:**

DAY 223

Today's Reading:
Luke 17:5–10

"Increase our faith!" It is a commendable request made by the apostles. They desired to be better and stronger in their lives and in their service to the Lord. They wanted to be able to do all the things that Jesus was commanding them. But Jesus, knowing their hearts, warns them against the danger of becoming prideful in their faith and service, lest they begin to think that they, in their goodness, deserve a reward from God for all that they have done. Jesus reminds them, and us, of the role of a servant and the relationship of that servant with the master. We must remember that a servant's role is to serve. He does not deserve or earn a reward for doing his duty. In our relationship with God, we are His servants. God has called us to serve Him, and we who are His children have answered that call and accepted that responsibility. We must remember that, no matter how much good we do, no matter how much knowledge or faith we have, we are still sinful creatures who have not earned a home in heaven. Our eternal reward is a gift of God's grace. We must not depend on ourselves, but rather trust in God's mercy and love for our eternal salvation.

How can we avoid trusting in ourselves for salvation?

DON'T FORGET TO PRAY AND HAVE A GREAT DAY!

⏳ THINGS TO PRAY FOR TODAY:

Day 224

Today's Reading:
Luke 17:11-19

This text is not as much about the miraculous healing of these ten lepers as it is about their gratitude, or lack thereof. Leprosy was a disease that not only robbed its victims of their health, but of their lives in every sense. With this dreaded disease came the loss of family, community, and every social tie and activity in the leper's life. In this miracle, these ten men's lives were restored. Not only was this fatal disease taken from them, but they could return to their families, friends, jobs, and places in society. It was truly a life-changing event. Can you imagine not saying thank you, not making your way back to Jesus to give thanks, honor, and praise to the One who had given you so much? Yet nine of these men did not. Shameful! But have you considered that so many do the same thing today? Jesus has given us so many blessings, the greatest of which is the healing of our souls from sin. We have been saved, rescued, redeemed. But so many never acknowledge the great mercy, grace, and love that God has shown toward us through Jesus. They never return to give thanks, honor, or praise to the One who has given them so much. May God help us to be ever grateful!

How do we show our gratitude to Jesus?

DON'T FORGET TO PRAY AND HAVE A GREAT DAY!

⏳ THINGS TO PRAY FOR TODAY:

DAY 225

Today's Reading:
Luke 17:20-37

This is a challenging text that has led to many interpretations and even false teachings. It would be impossible, in the few words that this thought allows, to adequately expound on all that has been said or thought about this passage. Nevertheless, the overall meaning of the text is pretty clear and provides a powerful lesson and exhortation for us. However, one might understand the details of Jesus' words, His message is clearly summed up in two words: Be Prepared! It is easy and natural for us to become comfortable in our lives and in this world and to see both as permanent and reliable. But Jesus reminds us that they are not. One of the central messages of this text and of the entire Bible is that this world is temporary. There is coming a day when Jesus will return, not to live or reign on the earth, but to bring this world to an end and to sit in judgment over all humanity. When that day comes, Jesus warns in this passage, there will be no more time or opportunity for preparation. Our eternal fate will be sealed. Therefore, we must prepare ourselves for that day, being ever watchful for our Lord's return!

How should we prepare ourselves for Jesus' return?

DON'T FORGET TO PRAY AND HAVE A GREAT DAY!

X THINGS TO PRAY FOR TODAY:

Day 226

Today's Reading:
Luke 18:1-8

Have you ever wondered if praying for the same thing over and over is displeasing to God? Does it show a lack of faith in God that we can't, or don't, take our concern or need to Him one time and consider it taken care of, never to be mentioned again? In this parable recorded only by Luke, Jesus gives the answer to those questions, and that answer is far different than the way we often feel. What we often view as a lack of faith or trust, God views as dependence and submission. Just as the widow in the parable goes repeatedly to the judge for help because she realizes that he is her only hope, we take our cares and needs to God in recognition of the fact that it is only in Him that we find our hope. God desires for us to pray to Him and not to cease in seeking His help and care. Of course, as we pray, we must do so in faith, trusting God to care for us in the way that is best for us according to His will. But given that stipulation, God is not bothered or displeased by our continual seeking of His consolation and blessings. His love for us is deep and abiding, and His desire is that we continually seek Him and a closer walk with Him.

Why is it important to God that we pray to Him?

DON'T FORGET TO PRAY AND HAVE A GREAT DAY!

⏳ **THINGS TO PRAY FOR TODAY:**

DAY 227

 Today's Reading:
Luke 18:9–14

While yesterday's reading dealt with the constancy of our prayer lives, today's deals with the attitude of our prayers. In this parable, Jesus contrasts the prayers and hearts of two men. One of them, a Pharisee (if his description of his life is accurate), had gone above and beyond in devoting his life to righteous living. But while his life was commendable, his attitude was not. He was haughty, arrogant, and self-serving in his prayer. His audience was not God, but those who might hear his prayer and be impressed with his righteousness. The other man, a tax collector, comes before God with a humble and broken spirit, confessing his sinfulness and begging for God's mercy. What is the lesson in this text for us? We must remember, unlike the Pharisee, that despite our best efforts and all the good that we might accomplish, we are sinners, unworthy of God's mercy and salvation. As we go to God in prayer, we must go before Him in humility, recognizing our dependence upon Him and His grace and mercy toward us.

Why is our attitude in prayer important?

DON'T FORGET TO PRAY AND HAVE A GREAT DAY!

 THINGS TO PRAY FOR TODAY:

Day 228

 Today's Reading:
Matthew 19:1–12

There is possibly no one issue in the church or in the religious world as a whole that has caused more controversy or trouble than the issue of marriage, divorce, and remarriage. But as we see from this reading, the controversy over this issue is not a new one. Even in Jesus' day (and in fact long before Jesus' day), it was a problem among God's people. The Jews come to Jesus to ask His opinion on the issue. In essence, what Jesus tells them is not to depend on men, whether it be Moses or rabbis of their own day, to guide their thinking on marriage, but rather to look at what God desired and designed when He created marriage in the very beginning. God's intention and plan for marriage was that it be a lifelong bond between one man and one woman. God creates that bond in marriage, and only God has the right to dissolve it. Oh, how much better our world would be if everyone would respect and abide by God's plan and design for marriage.

Why do you think faithfulness and
commitment in marriage matters to God?

DON'T FORGET TO PRAY AND HAVE A GREAT DAY!

⌛ **THINGS TO PRAY FOR TODAY:**

Day 229

 Today's Reading:
Mark 10:13–16

"C hildren are to be seen and not heard." Have you ever heard this statement made, or if you haven't heard it said out loud, you have perhaps seen it played out in the attitudes and actions of people. Children can be restless, active, and distracting at times. And we are often nowhere more intolerant of those qualities than at church. "Why can't they be quiet?" "Why can't they sit still?" "Why doesn't someone take them out?" When we adopt these attitudes, we come dangerously close to the behavior of the disciples who rebuked those bringing children to Jesus. They felt like the children were just getting in the way. Jesus had too many important things to do to be wasting His time with children. They forgot that each one of those children had a soul and was loved by God. Jesus was "indignant" with them and reminded them of the wonderful qualities and hearts that children have that we would all do well to emulate. Let us encourage those who are trying to bring their children to Jesus, and may we all strive to become like little children before God.

What qualities do children have that we should emulate?

DON'T FORGET TO PRAY AND HAVE A GREAT DAY!

 THINGS TO PRAY FOR TODAY:

DAY 230

Today's Reading:
Matthew 19:16-22

T his is, in my opinion, one of the saddest stories in the New Testament. Sadder still is the fact that it is played out over and over in our world today. The man at the center of this story was a good man, a religious man, a righteous man. He was better than most in his obedience to the law. But that wasn't enough. He wanted more. He wanted to have eternal life. Not only did he want eternal life, but he came to the right place to find it. He seemed to have all the pieces in place—obedience, desire, submission. He was almost there. But there was a problem. Jesus, knowing the young man's heart, instructed him to sell all that he had and come follow Him. Though this young man obeyed God's law, he worshipped his things. They had become his god. If he was to have eternal life, he would have to replace his god (worldly things) with the God of heaven and earth. It is still true today that many are not faithful to God because they worship their things instead. Even many who wear the name of Christ are guilty of serving the god of this world. But just like the rich young ruler, we cannot serve both. We must choose whether we will serve God or things.

Why can we not serve both God and things?

DON'T FORGET TO PRAY AND HAVE A GREAT DAY!

⏳ THINGS TO PRAY FOR TODAY:

Day 231

Today's Reading:
Matthew 19:23-30

This teaching of Jesus is not about the evil of riches or worldly things. It is about the hearts of those who would follow after Jesus. He has just finished a conversation with the rich young ruler. You can almost picture that young man walking away with his head bowed down in sorrow as Jesus turns to His disciples and begins to use that occasion to teach them. In that day, the wealthy were considered to be blessed and favored by God. If they could not be saved, then who could? But Jesus' words are not really about the rich at all, but about their (and our) attitude toward those things. Just as the rich young ruler's wealth could not buy him salvation, our material things cannot acquire salvation for us. Because we depend on worldly things so much in this life to provide all that we need, it is easy for us to believe that our worldly things might somehow provide for our spiritual needs as well. We may and should do many good and commendable works with our physical things, but none of those things can earn salvation for us. Salvation is only found in a faithful relationship with God through Jesus Christ that puts Him first and above all else in our lives.

What should our attitudes be toward worldly things?

DON'T FORGET TO PRAY AND HAVE A GREAT DAY!

⏳ THINGS TO PRAY FOR TODAY:

DAY 232

Today's Reading:
Matthew 20:1-16

This parable of Jesus paints a beautiful picture of the love and mercy of God toward all those who would enter the heavenly kingdom. The wondrous glory of heaven—rest from labors, freedom from anything that troubles, glorious presence of God—is prepared for all those who have been washed in the blood of Christ, and who have been faithful to Him. Those who are blessed to learn the truth at an early age and enjoy a lifetime of the blessings that come from a faithful relationship with God spend much time anticipating and longing for that heavenly home. Others come to God in midlife, having been convinced of the truth at a later time, and enjoy the security of knowing that their lives are safe in the hands of a loving Savior. Still others do not find the truth until the twilight of their lives and rejoice in knowing that they are finally free from sin and bound for that eternal home. Regardless of when one comes to Christ, the prize is set—the immeasurable glory of an eternity spent in the presence of God, His precious Son, and with all the saints. Thanks be to God for His overwhelming love and mercy!

What do you look forward to most about heaven?

DON'T FORGET TO PRAY AND HAVE A GREAT DAY!

⏳ **THINGS TO PRAY FOR TODAY:**

DAY 233

Today's Reading:
John 10:22-30

Jesus, in this passage, talks to the Jewish leaders about "His sheep." His statements here have caused some confusion and even false teaching. In reality, however, they are fairly straight-forward and easy to understand. He tells the Jewish leaders that they are not of His sheep and then adds, "My sheep hear my voice, and I know them, and they follow Me." Some have used these statements to support the doctrine of predestination, but is that what Jesus is teaching? Why are the Jewish leaders not of His sheep? Simply because they have not heard His voice and followed Him, for that is who Jesus says His sheep are. The "knowing them" that Jesus speaks of is an experiential knowing—He knows them because they have followed Him and obeyed His word (see Matthew 7:21-23). The sheepfold of Christ is open to all humanity. We each have the opportunity to be His sheep—to hear Him, follow Him, and be known and cared for by Him. But if we desire to be His sheep, we must, through our faith and obedience, come to Him and enter the fold through Him (see John 10:7-9). What a blessing it is to be sheep of the Good Shepherd.

How do we enter the fold of Christ?

DON'T FORGET TO PRAY AND HAVE A GREAT DAY!

 THINGS TO PRAY FOR TODAY:

Day 234

Today's Reading:
John 10:31–39

Isn't it interesting how we will so often rest on our own understandings and preconceived ideas and wholly reject something (or someone) without examining the evidence? The Jewish leaders had already made up their minds. Jesus was a blasphemer! He was a man who claimed to be God, and He was worthy of death. That was their belief. There would be no changing their minds. In His defense, Jesus simply tells them to look at His works. "If I am not doing the works of My Father, then do not believe Me; but if I do them...[then] believe the works, that you may know and understand that the Father is in Me, and I in the Father." It was a simple and straightforward argument. But there would be no convincing them. Their minds were made up. We are often much more like the Jewish leaders than we would like to think. We rest on our traditions and opinions and turn a blind eye to the evidence of Scripture. How much different would the religious world be today if we would all lay aside our preconceived ideas and simply allow the Bible to guide our thoughts and actions? May God help us all to be open to and accepting of His word.

Why do you think we tend to hold so tightly
to our traditions and preconceived ideas?

DON'T FORGET TO PRAY AND HAVE A GREAT DAY!

 THINGS TO PRAY FOR TODAY:

Day 235

Today's Reading:
John 10:40–42

Jesus retreated from the murderous Jews and came to a place that was familiar to Him. It was the place where John had spent so much time teaching and baptizing. People had come to this place in droves to hear John speak about the One who would come after him, the One whose shoes he was not worthy to latch, the One the prophets spoke of, the Messiah. Now many of those same people had come back to this spot, not to hear John, but to see Jesus. As they remembered the words that John had spoken concerning that special One that would come after him, and as they considered the signs that they had seen Jesus perform, they believed in Him. Ironically, Jesus had just rebuked the Jewish leaders, those who were supposedly the most religious among them, the ones who knew the law and prophets best of all, for ignoring the signs that He had done and not believing in Him, even though He did the works of God. What is the lesson for us today? The Bible provides all the evidence that anyone needs to be able to believe in Jesus and follow after Him. May we be like those who remembered what they had been taught and believed.

What evidence does the Bible provide of the truth about Jesus Christ?

DON'T FORGET TO PRAY AND HAVE A GREAT DAY!

 THINGS TO PRAY FOR TODAY:

Day 236

 Today's Reading:
John 11:1–16

Today, and for the next couple of days, we will be thinking about the beautiful story of the raising of Lazarus. There are so many lessons in these texts that give us great insights into the mind and heart of God, insights that I believe are relevant to us today. In the beginning of the story, Jesus receives word that His friend Lazarus is sick, but despite Lazarus' sisters' plea for help, Jesus tarries two days before making the trip to Bethany. Why? If Jesus had the ability to prevent the death of Lazarus and the overwhelming sorrow that it brought to Mary and Martha, why did He not go immediately? Why did He not speak the word that would have healed Lazarus of his sickness? So often in our own lives, we ask very similar questions: *Why isn't God answering my prayers? Why doesn't He help me? Doesn't He understand how urgent my need is?* The answer to our questions is found in Jesus' reason for not going immediately to Lazarus. For both him and us, the Lord works in His own time, knowing that our struggles are sometimes necessary for growth. He not only knows what we need but when we need it, and His timing is always perfect according to His will and purpose.

How can we grow from our struggles?

DON'T FORGET TO PRAY AND HAVE A GREAT DAY!

 **THINGS TO PRAY FOR TODAY:**

Day 237

 Today's Reading:
John 11:17–37

J esus wept." It is the shortest verse in the Bible and an incredibly simple, matter-of-fact statement. But it is filled to overflowing with meaning and significance. Have you ever wondered why Jesus wept? If He knew that He was going to raise Lazarus and what the final outcome was going to be, why feel sorrow? Why weep? The answer, I believe, is given in v. 33: "When Jesus saw her weeping, and the Jews who came with her also weeping, He was deeply moved in His spirit and greatly troubled." Jesus knew that Lazarus would be raised, but He felt sorrow because His friends felt sorrow. He wept because they wept. His tears were not for Lazarus, but for those who were brokenhearted and overwhelmed with grief. And so it is with us. The Hebrews writer says that Jesus is a high priest who is "touched with the feeling of our infirmity" (Hebrews 4:15 KJV). He hurts with and for us when we hurt. He understands our suffering as only someone who has experienced the same suffering can. He is a compassionate friend and Lord. What a blessing it is to serve Him!

Why is it important that Jesus understands our sufferings?

DON'T FORGET TO PRAY AND HAVE A GREAT DAY!

 ⏳ **THINGS TO PRAY FOR TODAY:**

DAY 238

Today's Reading:
John 11:38–44

As Jesus, and those who were with Him, gathered at the tomb of Lazarus, one thing was sure—Lazarus was dead. It had been four days. He had been wrapped and prepared for burial. He had been placed in a cave as his tomb, and the opening had been sealed. So sure was Martha of her brother's death that she objected to Jesus' instruction to remove the stone from the tomb's opening, concerned about the stench that would surely emanate from Lazarus' decomposing body. Why does any of this matter? While the power to heal sickness was amazing and unique to Jesus, He had certainly demonstrated His power over physical illness. Those who believed in Him had no trouble believing that He could heal the sick. In this case, both Mary and Martha stated that, if Jesus had been there in time, He could have healed Lazarus. But to raise the dead was another matter completely. It was a challenge to the faith of even the most faithful to believe that Jesus could raise from the dead one who had been dead four days. But once again, and in dramatic fashion, Jesus powerfully proved His authority over physical life, and Lazarus lived.

What encouragement do we gain from Jesus' raising of Lazarus?

DON'T FORGET TO PRAY AND HAVE A GREAT DAY!

⧗ THINGS TO PRAY FOR TODAY:

DAY 239

 Today's Reading:
John 11:45–57

"S o from that day on, they made plans to put Him to death." The raising of Lazarus was the final straw. Up until this point, the Jews' attempts to take Jesus had been reactionary and spontaneous. It was this event that sparked the Jewish leaders' organized plan to kill Him. It is interesting to me that, despite the goodness and power of Jesus, there were some who were always skeptical and suspicious of Him. While many believed in Him because of the raising of Lazarus, the text says that some went and told the Pharisees. They were looking to stir up trouble. They saw Jesus as a threat that had to be dealt with. Interestingly, as you look through the pages of history, there have always been people, governments, groups, and even religions that have followed in the steps of the Pharisees. Despite Jesus' goodness and power as displayed in God's Word, they have seen Him as a threat to their power, authority, or "freedom" and have plotted to destroy Jesus and His authority within their own time and realm of influence. It continues to happen today in our own world. May we all be willing to see and believe in Jesus.

Why do you think so many see Jesus as a threat?

DON'T FORGET TO PRAY AND HAVE A GREAT DAY!

 THINGS TO PRAY FOR TODAY:

Day 240

Today's Reading:
Matthew 20:20–28

Notoriety. Honor. Authority. They are some of the most sought-after achievements in our world today. We will work and sacrifice, and some will even lie and cheat to have them. But notoriety, honor, and authority are not new ambitions. They have always existed. Even with all of the influence and tutelage that Jesus offered, the apostles still struggled with these worldly pursuits. Even among the closest of Jesus' followers, James and John (and their mother) wanted to be the greatest. They had not yet learned the vital lesson of servanthood. They did not yet understand what it truly meant to be followers of Christ. In our dog-eat-dog world of corporate ladders and "might makes right" thinking, the value of being a servant is almost non-existent. There is no glory in helping others, no honor in putting others first. But it is still true that God desires for His people to be servants. To be humble and compassionate in our lives is a Christ-like trait that we must aspire to have. Why? Because in the eyes of God, the first truly shall be last and the last first.

What does it mean to be a servant in today's world?

DON'T FORGET TO PRAY AND HAVE A GREAT DAY!

⏳ THINGS TO PRAY FOR TODAY:

Day 241

Today's Reading:
Mark 10:32–45

This is a parallel passage to yesterday's, but Mark frames the request of James and John with some of the details of the conversation that prompted that request. Jesus is foretelling His coming suffering, death, and resurrection. He is trying to prepare them for the difficult events of the not-too-distant future. James and John (and probably the others also) have trouble seeing or understanding the suffering of Jesus but are wholly focused on His glory. In response to their request, Jesus reminds them that to continue to follow Him will mean that they will have to endure the same sufferings He does. But they fail to grasp the cost of discipleship—the service, the sacrifice, and the suffering that faithfully following Christ will bring into their lives. Likewise, we need to understand the cost of discipleship in our own lives. We may not ever be called upon to suffer as the apostles or other early disciples of Jesus did, but we are called to leave the world behind and to follow after Christ, to choose Him above everything else. That commitment will require us to serve and sacrifice. Are we willing to pay the price?

What kind of sacrifices do Christians have to make today?

DON'T FORGET TO PRAY AND HAVE A GREAT DAY!

 THINGS TO PRAY FOR TODAY:

DAY 242

Today's Reading:
Mark 10:46–52

"Go your way; your faith has made you well." These were Jesus' words to Bartimaeus. I want to focus your thoughts for a moment on the "Go your way" portion of Jesus' statement. Jesus was giving this man the freedom to go back to a normal life. He was free to go and experience and enjoy the aspects of life that blindness had taken from him. There was no obligation to Jesus, no price to pay, nothing else asked of him. But notice what Bartimaeus did: "And immediately he recovered his sight and followed Him on the way." He did not take advantage of the opportunity to go his way, to return to a normal life, to celebrate his healing. He did not rush off to let his friends and family know of the wonderful thing that had happened to him. In response to his healing, he chose to follow the One who had restored his sight and, in many ways, his life. Jesus had given him a new lease on life, and he chose to give that life back to Jesus. What a wonderful example of the kind of faith, gratitude, and commitment to Christ we should all have.

What does it mean to follow Jesus today?

DON'T FORGET TO PRAY AND HAVE A GREAT DAY!

 THINGS TO PRAY FOR TODAY:

Day 243

 Today's Reading:
Luke 19:1–10

Z acchaeus is a fairly well-known character in the New Testament, mainly due to the children's song about him. He has an extraordinary story because of the great change that took place in his heart and life as a result of his encounter with Jesus. In the course of these few short verses, Zacchaeus goes from being an unscrupulous tax collector to a benevolent disciple of Christ. He is a true example of repentance. But one of the most remarkable things about this man's story, in my mind, is the extraordinary effort he put forth in order to see Jesus. His short stature prevented him from seeing Jesus through the crowds, so he ran ahead, found a tree to climb, and positioned himself to be able to see Jesus as He passed by. He was not looking for a miracle or special attention. The text only indicates that he sought to see who Jesus was, but his interest level was great enough to motivate a tremendous effort. It was an effort that Jesus noticed and, calling him by name, showed interest in this man that had shown so much interest in Him. Oh, that we and the world around us could be so interested in Jesus Christ.

Why do you think Zacchaeus was so interested in Jesus?

DON'T FORGET TO PRAY AND HAVE A GREAT DAY!

 THINGS TO PRAY FOR TODAY:

DAY 244

Today's Reading:
Luke 19:11–27

T his parable is often equated or confused with the parable of the talents (Matthew 25), but it is a separate parable told at a different place and time. It seems this parable was probably told while Jesus was still at the home of Zacchaeus and was likely prompted by Zacchaeus' vow of repentance. The very similar parable of the talents will be discussed later, so with this text, let's think about the element of the story that is different. There are enemies of the master in this story who do not want him to rule over them, and who try to undermine his authority and leadership. The enemies obviously represent the Jewish leaders who had refused to accept Jesus as the Messiah and would eventually kill Him in an attempt to prevent Him from ruling. There have always been, and always will be, enemies of God and Christ who will refuse to submit to their rule and will try to thwart their plans. But just as with the Jewish leaders of Jesus' day, those efforts will be unsuccessful. Jesus reigns, and the day is coming when He will appear in the clouds and when every knee will bow and every tongue will confess that He is, indeed, Lord (Philippians 2:9-10).

What are some reasons people refuse to submit to God?

DON'T FORGET TO PRAY AND HAVE A GREAT DAY!

⌛ THINGS TO PRAY FOR TODAY:

DAY 245

Today's Reading:
John 12:1-8

It is hard to believe that one could spend so much time with Jesus and not be completely changed by Him. How could Judas be an apostle of the Lord and still be so enamored with worldly riches that he is characterized by John as "a thief"? Apparently, this was not a new problem for Judas. John says that it was his practice to take money out of the money box with which he had been entrusted. His mind and heart were given to physical things, so much so that he resented this act of love and honor that was being bestowed upon Jesus. Mark reveals that it was this event that prompted Judas to go to the chief priests for the purpose of betraying Jesus to them (Mark 14:10-11). Other than revealing the character of Judas, what can this text teach us? I believe that it is a grim reminder of the power and danger of the attraction of worldly things. If we allow them to, the things of this world can occupy our hearts in a way that leaves no room for Christ and causes us to betray Him just as Judas did. It is no wonder that Jesus warns us that we "cannot serve God and money" (Matthew 6:24).

Why do you think that worldly things
are such a powerful temptation?

DON'T FORGET TO PRAY AND HAVE A GREAT DAY!

 THINGS TO PRAY FOR TODAY:

DAY 246

Today's Reading:
John 12:9–11

It never ceases to amaze me to see the dark, devious attitudes and motives of the Jewish leaders. Even if their motives had been pure (which they were not), they were willing to lay aside the same law of God they claimed to be protecting in order to rid themselves of Jesus and anyone else that might cause others to believe in Him. Their deceitfulness knew no bounds as they plotted to kill, not only Jesus, but Lazarus as well. How could they have such disregard for the law that they professed to love and had devoted their lives to, and for the God that had given it to them? It is a sad testament to their hardness of heart and hypocrisy. It is a dangerous thing to become so hardened in heart that one cannot be touched by Jesus. That danger exists for us today, just as it did for the chief priests of Jesus' day. Though our means of rejection may be much more subtle and less violent than theirs, our hardness of heart can cause the same attitudes of denial and rejection toward Jesus. May God help us always to have soft and willing hearts in accepting and submitting to Jesus as Lord.

What are some things that can cause
our hearts to become hardened?

DON'T FORGET TO PRAY AND HAVE A GREAT DAY!

⏳ **THINGS TO PRAY FOR TODAY:**

Day 247

Today's Reading:
Luke 19:28–40

What a powerful passage! There were not many moments during Jesus' ministry when He was treated like the king and Lord that He was (and is). As you read through the gospels, the focus is often on His adversaries and all the doubts, accusations, rejections, and plotting that were constantly a part of His life. We can forget that there were a great many people who did believe in Jesus and who were sincere and devoted disciples. This passage reminds us of that fact. These disciples recognized Him as Lord and as the Son of God. They were excited to give honor and praise to Him and to treat Him like the King that He was. When He was commanded to rebuke His disciples for what the Pharisees saw as blasphemous behavior, Jesus responds with the powerful statement that, if they were to keep silent, even the stones would cry out. Jesus was the Son of God. That fact was undeniable and irrefutable. All of creation was a testament to the greatness of God, and even the stones would attest to the glory of Jesus as the only begotten of the Father.

What was significant about this entry into Jerusalem by Jesus?

DON'T FORGET TO PRAY AND HAVE A GREAT DAY!

⌛ **THINGS TO PRAY FOR TODAY:**

Day 248

Today's Reading:
John 12:12–19

L ook, the world has gone after Him!" This was the conclusion of the Pharisees. All their attempts to discredit, disparage, and find fault with Jesus had been ineffective. People had believed in Him and still had followed after Him in great numbers. Their desire and willingness to follow after Jesus had been greater than the Pharisees' plotting and schemes to destroy Jesus' influence. I believe that the world is not much different today. Despite the skepticism that often exists, and despite the many people and forces that would have us to believe that Jesus and religion is all a farce, the world is still filled with people who are willing to believe and follow the truth when they find it. The difference is that Jesus is no longer walking in this world, showing Himself to them in human form. He has, instead, called us to show Him to the world. Through our love and faithfulness, Jesus desires for the world to see and follow after Him. And they will. Through our lives and service, I believe that we can still say today that "the world has gone after Him!"

How can we show Jesus to the world today?

DON'T FORGET TO PRAY AND HAVE A GREAT DAY!

⏳ **THINGS TO PRAY FOR TODAY:**

DAY 249

Today's Reading:
Luke 19:41–44

Even though the Jewish leaders, those who should have been closest to God and the first to recognize Him as the promised Messiah, had rejected Him, Jesus' heart was still full of compassion for them. In this scene, Jesus weeps over the city of Jerusalem. In less than forty years, this great and holy city, which had represented God's people and been the center of their lives and nation, would be overtaken and destroyed. If only they had listened to Him. If only they had believed. In this sad scene, we see clearly the merciful and longsuffering love of God. Though these hard-hearted leaders had twisted and corrupted God's laws, though they had led God's people astray, though they had rejected His Son and would soon murder Him, yet God's love persisted. He mourned their downfall and wished for their return. It is no different in our day. Despite our world's own hard-heartedness and refusal to believe, God continues to love. He continues to desire salvation for mankind. And he continues to wait patiently, giving us time to repent and turn to Him before it is too late. What a loving and patient God!

Why do you think God is so long-suffering toward us?

DON'T FORGET TO PRAY AND HAVE A GREAT DAY!

 THINGS TO PRAY FOR TODAY:

Day 250

 Today's Reading:
Matthew 21:12–17

A s I read this passage, it strikes me as interesting that the Jewish leaders were more interested in what some children were saying than in what Jesus was doing. He had created havoc in the temple by running out the merchants who had set up shop there, condemning their corruption and wrongdoing. He had then proceeded to heal all who came to Him with infirmities. Surely these actions were worthy of the Jews' attention and reaction. But they had become accustomed to ignoring the great works of Jesus. They had made a habit of closing their eyes to His righteousness, compassion, and power. To recognize those things would force them to acknowledge Him. They chose rather to concentrate on what they considered to be the blasphemous language of children. Their words were words that could be used to accuse Jesus, to build a case against Him. Though the words were true, they could be used by the unbelieving Jewish leaders to condemn Jesus. So they chose to focus on what they wanted to see and ignore the truth.

Why were the Jewish leaders so upset by the children's words?

DON'T FORGET TO PRAY AND HAVE A GREAT DAY!

⌛ THINGS TO PRAY FOR TODAY:

Day 251

Today's Reading:
Matthew 21:18–22

What good is a fruit tree with no fruit? While Jesus' action here might seem to be harsh and impulsive, there is no doubt that He knew the condition of the tree before reaching it, and that He had a purpose and plan for His action. But what was that purpose? Obviously, this occasion provided Jesus with an opportunity once again to teach His apostles about the power of faith. But I believe that there is another lesson to be learned from this text. A fruit tree's purpose is to produce fruit. A tree that is barren is useless. As disciples of Christ, we are much like fruit trees. Our responsibility is to bear fruit for Him. But just as surely as a barren fruit tree is not fulfilling its purpose, if we are not bearing fruit for Christ, then neither are we fulfilling our purpose. Could it be that Jesus is attempting to impress upon His apostles, and us, the importance of fulfilling our purpose and the seriousness with which God views that purpose? May He help us to be about the business of bearing fruit for Him.

What does it mean to bear fruit for Christ?

DON'T FORGET TO PRAY AND HAVE A GREAT DAY!

⧗ **THINGS TO PRAY FOR TODAY:**

Day 252

Today's Reading:
Matthew 21:23–27

Jesus was trapped, or so the Jewish leaders thought. Though the text doesn't give any background information, you can imagine the plotting and scheming that had gone on prior to this encounter. The chief priests and elders had put their heads together and come up with the perfect trap. They had planned every detail carefully—the time, the place, the question. On the surface, the questions are simple and straight-forward, yet in their minds, there was no safe answer. If Jesus said that it was by God's authority that He did these things, they could seize Him immediately on the charge of blasphemy. If He claimed any other authority, He was guilty of working against the authority of the Jewish leaders. They had Him! But Jesus' wisdom was far greater than theirs. He immediately saw through their guise and knew their intent. He turned the tables on them and put them in the same situation. If they answered His question, He would answer theirs, but they could not. Once again, Jesus had proven Himself to be superior to them in wisdom and authority.

What impresses you most about how Jesus dealt with His enemies?

DON'T FORGET TO PRAY AND HAVE A GREAT DAY!

⏳ **THINGS TO PRAY FOR TODAY:**

Day 253

Today's Reading:
Matthew 21:28–32

This passage is really about the heart. In Jesus' teaching, and throughout the New Testament, it is continually expressed that God desires the hearts of sinners that are soft, aware of sin, and repentant over those hearts and lives that are haughty and hypocritical. The Jewish leaders were very often of the latter type. They placed themselves above others and above sin. They were self-righteous and judgmental. They were hard-hearted, refusing to see or believe in Jesus, and condemning of anyone who did. In this short parable, Jesus describes them as the son that agreed to obey his father but never did. In contrast, Jesus said it is those who had initially refused to obey the father (sinners), but who had afterward repented and obeyed, who were justified. God still desires for us to have soft hearts. We are all sinners, redeemed by the blood of Christ. We must be willing to recognize our shortcomings, repent of our sins, and submit to God. In doing so, we must put away the high-mindedness and hypocrisy that Jesus condemned the Jews for. It is only in this way that we find the forgiveness that we need and become pleasing to God.

What are some things that can cause
a person to become hard-hearted?

DON'T FORGET TO PRAY AND HAVE A GREAT DAY!

 THINGS TO PRAY FOR TODAY:

DAY 254

 Today's Reading:
Matthew 21:33–46

God had entrusted the Jews with His law and with the well-being of His people. He had blessed them with a name, an inheritance, His protection, and many great promises. In return, He had expected them to keep those laws faithfully, to guard His people against false gods and false religions, to submit to Him and Him only, and to teach His laws and precepts to His people. But they had gone their own way. They had taken the things that God had given them as their own and had forgotten who they truly belonged to. They had perverted and misused them. They had mingled God's commands with traditions of their own, and they had led many astray. They had rejected God's prophets and messengers who had tried to correct them. They had even rejected His own Son and would eventually kill Him. So as Jesus teaches through this parable, God had rejected them. He would establish a new covenant and open up His kingdom to a new people, all people. This text should serve both to encourage and warn us. God's covenant and kingdom are open to us through Christ, but we must be careful to be found faithful in what God has entrusted to us.

What is involved in being a faithful servant of God?

DON'T FORGET TO PRAY AND HAVE A GREAT DAY!

 THINGS TO PRAY FOR TODAY:

DAY 255

Today's Reading:
Matthew 22:1-14

When I read this parable, my initial reaction to it is one of sadness. The king had prepared a great feast because of this joyous occasion, the marriage of his son. He is happy, excited, overjoyed, and he wishes to share his joy with his friends and neighbors. He initially invites people to the feast who he has a relationship with, those whom he knows and cares for. But they all reject him. They do not desire to share in his joy or have enough respect for him to accept his invitation. They even beat and kill the servants that are sent to him with the invitation. How saddened and hurt the king must have felt at being treated so shamefully by those who were supposed to be his friends. Obviously, the king represents God, and the friends are the Jews. God had desired to share with His chosen people this great and joyous event, but they were not willing. So He rejected them and opened the feast to any who would answer the invitation and prepare themselves for the wedding feast. May we be found dressed (see Galatians 3:27) and ready when the bridegroom appears.

How should we prepare ourselves for this wedding?

DON'T FORGET TO PRAY AND HAVE A GREAT DAY!

 THINGS TO PRAY FOR TODAY:

Day 256

Today's Reading:
Matthew 22:15–22

Despite all their attempts, the Jewish leaders could not find fault with Jesus within their own law. He was flawless in His conduct and in His understanding of the law of Moses. So they turned to the Roman law to try and trap Him. They sent men to question Him on the issue of taxation, a hotly debated topic among the Jews. The Herodians agreed with submission to the Roman emperor and paying taxes to that government, while the Pharisees saw taxes as a violation of the Jewish law. Again, whichever side Jesus chose, He would have trouble with someone. Knowing their hearts and evil intent, Jesus responds by calling for a Roman coin engraved with the image and name of the Caesar. His teaching is that it is right to give to Caesar what belongs to Him, but that they must also remember to give to God those things that belong to Him. It may be that He was speaking of the Jewish taxes due to the temple. But more likely, Jesus was telling them to give God the honor, love, and obedience that was due Him. We likewise must give to God the love and devotion that we owe Him.

How do we give God the love and devotion that we owe Him?

DON'T FORGET TO PRAY AND HAVE A GREAT DAY!

⏳ **THINGS TO PRAY FOR TODAY:**

DAY 257

 Today's Reading:
Luke 20:27-40

It must have been a wondrous thing to watch Jesus spar with the Jewish leaders. The Sadducees took the next turn, as one came to Jesus with a riddle in an attempt to prove what they believed to be the absurdity of the resurrection. Taking another "unanswerable question," Jesus teaches another great truth, this time about the resurrection. The Sadducees, like many today, had trouble differentiating between the physical and the spiritual. How would physical relationships exist in the same way when all of humankind was resurrected? It was impossible. But Jesus distinguishes between the physical and spiritual by teaching that, in the resurrection, there will be no marriage. Marriage is a physical union that exists only in the physical world. In the resurrection, we will take on spiritual forms and will no longer be subject to physical relationships. It is a concept that is difficult to grasp because of our physical nature, but in order to put on the spiritual, we must put off the physical with all of its elements and relationships. What a glorious transformation that will be!

When will the resurrection take place?

DON'T FORGET TO PRAY AND HAVE A GREAT DAY!

 THINGS TO PRAY FOR TODAY:

Day 258

Today's Reading:
Mark 12:28-34

Matthew records that this scribe came to Jesus to "test" Him, that is, to put him to the test. It was another attempt to entrap Jesus in His own words. The Law of Mosses contained some 613 individual laws and commands. How could He pinpoint one as the most important? Jesus' answer is a simple one: love God with all your heart, soul, mind, and strength. He then goes a step further to name the second most important law—to love your neighbor as yourself. If one keeps these two commands, Jesus says, he will have been faithful to the entire law. At this point in the text, an interesting thing happens. This scribe who came to test Jesus realizes the wisdom and truthfulness of Jesus' answer. He agrees with Him, commends His answer, and even expounds on what Jesus says. This doubter has seemingly become a believer. He has been won over by the unavoidable truth of what Jesus has taught. In response, Jesus commends the scribe by telling him: "You are not far from the kingdom of God." What a testament to the wisdom and truthfulness of Jesus.

What does it mean to love God with
all your heart, soul, mind, and strength?

DON'T FORGET TO PRAY AND HAVE A GREAT DAY!

 THINGS TO PRAY FOR TODAY:

DAY 259

Today's Reading:
Matthew 22:41–46

This text demonstrates the misunderstanding and ignorance of the Jewish leaders concerning the prophesied Messiah. This time, it is Jesus who questions the Pharisees asking them, "What do you think about the Christ? Whose Son is He?" They correctly answered, "the Son of David." Ironically, Jesus' followers had, just a few days before, praised Jesus, calling Him the Son of David (Matthew 21:9, 15) to which the Pharisees adamantly protested. The Jews had taken the prophecies literally and thought the coming Messiah to be only of the physical lineage of David. "Why then," Jesus asked, "did David call Him Lord?" The point is, if David called the Messiah Lord, it stands to reason that He must be more than just the physical descendant of David. In fact, He must be more than merely human. He must be from God. For this reasoning, the Jews had no response and, in fact, did not question Him again until the night that He stood on trial before them.

Why do you think the Jews continued to refuse to believe in Jesus?

DON'T FORGET TO PRAY AND HAVE A GREAT DAY!

 THINGS TO PRAY FOR TODAY:

DAY 260

Today's Reading:
Mark 12:35-37

This is the same event that we considered in yesterday's reading, but Mark adds a different dimension to it. While Matthew (writing to the Jews) focuses on the Jewish reaction to Jesus' statements, Mark (writing to a Gentile audience) chooses to focus on the reaction of "the common people." These common people were the poor of society, the ones without wealth, notoriety, or position. They lacked the level of education or understanding of the Law of Moses that the Pharisees and Scribes enjoyed, but they understood the teaching of Jesus. Not only did they understand it, they received it "gladly." They rejoiced in knowing that the prophecies had been fulfilled, the Messiah had come, and that He stood before them in the person of Jesus. Though their lives were simpler and their education inferior, their faith was stronger, and their hearts were open to receiving Jesus as the Son of God. They, and not the religious elites of the day, stand as patterns and examples for our lives today.

Why do you think "the common
people" were more willing to believe?

DON'T FORGET TO PRAY AND HAVE A GREAT DAY!

 **THINGS TO PRAY FOR TODAY:**

DAY 261

 Today's Reading:
Matthew 23:1–12

In this text, Jesus never calls the scribes and Pharisees "hypocrites" (though He will several times in the next few verses), but He does describe their actions and, in so doing, certainly characterizes them as truly hypocritical. Do as they command, He teaches, because they sit in positions of authority, but do not follow their example because they do not even follow their own teaching. The actions of the scribes and Pharisees were not motivated by their deep love for God or their firm devotion to God's law, but rather by their love of praise and notoriety and by their cravings for power and authority. Though they exalted themselves and claimed to be closer to God than the average man, they were in fact very far from what God wanted them to be. As we live our lives in Christ, we must be careful not to fall into the path of the Pharisees, practicing religion for the sake of appearances, and exalting ourselves in the eyes of men. We must instead humble ourselves, understanding that we are all sinners redeemed by the blood of Christ and saved only by the grace of God.

How can we avoid following in the ways of the Pharisees?

DON'T FORGET TO PRAY AND HAVE A GREAT DAY!

 THINGS TO PRAY FOR TODAY:

Day 262

 Today's Reading:
Matthew 23:13–22

A fter warning His listeners not to follow the example of the
scribes and Pharisees, Jesus turns His attention to the Jewish
leaders as He speaks to them directly. "But woe to you, scribes and
Pharisees, hypocrites!" Consider the seriousness of the accusation
that Jesus levies against them in this text. They have shut up the
kingdom of heaven. For those who were in leadership positions
among God's people, those who were to be examples of righteousness
and spiritual leaders among the Jews, their responsibility was to lead
the people toward God and salvation through obedience to the
Law of Moses. But by their actions and example, they had actually
done the opposite. There were leading people away from God and
denying them entrance into the kingdom of heaven. For a leader
of God's people, could there be any worse testimony given against
him than that he has shut up the kingdom of heaven to the very ones
that he is supposed to be leading into that kingdom? What a difficult
accusation it must have been for the scribes and Pharisees to hear
and consider.

Can we shut up the kingdom of heaven for people today? If so, how?

DON'T FORGET TO PRAY AND HAVE A GREAT DAY!

 ⏳ **THINGS TO PRAY FOR TODAY:**

DAY 263

Today's Reading:
Matthew 23:23–28

These condemnations of the scribes and Pharisees all deal with the outward actions vs. the inward attitudes. God is certainly concerned about our outward lives—the things that we teach, practice, say, and do. He desires that our actions be godly and obedient. But there is more to being what God would have us to be than just the outward actions. God also cares about where those actions come from—the heart. He cares about our attitudes, motives, and thoughts. He wants the outward man to be a reflection of what the inside looks like. How often do we read in the New Testament about the importance of having both the proper heart and actions involved in our worship (John 4:24), teaching (Ephesians 4:15), and lives (1 Peter 1:22)? It is easy for us, like the scribes and Pharisees, to become so consumed with maintaining the outward appearance of righteousness that we can neglect the heart and spirit that is to motivate our Christian lives. May we ever strive to have hearts that are filled with love and faith and that motivate lives of obedience and service.

Why is the heart so important to God?

DON'T FORGET TO PRAY AND HAVE A GREAT DAY!

⏳ **THINGS TO PRAY FOR TODAY:**

DAY 264

Today's Reading:
Matthew 23:29–36

How ironic is the statement of the scribes and Pharisees that Jesus highlights in this condemnation. The Jewish leaders speak against their forefathers who persecuted the prophets, saying that they never would have done what those of old did. But they have already in their hearts made the decision to put to death the Messiah, the Son of God. That atrocious event is only days away, and Jesus brings to light the murder that is in their hearts and foretells of their persecution and murder of many servants of God. They are in fact worse than their fathers, and Jesus warns them that the blood of all the faithful servants of God who have ever been slain is on their hands. What a sobering charge this was that Jesus made against them. But as the scribes and Pharisees heard these words proclaimed by Jesus, they knew in their heart of hearts that He spoke the truth. They knew their intent and their plans. Though they no doubt kept up a pretense of righteousness before the people, they were well aware of the malice and hatred that had taken over their hearts. Their course had been laid, and their fates sealed.

How do you think the scribes and Pharisees justified their hypocrisy?

DON'T FORGET TO PRAY AND HAVE A GREAT DAY!

⧗ THINGS TO PRAY FOR TODAY:

Day 265

 Today's Reading:
Matthew 23:37–39

How beautiful, and yet how sad, are the words of Jesus as He looks over the city of Jerusalem and mourns over her rejection of Him and His Father. In this short statement, we catch a glimpse of the heart of God—how badly He wants to be a Father to His people, to care for them, protect them, provide for them, and love them. But in Jesus' words, they "were not willing." They had chosen another path, other ways, and other gods. They had devoted themselves to their traditions, to earthly powers, and to their own selfish desires instead of being devoted to God. They were not willing to submit to God and put themselves under His care. They were not willing to put Him above all else. So God, with sadness in His heart, allowed them to follow the path that they had chosen. He had removed His protective and benevolent care from them and had removed them from their place as His special people. It was not His choice but theirs. God's desire for us is the same—to protect, provide for, care for, and love us as His dear children. We must decide whether we are willing to be His children. The choice is ours. May we choose God!

What is involved in choosing to be children of God?

DON'T FORGET TO PRAY AND HAVE A GREAT DAY!

 THINGS TO PRAY FOR TODAY:

Day 266

 Today's Reading:
Mark 12:41-44

How does God judge the things that we give to Him, and the way in which we give those things? This observation made by Jesus as He watches people put money into the treasury gives us some insight into the answers to those questions. First of all, Jesus does not judge or condemn the giving of those who gave out of their abundance. They had been greatly blessed with many things and gave a portion of those things that the gospel writer describes as "much." But because of their wealth, their giving was not necessarily sacrificial. In contrast, the poor widow that Jesus points out had given "her whole livelihood." In a great act of devotion and faith, she had given to God literally all that she had from a monetary standpoint. Though it was a minuscule amount of money, Jesus commends her as giving more than all others who had given to the treasury. This text reiterates the point that it is our hearts that God desires more than anything else. As we give to God of our time, talents, or things, whether we can give much or only a little, He desires for us to give with a whole-hearted devotion and faith.

Why is God concerned with the heart with which we give?

DON'T FORGET TO PRAY AND HAVE A GREAT DAY!

 ⏳ **THINGS TO PRAY FOR TODAY:**

DAY 267

 Today's Reading:
Mark 13:1–13

For the Jews, the city of Jerusalem (and the temple in particular), was a great source of pride. It was seen as a permanent and untouchable symbol of their glory as God's chosen people. But in just a few short years, it would be completely destroyed. However, for Jesus' disciples, there were even greater challenges that lay ahead. The path of faithfulness was going to prove to be a very difficult one, riddled with false teachers, persecution, and betrayal. They were not going to be alone, for the Holy Spirit would be with them to guide them. But their faithfulness would require commitment and endurance. Two thousand years have passed since Jesus spoke those words, yet they are just as true today as they ever were. Faithful discipleship is still a difficult path that demands commitment and endurance. It requires that our love for Christ be greater than our love for anything else. But at the end of that difficult road, there is a great prize. Jesus' promise is a great one, and one that is sure: "But the one who endures to the end will be saved."

Why is the Christian life often a difficult one?

DON'T FORGET TO PRAY AND HAVE A GREAT DAY!

⧖ THINGS TO PRAY FOR TODAY:

DAY 268

Today's Reading:
Mark 13:14–23

The prophet Daniel had foretold a progression of kingdoms and empires that would come, conquering and possessing the land. It was a foregone conclusion that Jerusalem would be invaded and destroyed. Beginning in the mid 60s A.D., the city was partially surrounded and was ultimately completely overrun and destroyed in A.D. 70. It is this event that Jesus is warning about in this text. He gives His disciples (who will be Christians at the time of the invasion) instructions of what to do in order to survive: don't take time to gather your things and flee the city. Jesus' sole interest is in the preservation of His people. That was true of the destruction of Jerusalem, and it is true today. The New Testament warns us of an enemy with a mission of destroying us. It is not a physical enemy but a spiritual one. But Jesus gives us instructions concerning how to survive the attacks, just as He did for those living in His own day. If we will listen to His teaching and follow His precepts, we will survive and stand victorious in the end.

What has Jesus instructed us to do to survive our enemies' attacks?

DON'T FORGET TO PRAY AND HAVE A GREAT DAY!

⏳ THINGS TO PRAY FOR TODAY:

DAY 269

Today's Reading:
Mark 13:24–27

In the minds of the Jews, there was no worse fate to consider than the destruction of the temple and holy city. But in this part of the text, Jesus turns His attention to a much more final destruction, the true end of time. While a physical invasion from an earthly army might have power to kill and destroy, that power is only limited and temporary. However, Jesus foretells a time when He will appear to bring an end to all things for all time. He will send His angels to gather together those who belong to Him and to bring the world to judgment. What is His purpose? Maybe to bring perspective to this situation, to remind His disciples that there are things that are more important than this world and its cares, to remind them of what it is that they are truly living and fighting for. There are times when we all need perspective, to remind us of what is truly important. Just as Jesus did on this occasion, God constantly through His word gives us those important reminders.

How does God remind us of what is truly important?

DON'T FORGET TO PRAY AND HAVE A GREAT DAY!

 THINGS TO PRAY FOR TODAY:

Day 270

Today's Reading:
Mark 13:28-31

After reminding them of what is truly important, Jesus returns to the physical circumstances the disciples face. The physical destruction of Jerusalem is coming. It will take place during their lives. They must ready themselves and be prepared. They must watch for the signs and know when it is time to act. As this text concludes, there is the reminder of the sovereignty of God's will. "Heaven and earth will pass away, but My words will by no means pass away." It was God's will and purpose that Jerusalem be destroyed. Though it may have been hard for many of that day to understand, there was a grander purpose and plan in place. God's desire, as it always has been, was for the salvation of His people, the church. Through the events of history, God would providentially cause the spread of the gospel and the growth of His church. What a wonderful thing it is to worship and serve a God Whose will rules the universe and Whose word will never pass away.

Why is it important that God's Word will never pass away?

DON'T FORGET TO PRAY AND HAVE A GREAT DAY!

⏳ **THINGS TO PRAY FOR TODAY:**

DAY 271

Today's Reading:
Matthew 24:36–44

When will the Lord return? For centuries, men have searched for the answer to this question. Many have theorized, some have predicted, but none have been successful. Jesus clearly teaches that the time of His return is appointed by the Father and is only known to Him. There will be no signs or precursors. Until that day, the world will continue to function, and life will go on as it always has. People will work, rest, play, and carry on relationships. All will be as normal until the moment when Jesus returns to judge the world and to deliver His church up to the Father. So considering the unknown time of Jesus' return, what is His advice? "Stay awake" and "be ready." To "stay awake" simply means to be aware and conscious of the possibility of His return at any moment. Don't be caught off-guard. To "be ready" means just what it says—to constantly be in a state of preparedness to meet the Lord. We may not know when the Lord is going to return, but we have certainly been told how to be prepared for that great event. May God help us all to watch and be ready!

Why do you think God has not told us when His Son would return?

DON'T FORGET TO PRAY AND HAVE A GREAT DAY!

⏳ **THINGS TO PRAY FOR TODAY:**

DAY 272

 Today's Reading:
Mark 13:32–37

This, of course, is the same conversation that we read of from Matthew's account yesterday. In his account, Mark alludes to the stewardship principle that Jesus so often focuses on in His teaching. Jesus' return is tantamount to the return of the master to take account of the things that his servants have been left in charge of during his absence. In this present age, while we await the return of our Lord, we are indeed stewards of His kingdom, the church. We are responsible for using our things, our talents, and our time in a way that will allow us to be pleasing to Him and that will allow His church to fulfill its purpose and mission in this world. In caring for the Lord's kingdom, we must remember that His return is imminent. Our goal and aim must be to be pleasing to Him and to be faithful stewards of those things that He has entrusted to us. And knowing that His return will be without warning, we must work to be ready for that great event.

Why has God given us the responsibility of being stewards?

DON'T FORGET TO PRAY AND HAVE A GREAT DAY!

 **⧗ THINGS TO PRAY FOR TODAY:**

Day 273

 Today's Reading:
Luke 21:34-38

A s I read this passage, my eye is immediately drawn to the phrase, "Lest your hearts be weighed down." Jesus, still speaking about the end of time and His return, is warning His listeners not to become distracted by the things of this world so that they are not prepared for His coming. But this phrase indicates that Jesus was warning about more than just a simple lack of awareness or watchfulness. He was warning about the danger of allowing the cares and temptations of life to fill up their hearts and keep them from being devoted to God. Once again, the focus of Jesus' teaching is on the heart. It may be that we don't often see how participating in the pleasures of life can be detrimental to our spiritual well-being. We make a distinction between the physical and spiritual and don't understand the close connection. But as Jesus teaches, the physical things that we participate in and make a part of our lives have an indelible impact on our hearts. What we do affects where our hearts are, and where our hearts are define our lives and relationship with God.

How can the cares of life "weigh down" our hearts?

DON'T FORGET TO PRAY AND HAVE A GREAT DAY!

 THINGS TO PRAY FOR TODAY:

DAY 274

Today's Reading:
John 12:20-26

"We wish to see Jesus." What a wonderful attitude and powerful request. The language indicates that these God-fearing Greeks wanted to do more than simply to see Him; they wanted to speak with Him, to get to know Him. They had heard about Jesus and wanted to know the Messiah. Jesus' response was not to these men specifically, but to the entire crowd in general. Throughout Jesus' ministry, He had often said that His time had not yet come. His purpose on the earth was not complete, and the time for His atoning death had not come yet. But the coming of these Greek men is another indication that things have changed. Jesus' time has now come. He has accomplished all that was needed with the exception of the shedding of His blood for the sins of the world. It was time for God's saving grace to be extended to all nations and people. It was time for sin's power to be vanquished and Satan's hold to be broken. Jesus' death was imminent, and the world would never be the same. It was time.

What do you think v. 25 means?

DON'T FORGET TO PRAY AND HAVE A GREAT DAY!

⏳ THINGS TO PRAY FOR TODAY:

DAY 275

Today's Reading:
John 12:27–36

Lest we think that, because Jesus was God in the flesh, He was above the human emotions of fear, dread, and sorrow, we are reminded by our Lord that, as He contemplated His coming suffering and death, His soul was troubled. But we are also reminded in those same words that it was for this very purpose that He had come. To become the Lamb of God, the perfect sacrifice for sin, was His ultimate purpose in this world. His only prayer and request was that God and His name be glorified through Him. In this third recorded time during Jesus' ministry that God's voice is heard from heaven, Jesus is assured that God's name will be glorified through Him. Throughout the ages, God's name had been glorified through His many mighty acts, and through the godly and faithful lives of His servants. The God of heaven had proven time and again to be far above every principality and power, and above every false god that had been named by mankind. But in Jesus Christ, God would be glorified in a greater way than ever before. Jesus, the suffering servant, would be God's greatest demonstration of His power, love, righteousness, and mercy. To God be the glory!

How did Jesus' sacrifice glorify God?

DON'T FORGET TO PRAY AND HAVE A GREAT DAY!

 **⏳ THINGS TO PRAY FOR TODAY:**

Day 276

Today's Reading:
John 12:37–41

It is hard to believe that, at this point in Jesus' life, there were still those who remained unconvinced. Having seen all the wonderful works and authoritative teaching that saturated His days, how could so many still not believe. But we are reminded that it had always been known to God that this would be the case. Isaiah had prophesied long ago that many would not believe, and that God had allowed their disbelief for the carrying out of His will in the life of Jesus. What is truly amazing to me as I consider this passage is that, despite God's knowledge of the hard-heartedness of men concerning His Son (both then and now), He provided Him as a sacrifice, even for those who would never believe. What amazing love and overwhelming mercy it required for God to allow His Son to be nailed to a cross, shed His blood, and die for the sins of a world that would largely reject Him. That kind of love and mercy is beyond me, but I am so thankful that God saw fit to offer us salvation through Christ!

Why do you think God was willing to allow
Christ to die for those who would reject Him?

DON'T FORGET TO PRAY AND HAVE A GREAT DAY!

⌛ THINGS TO PRAY FOR TODAY:

Day 277

 Today's Reading:
John 12:42–50

There are different kinds of unbelief. Yesterday's reading was about those who totally rejected Jesus as the Savior. Today's reading is about the reluctant believer—the one who believes but is not willing to give up his present life to have the Life that Jesus offers. There were some among the rulers who fit this description. They believed in Jesus, but given the extreme hatred for Jesus among their peers, confessing that belief would surely bring dire consequences. They would lose their positions and all the honor and praise that went with them. It was a price that they were not willing to pay, so they kept their belief to themselves. One has to wonder how many of these rulers who believed in Jesus went along with the plans and efforts to crucify Him. In the end, there is no difference between the absolute unbeliever and the reluctant believer. They both will be judged by the words of Christ in the last day.

Why is being a reluctant believer just as bad as rejecting Christ?

DON'T FORGET TO PRAY AND HAVE A GREAT DAY!

 THINGS TO PRAY FOR TODAY:

Day 278

 Today's Reading:
Mark 14:1–11

Most commentators believe that this text refers to the same events as John 12:1-8, with Mary, the sister of Lazarus, being the unnamed woman who anointed Jesus' head (Mark) and feet (John) with a costly oil. This she did to honor Him and, as Jesus says, to symbolically prepare His body beforehand for burial. One of the highlights of this passage is the storm that is brewing around Jesus regarding His enemies. There are the chief priests and scribes who have firmly decided to "take Him by trickery and put Him to death" and are looking for the right opportunity. There are those who were indignant and very critical of such an extravagant act of honor being bestowed upon Jesus by Mary. And then there was Judas, the apostle of Jesus, whose love for money had taken precedence over His love for Jesus. This "wasteful" act of anointing Jesus' body was more than Judas could stand. He joined the ranks of Jesus' enemies and would look for the perfect opportunity to betray Him. The stage had been set, and it was only a matter of time.

What was the significance of Mary anointing Jesus?

DON'T FORGET TO PRAY AND HAVE A GREAT DAY!

⏳ **THINGS TO PRAY FOR TODAY:**

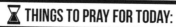

Day 279

Today's Reading:
Mark 14:12–16

For the Jews, the Passover represented one of their most cherished feast days. Memorializing the gracious mercy of God in sparing them from the final deadly plague that had sealed the deliverance of their ancestors from Egyptian bondage, it was a feast that was kept annually by God's command. But that feast, and in fact, the entire chain of events that had taken place so long ago in Egypt, had a much deeper meaning within the mind and purpose of God. It was to be a shadow of a much greater "passing over" and deliverance that God had in store for mankind. Through the shed blood of His perfect sacrifice, His Son, God would spare all those who were covered by that blood from spiritual death, the penalty of sin. As Jesus prepared to gather with His apostles to observe the Passover feast one final time, it would be an especially meaningful time of reflection and communion in view of the soon-to-come sacrifice that He was to make.

Why do you think it was so important to
Jesus that He spend this time with His apostles?

DON'T FORGET TO PRAY AND HAVE A GREAT DAY!

 ## THINGS TO PRAY FOR TODAY:

DAY 280

Today's Reading:
Luke 22:14–23

The time that Jesus spent with His apostles in the upper room on the night of His betrayal was special. But it's unlikely that anything done or said was more special than the event recorded here. For centuries, the Jews had observed the Passover to commemorate God's mercy and care as He worked to deliver them from Egyptian bondage. Following that pattern established by God so long ago, Jesus instituted a new memorial feast to commemorate His upcoming sacrifice and the deliverance that it would bring to mankind from sin and death. This memorial was to be observed by all those who accepted the new covenant offered by God through Christ and done in remembrance of Jesus and His sacrifice. It is this beautiful memorial that we still take part in each Lord's day as we come together. With hearts full of gratitude and love, we are reminded by the unleavened bread and fruit of the vine of the body and blood of our Lord, offered up as the atoning sacrifice for our sins. What a special time it is to be able to commune with our Lord in the memorial that He Himself established.

Why do you think Jesus desired
for us to take part in this memorial?

DON'T FORGET TO PRAY AND HAVE A GREAT DAY!

⏳ THINGS TO PRAY FOR TODAY:

Day 281

Today's Reading:
Luke 22:24–30

After all of their time with Jesus, and all the teaching and training that they had received from Him, there is still a somewhat selfish spirit displayed by the apostles. I see this as a testament to the propensity of our human bodies and minds toward fleshly desires. It is also no doubt the product of Satan's work to produce strife and division among Jesus' closest followers. The desire to be great is a powerful one—one that has led many away from God and into sin. But Jesus teaches His apostles, and us, that true greatness is not what the world defines as greatness. To be great in the eyes of God is to be a servant. Humility and submission are qualities that God prefers and in fact commands of His people. For those who are willing to submit humbly to God and to be servants to those around them, God will exalt in His heavenly kingdom and allow to share in all the wondrous glory of that eternal home. May we always choose to be faithful servants to God over the temporary greatness this world might offer.

Why does God desire for us to be servants?

DON'T FORGET TO PRAY AND HAVE A GREAT DAY!

 THINGS TO PRAY FOR TODAY:

Day 282

Today's Reading:
John 13:1–17

Jesus had often taught His disciples of the importance of humility and service, but as they met together in the upper room, Jesus gives them a powerful demonstration and example of those attributes. The job of foot-washing was reserved for the lowliest servant of the household. It was a demeaning and thankless job that no one wanted to do. But as the apostles are sitting around the table arguing over who will be the greatest (see yesterday's reading), Jesus dons a towel and begins to serve the apostles in a remarkably humble way. What lesson does He hope to teach them through this act of service? That if He, their teacher and Lord (not to mention the Son of God), can humble Himself to perform this act of service, then they (and we) certainly should be willing to serve one another in whatever way we can. For the servant of God, no work is so lowly that it is beneath us. If we can show the love of God to others and bring glory to Him through our service, then we should always be ready and willing to take on the role of a servant.

Why is it so important to God that we be servants?

DON'T FORGET TO PRAY AND HAVE A GREAT DAY!

⧗ **THINGS TO PRAY FOR TODAY:**

DAY 283

Today's Reading:
John 13:18–30

A s we have read previously, Judas has already decided to betray Jesus and has in fact already come to an agreement with the Jewish leaders concerning that deed. He remains with Jesus, but with the motive of finding the perfect time to betray Him into their hands. There were many attitudes that were driving Judas—greed, bitterness, unbelief—but behind them all was Satan. He had used Judas' love for money, his disdain for Jesus' attitude toward worldly things, his lack of true faith against him, and had led him down the path toward destruction. Judas serves as a vivid reminder to us that we are all susceptible to Satan's attacks. If one so close to Jesus—chosen to be an apostle, a daily eyewitness to His wisdom, power, and love—could fall to temptation and betray the Lord, surely any of us could be led down that same road. The example of Judas reminds us all of the diligence with which we need to resist Satan and pursue godliness.

What are some of the things we can do to help us resist Satan?

DON'T FORGET TO PRAY AND HAVE A GREAT DAY!

 THINGS TO PRAY FOR TODAY:

DAY 284

Today's Reading:
John 13:31–35

We are familiar with Jesus' command in this text concerning our loving one another. It is that mutual love that Jesus points to as the identifying mark of His disciples (Christians). But how is loving one another a "new" command? Under the old covenant, God's people were bound together by heritage. They had a common father in Abraham and a common history as a people and nation. It was these bonds that held them together and sealed their devotion to one another. They were taught to love God and to have a love for mankind in general, but the kind of love that Jesus refers to in this passage was not commanded. Under the new covenant, disciples of Christ would come from all different backgrounds and heritages. There would be no common bloodline except that of Christ. Their bond was to be found in the love that Christ showed for them and in the love that they had for one another. The deep, mutual, brotherly love that Christ taught and desired for His church was new and would set them apart from the rest of the world. That love among Christians is still a command, and should still be a special identifier of God's people wherever they are.

How do we demonstrate the kind of love Jesus commanded?

DON'T FORGET TO PRAY AND HAVE A GREAT DAY!

 THINGS TO PRAY FOR TODAY:

Day 285

Today's Reading:
John 14:1–6

T his beautiful passage is one that is very familiar to us. It is a beautiful and hopeful promise of Jesus concerning His return and the eternal home that He is preparing for each of us. But consider for a moment the context of His words—the mood and tone of the upper room that night is somber and melancholy. Jesus has revealed the presence of a traitor among them and has then talked about going away. The apostles are confused, concerned, and probably visibly upset. His words, recorded in John 14, are meant to lift them up, to encourage them, to give them comfort and hope. His going away is not forever. It is only for a time, and it is for a great purpose. He is going to prepare a place for them. His desire is for them to be with Him forever, and He is going to make the way ready. Jesus' words to His apostles are meant for us also. Just as He did for them, He wants all of us to be with Him for eternity. A home in heaven awaits all those who have come to the Father through Him. The way has been prepared. What a wonderful promise, full of hope and comfort!

How do we come to the Father through Christ?

DON'T FORGET TO PRAY AND HAVE A GREAT DAY!

⧖ THINGS TO PRAY FOR TODAY:

Day 286

Today's Reading:
John 14:7–11

Make no mistake: Jesus came into this world to save sinners through His atoning death. That was His purpose. But as you recognize that truth, do not miss the fact that Jesus accomplished more than that while here. During His life, and especially the three years of His earthly ministry, He set a perfect example of how to live a life of service and compassion and godliness. He never faltered or failed, but illuminated brilliantly the path that leads us to God. During His life, Jesus also accomplished another important feat—He showed us God. As we read and study these accounts of the life of Christ, we get an unprecedented view of the mind and heart of God the Father. We see His righteousness, His love, His compassion, His mercy, and His holiness. In the person of Jesus Christ, God walked among men and gave us the opportunity to experience Him and know Him in a way that had never been possible before. It is truly amazing to think about all the ways God has shown His love toward us!

What have you learned about God by studying Jesus' life?

DON'T FORGET TO PRAY AND HAVE A GREAT DAY!

 THINGS TO PRAY FOR TODAY:

DAY 287

 Today's Reading:
John 14:12–14

Jesus makes a great promise to His apostles about the things that their belief will allow them to do in His absence. They will be powerful warriors in His kingdom, displaying the wondrous works of God through the power of Christ working in them and, through those works, will bring glory to God. With Jesus as their constant help, they will have an eternal impact on the world. Belief in Jesus is still empowering! As our belief motivates us to obey His word and give Him our lives, we are transformed into His image by the saving power of His blood. Our fear is defeated by faith, and our hopelessness gives way to eternal hope. As we work and serve and live in this world, we do so by the power of Christ, shining as lights in a dark world, and bringing glory to God by our good works (Matthew 5:16). Our belief in Christ and the saving power of His blood make us infinitely more than we are capable of being on our own. As Paul says, "I can do all things through him who strengthens me" (Philippians 4:13).

How does our belief in Christ strengthen us?

DON'T FORGET TO PRAY AND HAVE A GREAT DAY!

 THINGS TO PRAY FOR TODAY:

DAY 288

Today's Reading:
John 14:15–18

It is amazing to read of the great love Jesus had for His apostles. He is preparing to leave them. He knows that it will be a devastating loss for them and a difficult situation to deal with, but He gives them the assurance that He will not leave them alone and helpless. He will continue to be with them through the Spirit of truth, to dwell with them and in them, bringing comfort to their hearts and understanding to their minds. As they continue to walk in His commandments, He will continue to be with them, guiding and teaching them. But the Spirit of truth Jesus promised to His apostles was not meant only for their benefit. That Spirit endowed them with the knowledge and understanding that produced the written Word of God, and that Word continues to teach and benefit every generation of humanity. Through His Spirit, God has provided a guide in His Word for all who will read it, believe it, and apply it to their lives. It is a great testament to God's love for all of us!

How does God's Word demonstrate His love for us?

DON'T FORGET TO PRAY AND HAVE A GREAT DAY!

⏳ **THINGS TO PRAY FOR TODAY:**

Day 289

 Today's Reading:
John 14:19–24

Relationship—it is at the core of everything God has ever done. He created mankind for the purpose of having a relationship with them. After sin entered the world, everything God did as recorded in the Scriptures was for the purpose of restoring the relationship that had been severed by sin. This passage reminds us of the purpose of the suffering and death that Jesus was preparing to go through. Relationship. If we will love Him and keep His words, then He and the Father will love us and dwell with us. That is all that God ever wanted, a relationship that will last for all eternity. Jesus was about to die to make that relationship possible. After that, it is up to us. We have to choose Him. We have to come to Him in faith and obedience, establishing a relationship with Him through baptism, and loving Him and devoting ourselves to keeping His word. God's love for us is clearly seen in the cross of Christ. His desire for a relationship with us is obvious. The choice is ours.

Why is our obedience necessary in
order to have a relationship with God?

DON'T FORGET TO PRAY AND HAVE A GREAT DAY!

 THINGS TO PRAY FOR TODAY:

Day 290

Today's Reading:
John 14:25–31

The events that were going to transpire in the coming hours and days would be very difficult for the apostles to understand. They could not imagine life without their Master and Teacher, much less all the terrible things that He was about to endure. The questions must have flooded their minds: *Where is He going? Why is He going away? Why can't we go with Him? What will we do without Him? When will He return?* Jesus, understanding their trepidation, tries to encourage them with words of consolation and hope. It seems as though His very heart hurts for them in contemplation of the confusion that they are experiencing and the heartache that is sure to follow. His care and concern for them speaks volumes about the care and concern God has for each of us. He does not want any of us to be plagued by fear, hopelessness, or despair. The story of Jesus is one of hope and love intended to comfort and encourage all those who hear and accept it.

Why do you think God is so concerned about us?

DON'T FORGET TO PRAY AND HAVE A GREAT DAY!

⏳ THINGS TO PRAY FOR TODAY:

Day 291

Today's Reading:
John 15:1-8

This passage has been often misused to justify doctrinal differences among denominational groups, but what is the true meaning of Jesus' words in this text? Jesus says that He is the true vine. As such, He is the source of life and nourishment for all the branches that are in Him. Apart from the vine, the branches will wither and die. He alone is the life-giving force for all those who belong to Him. As the vine, He is also the One who defines the branches so that the branches are identified by their attachment to the vine. Just as a grapevine only contains branches that produce grapes, so Jesus only contains branches (Christians) who produce proper fruit. There is, in this truth, a great responsibility placed upon those of us who are branches of the vine. If we are to be in Christ, then we must produce fruit pleasing and acceptable to God, the vinedresser, lest we be pruned away. Could there be any better image to describe the importance, not only of bearing fruit, but of bearing acceptable fruit for God?

Why is it important to God that we bear fruit?

DON'T FORGET TO PRAY AND HAVE A GREAT DAY!

⌛ **THINGS TO PRAY FOR TODAY:**

Day 292

Today's Reading:
John 15:9–17

Within these endearing words of Jesus toward His apostles, there is a great principle for each of us. "This is my commandment, that you love one another as I have loved you." With His imminent departure, Jesus was concerned that His apostles continue to love and care for one another in His absence. His desire was not that they simply love one another, but that they love one another in the same way that He had loved them—in a selfless, sacrificial way that always looked out for each other's best interest. What Jesus desired for His apostles, He desires and commands of all of His disciples in any age. His love for us is great and unconditional, and His command to us is that we replicate that love in our relationships with one another. He wants us to care for one another in a way that puts other's needs and concerns before our own, to sacrifice our own interests for the best interests of our brothers and sisters. May God help us to love others as He loves us!

Why is it important to God that we love one another?

DON'T FORGET TO PRAY AND HAVE A GREAT DAY!

⏳ **THINGS TO PRAY FOR TODAY:**

DAY 293

Today's Reading:
John 15:18-25

The life of a Christian is not always an easy one. It is a life of uncompromising commitment and fellowship of Christ. Many will not understand you or the reasons why you choose a life of faith. Many will belittle, disparage, and mock you for the life you have chosen. Some will hate you and desire to do harm to you because of the values you uphold. Jesus reminds us in this text that the world that hates and mistreats His people, hated and mistreated Him first. As we consider the suffering that Jesus endured during His life and especially in His death, we are reminded that the world has always been and always will be a world that is largely opposed to what Jesus stands for. It is a world that does not appreciate the value of virtue or the significance of service. It is a world that does not understand true love, nor does it believe in faith. Ultimately, it is a world that has rejected God and put its trust only in the physical. Therefore, Christ has called His people out of the world, to live by faith, and walk in His light. No, it is not always an easy life, but it is by far the best life!

Why do you think that so many in the world have rejected God?

DON'T FORGET TO PRAY AND HAVE A GREAT DAY!

 THINGS TO PRAY FOR TODAY:

DAY 294

Today's Reading:
John 15:26–16:4

The Helper that would be sent in Jesus' absence is a recurring theme of Jesus' words to His apostles in this, their last gathering before His death. This Helper, the Spirit of truth, would come to them from the Father to testify of Jesus and to guide them into all truth. But significant to this passage is the price that they would have to pay for testifying of Jesus. Jesus tells them that they would be cast out of the synagogue and in fact be killed for their belief in and proclaiming of Jesus. Considering these circumstances, Jesus does not want them to "be made to stumble." He wants them to understand that, despite their hardships and suffering for the cause of Christ, they are not alone. God is with them. He will send His Spirit, the Helper, to them to comfort and guide them. By extension, we need to understand that the same is true for us. Whatever this life might hold, we are not alone. God, in His indescribable love, is always with us to comfort and help us in our trials, so that we also may never be made to stumble.

How does God strengthen and comfort us?

DON'T FORGET TO PRAY AND HAVE A GREAT DAY!

 **THINGS TO PRAY FOR TODAY:**

DAY 295

Today's Reading:
John 16:5-15

Occasionally, throughout this discourse by Jesus, something is said to remind us of the scene. It is somber and saddening. So disheartened are the apostles by Jesus' revelation that He is about to leave them that they don't even think to ask where He is going. They are overwhelmed with sorrow. Their minds are cloudy and reeling with the thoughts of life without their Master and friend. It is against this backdrop that Jesus continues to speak about the Helper that is being sent to them. This Helper, the Spirit of truth, will guide them into all truth, empowering them, working through them to accomplish God's will and work on the earth. The language here suggests that the Spirit will work as a prosecutor, presenting the truth of God's word as evidence and convicting the world of sin, righteousness, and judgment. What a powerful statement about God's Word, the product of the Spirit's work and inspiration! That Word continues to lead many to God and convict those who reject its truths.

How does God's Word convict people today?

DON'T FORGET TO PRAY AND HAVE A GREAT DAY!

 THINGS TO PRAY FOR TODAY:

DAY 296

Today's Reading:
John 16:16–24

Jesus is going away. He has made that point abundantly clear to the apostles. They are devastated by this revelation, as we have seen. His leaving will fill them with sorrow, but His leaving will not be the end of the story. In this text, He tries to make them understand "the rest of the story." They will see Him again. Their sorrow will be turned into joy. Understandably, the apostles struggled with these words and this concept. If His going away was referring to His death, then how could they see Him again? And what did He mean by "a little while"? Jesus' death, while agonizing for Him and disheartening for His apostles, was not final. He would overcome it, just as the prophets and even He had foretold. He would turn their sorrow into joy. Maybe the lesson for us in this text is that God is not a God of sorrow, but of joy. Despite the fact that life often involves hardships and sorrows, for the child of God, the story always ends with joy. Our salvation and eternal home in heaven guarantees it!

How can we find joy even in difficult times?

DON'T FORGET TO PRAY AND HAVE A GREAT DAY!

⏳ THINGS TO PRAY FOR TODAY:

DAY 297

Today's Reading:
John 16:25–33

The final sentence of this reading offers a wonderful piece of encouragement and hope for all those who have committed their lives to Christ. Just a few hours after this statement is made, Jesus will be arrested, the apostles will scatter, and all will seem lost. But despite those events, Jesus wants them to know that He is not defeated. In fact, He has overcome. What seemed to be defeat was in fact God's plan, and what seemed to end with His death would give way to eternal life through His resurrection. Yes, He had overcome. And because He has overcome, all those who follow Him can overcome as well. Despite lives marked with tribulation and trial, we have reason to be cheerful. Jesus has overcome and has given victory to His disciples. As those who have been bought with the precious blood of Christ, we can live lives of peace, joy, and hope, knowing that we have a Savior that has overcome and gained victory for Himself and for all who belong to Him.

How has Jesus overcoming the world affected your life?

DON'T FORGET TO PRAY AND HAVE A GREAT DAY!

 **THINGS TO PRAY FOR TODAY:**

DAY 298

Today's Reading:
John 17:1–5

O ver the next three days, we will consider the prayer offered by Jesus in the upper room. It is a beautiful prayer to God concerning the events that are to come and the effect that those events will have on His followers. In this first part of the prayer, Jesus prays for Himself, but the focus of His thoughts is not really on Him, but on His Father. His desire at this moment is what it has always been—for God to be glorified and for His will to be accomplished. Jesus has spent His entire life glorifying God and now, in His death, His desire and intent are no different. His prayer for Himself is simply that through Him God's will and plan will be accomplished, and that God will be glorified. At this point in His life, the humility and commitment to God's purpose that Jesus displays is remarkable. Knowing the agony, suffering, and humiliation that stands before Him, He continues to put God's will and plan before His own human emotions. What a great lesson for us to learn from the Master Teacher!

How was God glorified through the death of Christ?

DON'T FORGET TO PRAY AND HAVE A GREAT DAY!

⏳ THINGS TO PRAY FOR TODAY:

DAY 299

Today's Reading:
John 17:6-19

The care and concern Jesus has shown for His apostles during this time in the upper room is undeniable. He has spent every day of the past three years teaching, training, and leading them. He has kept them and protected them. He has nurtured and cared for them. Now as He prepares to leave them, He is concerned for them. He is concerned for how they will deal with His loss and absence. He is concerned for how they will react to a world that will hate and abuse them. He is concerned for their faith and their faithfulness. So He prays. He prays that God will continue to keep them in His care as Jesus has done during His life. He prays that God will keep them from the evil one—that is, protect them from undue temptation and trial from Satan. He prays that God will sanctify them, that He will set them apart by His word. As we see throughout the remainder of the New Testament, God answers Jesus' prayer. The apostles go on to become courageous and powerful warriors for the kingdom, ushering in the church and leading in the spread of the gospel throughout the world.

What lessons can we learn from the apostles?

DON'T FORGET TO PRAY AND HAVE A GREAT DAY!

 THINGS TO PRAY FOR TODAY:

DAY 300

Today's Reading:
John 17:20–26

J esus prayed for us! What an amazing thought to consider that Jesus, at such a pivotal time in His life and mission, was thinking of us. His prayer for us was that we might be one. You have to wonder if Jesus in His foreknowledge looked down the corridors of time to see all the doctrinal error and division that would characterize those who believed in Him through the ages, and would, with pain in His heart, simply pray that we might be one. But notice that He did not simply pray for unity among His followers, but that our unity be defined by a unity with Him and God the Father. True unity, the kind of unity that Jesus prayed for, cannot be achieved without a submission to God's will and a following of His word. If all those who believed in God and Jesus would do away with human creeds and traditions and simply follow the teachings of God's word, then we would be united as Jesus prayed. What a wonderful thing it would be to be able to fulfill Jesus' desire and prayer for unity among His disciples!

How does Jesus' idea of unity differ from that of many today?

DON'T FORGET TO PRAY AND HAVE A GREAT DAY!

⏳ THINGS TO PRAY FOR TODAY:

Day 301

 Today's Reading:
Mark 14:26–31

Peter's confidence is admirable, even if he doesn't prove to be as steadfast as he thought. Peter is often impetuous and quick-tongued, rash and impulsive. But despite those characteristics that we might consider to be flaws in his character, Jesus saw great potential in him. In a firm yet gentle way, and with a great deal of patience, the Master Teacher was working to harness Peter's enthusiasm and passion and turn his weaknesses into strengths. Despite his shortcomings, Peter's love for Christ was undeniable! Over and over, throughout his time with Jesus, Peter demonstrated a desire to be near Him, to honor Him, and defend Him. While his methods may have been questionable at times, his motives were always pure. I believe Peter provides a great lesson for us. Despite his obvious imperfections, God was able to use him to do great things. When I look at myself in a mirror, I am made painfully aware of my own shortcomings, but Peter reminds me that if my love for God is pure, God can still use me to accomplish His will. What about you?

How can God use you in spite of your shortcomings?

DON'T FORGET TO PRAY AND HAVE A GREAT DAY!

 THINGS TO PRAY FOR TODAY:

DAY 302

Today's Reading:
Luke 22:31–34

Luke gives us further detail into the discussion between Jesus and Peter concerning Peter's denial of Christ. In discussing Mark's account of this event yesterday, we pointed out Peter's imperfections, but Luke reminds us that there was more involved in Peter's denial of Christ than just his rash overconfidence. Peter's denial was the result of Satan's tempting work in his mind and life. As Jesus told the apostles of the coming difficulties and their impending desertion, Satan was busy convincing Peter that there were no circumstances that would cause him to run away. Maybe if Peter had listened to Jesus more than to Satan, he would have avoided the circumstances that precipitated his denial. Satan then easily turned up the heat on Peter in what was already a very tense situation by using people to question his relationship with Jesus. Just as Peter did, we often underestimate the ability of Satan to tempt and trouble us and trust too much in our own ability to withstand. We would do well to learn the lesson that we must always be on guard and seek God's help in overcoming the temptations that Satan places before us.

What can we do to help us overcome temptation?

DON'T FORGET TO PRAY AND HAVE A GREAT DAY!

⏳ THINGS TO PRAY FOR TODAY:

Day 303

Today's Reading:
Luke 22:35-38

As He reminds them, Jesus had earlier sent his apostles out without any supplies so that they might learn to depend on God's care and provision through the generosity of fellow-disciples. But now the circumstances have changed. Jesus is going away, but they are to remain in this world. With His death, life for the apostles is going to become much more difficult. Jesus' instruction to the apostles here, in simple terms, is to prepare themselves for the difficult and dangerous times ahead. Much has been made of Jesus' instruction for them to arm themselves with swords. What are we to think of this command? Certainly, Jesus is not suggesting that they become militant in their defense of Him or His teachings (see Matthew 26:51-53; John 18:36). It was not uncommon for men of that day to carry swords, not only for protection against robbers and thieves that they might encounter as they travelled from one place to another, but also as a general tool to be used for a variety of purposes. Jesus' instruction is simply that they should supply and prepare themselves for the difficulties and dangers that would surely come upon them after His departure.

What can we learn from this text about our Christian lives today?

DON'T FORGET TO PRAY AND HAVE A GREAT DAY!

 THINGS TO PRAY FOR TODAY:

Day 304

 Today's Reading:
Matthew 26:36–46

The time of His suffering is at hand, and as Jesus goes to God in prayer, He is overwhelmed by the emotion of the moment. The scene at Gethsemane is full of imagery that is both beautiful and powerful. We see in this scene Jesus the man—filled with dread and trepidation because of the pain, suffering, and humiliation He knows is coming. As important and necessary as Jesus knows His sacrifice to be, His human side does not want to go through the coming events, and He prays to be saved from this moment. On the other hand, we see Jesus as One wholly committed to His Father and His plan. Even in His overwhelming dread, Jesus denies His own human desire and commits Himself to God's will. As He pours out His heart to God in prayer, His will becomes one with the Father's. In that moment, as Jesus releases His own will and entrusts His life into the hands of His Father, He finds the strength to overcome His fear and face with courage and resolve His appointed role of atoning sacrifice. What a beautiful picture of faith and faithfulness!

What can we learn from Jesus' prayers in the garden?

DON'T FORGET TO PRAY AND HAVE A GREAT DAY!

 **THINGS TO PRAY FOR TODAY:**

Day 305

 Today's Reading:
Luke 22:39–46

We typically think of the suffering of Jesus beginning after He falls into the hands of His enemies. What Luke uniquely shows us about this scene is the immense suffering of Jesus even before His arrest. The prayers of Jesus show us, not just a dread of the difficulty of coming events, but a human mind and body that succumbs to the extraordinary stress of His circumstances. It has been suggested that Luke's description of sweat that "became like great drops of blood" was a literal statement, not a figurative one. If that is the case, it is evidence of the intense suffering and pressure that Jesus was experiencing as He anticipated His coming sacrifice. Luke also reveals that an angel appeared from heaven to strengthen Him, adding credence to the statement that Jesus makes in Matthew 26:38, "My soul is very sorrowful, even to death." So great was Jesus' suffering in Gethsemane that He was literally close to death. Oh, the price that He was willing to pay for us!

Why do you think Jesus' suffering was so great in Gethsemane?

DON'T FORGET TO PRAY AND HAVE A GREAT DAY!

 THINGS TO PRAY FOR TODAY:

Day 306

Today's Reading:
Matthew 26:47–56

From this point forward, we will look at every account of every event. As the mob comes to arrest Jesus, Peter draws his sword in defense of His Master. In Matthew's account of these events, He is alone in highlighting a statement made by Jesus to Peter as He commanded him to put away his sword. Jesus reveals that, despite the armed men who have come to take Him, He is in complete control of all things. Just a word and His Father will send an army of angels to His rescue. There is no man and no mob that can forcibly take Jesus' life from Him. His death is to be completely voluntary. If it is not, then He is not truly a sacrifice. What a sobering thought to understand that, at any point, it was within Jesus' power to stop the suffering and demonstrate His power and glory. But He did not say that word. He willingly endured all the suffering and allowed Himself to be made a sacrifice for us. What a wonderful Savior!

Why is it important that Jesus' death was voluntary?

DON'T FORGET TO PRAY AND HAVE A GREAT DAY!

⏳ THINGS TO PRAY FOR TODAY:

DAY 307

 Today's Reading:
Mark 14:43–52

As we consider Mark's account of Jesus' arrest, I want to focus on Judas, the betrayer of Jesus. He had been a hand-picked apostle of the Lord. He had spent every day of three years with Him, witnessing His love, compassion, and wisdom, learning from His teaching, and experiencing His power. But Judas' heart belonged to the world, and he had sold His Lord for a mere thirty pieces of silver. As he leads the mob into the garden to take Jesus, notice that Judas addresses Jesus as "Rabbi Rabbi," a term of respect and reverence. He then identifies Jesus to the mob with, of all things, a kiss—a show of love and friendship. Oh, the depths of Judas' betrayal! To not only lead Jesus' enemies to Him, but to make a mockery of the friendship and tutelage that Jesus had extended toward Him was the very epitome of disregard and betrayal. What a powerful force greed and sin can be when they are allowed to take root in the heart!

What can we learn from Judas and his betrayal of Jesus?

DON'T FORGET TO PRAY AND HAVE A GREAT DAY!

 THINGS TO PRAY FOR TODAY:

DAY 308

Today's Reading:
Luke 22:47-53

The scene was tense and chaotic. Judas arrives with a band of soldiers and officers who are armed and ready for a fight. The apostles are confused and not sure how they should react. Should they fight? Should they run? Should they just do nothing? While some of the apostles turn to Jesus for guidance, Peter takes matters into his own hand and draws his sword, striking the servant of the high priest. But what happens next is truly amazing. As He had done on other occasions throughout His ministry, Jesus brought calm to the chaos. He puts a stop to the violence and bloodshed as quickly as it begins and, in an incredible act of mercy and compassion, heals the injured servant. Can you imagine being Malchus? You are there to take Jesus into custody and lead Him to what will surely end in His death. But He shows nothing but kindness and love toward you. What would you do? How would you respond? Could you continue with your duty, or would you be forced to change your mind? We read nothing more of Malchus and do not know what became of him, but it is difficult to believe that He wasn't changed by His experience with Jesus on that night.

What would you have done if you had been in Malchus' place?

DON'T FORGET TO PRAY AND HAVE A GREAT DAY!

⏳ **THINGS TO PRAY FOR TODAY:**

Day 309

 Today's Reading:
John 18:1-11

John records an interesting detail of this event that the other writers do not. When the band of armed soldiers and officers recognized that it was Jesus who stood before them, John records that they "drew back and fell to the ground." How do you explain this uncharacteristic response of well-trained and armed men? As Jesus pointed out to them (in other accounts), He had been with them daily in the temple. They knew Him, His character, and His temperament. But they also knew His power. If they had not witnessed it in person, they had certainly heard the stories of Jesus' power over nature, disease, and even life. They could only imagine what He was capable of if He felt that His life was in danger. Would He strike them down? Would He call fire down from heaven to consume them? Would He inflict them with some terrible disease? Their minds must have reeled with thoughts of what this man could or would do when they confronted Him. As they stand face to face with Jesus, they are for the moment filled with fear and awe to be in His presence.

Is there any lesson we can learn from the soldiers in this text?

DON'T FORGET TO PRAY AND HAVE A GREAT DAY!

 **THINGS TO PRAY FOR TODAY:**

DAY 310

Today's Reading:
Matthew 26:57–68

It would be difficult to overstate the level of hatred and disdain the Jewish leaders felt toward Jesus. He had questioned their authority, condemned their hypocrisy, and threatened their power. Despite His wisdom, power, and claims to the Son of God, they had made a firm decision that Jesus must be done away with. Their purpose and goal was clear—to see that Jesus was put to death. As they bring Him to the home of Caiaphas in the middle of the night, they search for false witnesses to testify against Jesus. Driven by hatred and treachery, it was not the truth that they were interested in, but only incriminating testimony. However, the flawless character of Jesus' life is seen in the fact that they could not find even false witnesses who were agreed in their lies concerning Jesus. Finally, when two witnesses recount Jesus' statement concerning the tearing down and rebuilding of the temple (a prophetic statement about His death and resurrection), the Jewish leaders had their evidence—a statement that they considered to be blasphemous. They were ready to deliver Him to death.

How do you think the Jews were able to justify their actions?

DON'T FORGET TO PRAY AND HAVE A GREAT DAY!

 THINGS TO PRAY FOR TODAY:

Day 311

Today's Reading:
Mark 14:53–65

To properly understand the events that led to Jesus' death, we must consider the circumstances of His trials. In yesterday's reading, we considered the hatred the Jews felt toward Jesus and the hard-hearted determination with which they pursued His death. But to fully realize the lengths to which they were willing to go, we must remember that these religious leaders and teachers of the day were in violation of their own laws with practically every action on the night of Jesus' arrest. From trying Jesus at night, to the involvement of Annas and Caiaphas, to the lack of opportunity for defense to the physical abuse that Jesus suffered—every element of these trials was a travesty of justice. It boggles the mind to consider how these men who had devoted their lives to upholding the law of God could, on this occasion, treat it with such abuse and disregard. It is a testament to the depths of depravity to which greed and jealousy had taken them, and it serves to warn us against allowing those same attitudes to take root in our hearts.

Why did the Jewish leaders feel such hatred toward Jesus?

DON'T FORGET TO PRAY AND HAVE A GREAT DAY!

 THINGS TO PRAY FOR TODAY:

DAY 312

Today's Reading:
Luke 22:63-71

"Are You then the Son of God?" It was the right question, the most important question. But it was asked with the wrong heart and motive. The Jewish leaders were not interested in believing in Jesus as the Son of God and promised Messiah. They were not interested in following Him as disciples. Their only desire was to find fault and a reason to accuse Him of blasphemy. Their question was nothing more than a means of finding guilt. Nevertheless, their question was the right question. It is that question that can still make all the difference. Is Jesus the Son of God? If He is, then He is surely worthy of our faith and obedience and our very lives. Still in our own time, if honest and searching hearts are willing to ask the question and accept the obvious answer, then Jesus the Son of God is still able to change their lives and give them salvation. What a Savior!

Why is believing in Jesus as the Son of God so important?

DON'T FORGET TO PRAY AND HAVE A GREAT DAY!

⏳ THINGS TO PRAY FOR TODAY:

Day 313

Today's Reading:
John 18:12–14, 19–24

John is alone in mentioning the scene at the home of Annas on the night of Jesus' arrest. Before He is taken to Caiaphas the high priest, the soldiers escort Jesus to the home of Annas, the former high priest and father-in-law of Caiaphas. The Romans had dictated a limit to the amount of time one could serve as high priest, but under Jewish law, the office of high priest was to be a lifetime appointment. So while, as the former high priest, Annas had no official position or authority, he may have, in the eyes of the Jews, still been considered the rightful high priest and thus continued to have a great deal of influence. Only Caiaphas, as the official high priest, could bring charges upon Jesus before the Roman governor, but it is Annas who performs the preliminary examination. It is in the home of Annas that we have the first recorded act of abuse against Jesus, as He is struck by one of the officers for what was considered disrespect toward the high priest. With that act, the physical suffering of Jesus at the hands of His enemies had begun.

Was Jesus disrespectful to Annas? Why or why not?

DON'T FORGET TO PRAY AND HAVE A GREAT DAY!

 THINGS TO PRAY FOR TODAY:

DAY 314

Today's Reading:
Matthew 26:69–75

In real time, it had only been a few hours since Peter had stood before Jesus, adamantly denying Jesus' warning that he would deny Him. In Peter's mind, there was nothing that could happen that would cause him to shrink from his commitment to His Lord and friend. But he never imagined things would go as they had. When the armed mob showed up in the garden to take Jesus, he had tried to fight in defense of Jesus, but had been rebuked. Jesus had allowed them to bind Him and take Him away. Peter, along with all the others, had fled the scene, but he hadn't gone far. He was confused and concerned. He wanted to see what would happen, and he was willing to go into harm's way to follow Jesus. But before he knew it, Peter found himself being confronted. "You were with Him." Fear took over and—not once, not twice, but three times—Peter heard himself denying his relationship with Jesus. Then, as he heard the rooster crow, Jesus' words came flooding back into his memory, crushing his spirit and sending shockwaves of guilt and shame through his body. "And he went out and wept bitterly."

What do you think motivated Peter to follow Jesus into the city?

DON'T FORGET TO PRAY AND HAVE A GREAT DAY!

⏳ THINGS TO PRAY FOR TODAY:

DAY 315

Today's Reading:
Mark 14:66–72

As Peter came to the place where Jesus was being interrogated, he did all he could to blend in. He wanted to see what was going to happen to Jesus, concerned for the welfare of his friend and Lord, but he did not want to put himself in danger. Instead of hiding in a dark corner, he warms himself by the fire. He not only denies being with Jesus, but even denies understanding what they are talking about. He even stoops to cursing and swearing in order to avoid suspicion. It occurs to me that we often follow a similar pattern in our own lives. We want to be close to Jesus, maintaining a relationship with Him, but we do not want that relationship to endanger our place in this world. So just as Peter did, we work hard to blend in—to look like, sound like, and act like the world around us, hiding our relationship with Christ. But just as it did in the life of Peter, those actions can only result in our sinful denial of our Lord.

How did Peter's blending in contribute to his denial of Jesus?

DON'T FORGET TO PRAY AND HAVE A GREAT DAY!

 THINGS TO PRAY FOR TODAY:

Day 316

Today's Reading:
Luke 22:54–62

Luke reveals a detail of this event that adds a powerful and emotional element to the story. As the rooster crows following Peter's third denial of Jesus, Luke tells us that Jesus turns and looks at Peter. From this statement we can infer that, at least during this part of the proceedings, Jesus was in view of Peter. As he denied his Lord, he could see the questioning and abuse Jesus was enduring. Can you imagine what Peter must have felt as he heard the rooster crow and looked toward Jesus only to see His Lord, teacher, and friend looking back at him? As their eyes met, Peter remembered the words Jesus had spoken to him just a few hours before and the bold confidence he had displayed in response. What must he have seen in Jesus' eyes— sadness and disappointment? Possibly, but if so, he certainly also saw love and forgiveness. Peter had failed on this night, but it certainly would not be the end of his relationship with Jesus.

How does this detail affect your view of this story?

DON'T FORGET TO PRAY AND HAVE A GREAT DAY!

 THINGS TO PRAY FOR TODAY:

DAY 317

 Today's Reading:
John 18:15–18, 25–27

John's account of this event includes several interesting details that the other writers do not. One of those details is in the wording of the questions asked of Peter. The first two of those queries are phrased negatively—"You also are not one ... are you?" Consider two quick observations about this wording. First, the negative wording of these questions suggests an attitude of disrespect toward Jesus. "Why would anyone be His disciple? Surely you are not!" Second, the negative wording of the questions encourages Peter to deny Jesus and makes that denial easier. Peter doesn't have to defy the accusers, but simply has to acknowledge that he is not a disciple. Peter was certainly responsible for his own actions, but Satan was cunning in the way he used those around him to tempt him. What's the lesson for us? Satan is still cunning. He still uses people and situations and even the wording of questions to tempt us to deny Christ and forfeit our relationship with Him. If we are to withstand, we must be strong and courageous.

*How would you respond if someone
questioned your relationship with Christ?*

DON'T FORGET TO PRAY AND HAVE A GREAT DAY!

 THINGS TO PRAY FOR TODAY:

DAY 318

Today's Reading:
Matthew 27:1–2, 11–14

According to Jewish law, one suspected of a crime could not be tried at night. All of the hearings, interrogations, and abuse that Jesus had endured the night before had been unlawful. But now the morning had come and the underhanded overnight tactics of the Jewish leaders gave way to the more "official" act of delivering Jesus to Pilate for trial. Pilate, the Roman governor, was not interested in Jewish law or in whatever infractions of that law Jesus might have been guilty of. He seemingly questioned Jesus more out of curiosity than anything else, but the thing that intrigued Pilate most was the silence of Jesus in the presence of His accusers. Why did He not speak up? Why did He not defend Himself? Pilate marveled at the quiet and humble spirit of Jesus in the face of such hatred and malice. This Man was no ordinary criminal. There was something special about Jesus.

Why do you think Jesus did not respond
to the accusations of the Jews?

DON'T FORGET TO PRAY AND HAVE A GREAT DAY!

⏳ THINGS TO PRAY FOR TODAY:

DAY 319

Today's Reading:
Mark 15:1–5

"Are You the King of the Jews?" The Jews were hoping this charge would be seen as an act of insubordination against the Roman government, one punishable by death. In the eyes of Pilate, it was the only accusation levied against Jesus with any substance. Jesus was in fact the King of the Jews. No, He was not the Jewish king that had been condoned by the Roman government. Rather, He was the King of kings and Lord of lords, the One foretold and promised by the prophets of old. Ironically, the greatest promise of God, the greatest source of hope for God's people, was the very thing that the Jewish leaders held against Jesus and used to accuse Him before Pilate. When asked about this charge, Jesus did not deny it but responded simply, "You have said so." Neither the unbelief and rejection of the Jewish leaders, nor the condemnation of the Roman government could change the undeniable fact that Jesus Christ was, and is, the King of kings and Lord of lords!

What does it mean to say that Jesus is King of kings?

DON'T FORGET TO PRAY AND HAVE A GREAT DAY!

 THINGS TO PRAY FOR TODAY:

DAY 320

 Today's Reading:
Luke 23:1-5

As the Jews bring Jesus before Pilate, they do so with a flurry of charges of crimes against the Roman government. They wanted Jesus to be viewed as an enemy of the state, One who had no regard for the Empire or its leaders. Of course, Jesus had done nothing to violate Roman law. He had shown due respect for those in authority and had instructed His disciples to give to Caesar what was due him (pay taxes). As was mentioned in yesterday's reading, the only charge that Pilate finds credible seems to be the charge that Jesus claimed to be the King of the Jews. It is the only charge that he questioned Jesus about, but even in that charge, Pilate sees no guilt in Him. He quickly sees through the ploy of the Jews and declares publicly that He finds no fault in Jesus. But the Jews had come too far to turn back now. They will not take "no" for an answer. In response to Pilate's verdict, they simply become more fierce and demanding, declaring the guilt of Jesus.

Why did the Jews need Pilate to find Jesus guilty?

DON'T FORGET TO PRAY AND HAVE A GREAT DAY!

⏳ THINGS TO PRAY FOR TODAY:

Day 321

 **Today's Reading:**
John 18:28–38

"What is truth?" It is a profound question, even if Pilate didn't mean for it to be. While Jesus represented (and in fact embodied) truth, every tactic and accusation employed by His enemies was untruthful. Truth has always made the difference between right and wrong, righteousness and disobedience. To know and obey the truth makes one faithful and pleasing to God. Truth is important! Jesus came to once and for all bring truth to the world. He came into the world, bringing "grace and truth" (John 1:17) and in fact claimed to Himself be "the way, the truth, and the life" (John 14:6). In a religious world that is still today filled with confusion, misunderstanding, and inaccurate teaching, Pilate's question, "What is truth?" is a question that, if asked by an honestly seeking heart, can make all the difference, leading him away from the teachings and ideas of men and to the source of truth, God's Word.

Why do you think there are so many different "truths" taught today?

DON'T FORGET TO PRAY AND HAVE A GREAT DAY!

⏳ **THINGS TO PRAY FOR TODAY:**

Day 322

Today's Reading:
Matthew 27:3–10

Matthew is alone in recording the tragic end to Judas' life, and he does so seemingly for the sole purpose of demonstrating the fulfillment of Old Testament prophecy in every detail of Jesus' death. I still believe there is a valuable lesson to be learned from this text. As Judas saw the result of his betrayal of Christ, he was overwhelmed with remorse; so much so that this man, who was driven by greed and love of money to hand Christ over to His enemies, went back to the chief priests and elders to return the thirty pieces of silver that had been the price of his betrayal. He was well aware of his sin and was filled with sorrow because of it. Many have asked the question, "Could Judas have been forgiven and saved?" While I believe the answer to this question is a resounding, "Yes!"—sadly, Judas did not choose the path of forgiveness and restoration. He chose rather to try to escape his guilt by taking his own life, and in so doing, robbed himself of the opportunity to overcome his failures. The lesson? We must remember that there is no sin that is unforgivable except the one that we are unwilling to seek forgiveness for and restoration from.

Why do you think Judas did not seek forgiveness?

DON'T FORGET TO PRAY AND HAVE A GREAT DAY!

 THINGS TO PRAY FOR TODAY:

DAY 323

 Today's Reading:
Luke 23:6–12

Jesus was a problem for Pilate. On the one hand, Pilate saw no wrongdoing in Him and knew that He ought to be released. On the other hand, there was an angry and determined group of people who would have it no other way but to see this Man killed. When Pilate heard that Jesus was from Galilee, he wasted no time in sending Him to Herod, the ruler of that province who happened to be in Jerusalem at the time. Let Jesus be his problem. Then there was Herod, who had no interest in fairness or justice, but who was very interested in seeing Jesus out of curiosity. He desired to see one of the miracles that he had heard so much about, but Jesus gave him not so much as a reply to satisfy his curiosity. What strikes me most about this scene is the complete lack of integrity and justice displayed by both of these government officials. Being commissioned to rule over the people and uphold the law of the land, both of them are completely unwilling to do what is right and just. Though Jesus' death was ultimately by the will of God, it was made possible by the cowardly acts of men like Pilate and Herod.

How did these men fit into God's plan?

DON'T FORGET TO PRAY AND HAVE A GREAT DAY!

 THINGS TO PRAY FOR TODAY:

DAY 324

Today's Reading:
Matthew 27:15–26

We see in this text another attempt by Pilate to weasel out of his responsibility in regard to Jesus. In fulfilling the standing tradition of releasing a Jewish prisoner during this feast week as a goodwill gesture toward the Jews, Pilate placed Jesus, a man who was innocent and only before him because of envy, alongside Barabbas, a notorious prisoner that was known to them to be violent and dangerous. Pilate was confident that he had found a way to release Jesus while staying in the good graces of the Jews; surely they would choose Jesus. Surely they would not want a dangerous criminal like Barabbas back on the streets. But Pilate underestimated the hatred and malice the Jewish leaders felt toward Jesus. They would gladly accept the robber and murderer rather than have Jesus released. Jesus' death was the only outcome acceptable to these men who were determined to destroy Him. Despite Pilate's desire to release Jesus, his fear of the crowds and of the backlash of doing the right thing caused him to give in and deliver Jesus to be crucified.

Why do you think Pilate was afraid to release Jesus?

DON'T FORGET TO PRAY AND HAVE A GREAT DAY!

⌛ **THINGS TO PRAY FOR TODAY:**

DAY 325

 Today's Reading:
Mark 15:6–15

Can you for a moment put yourself into the shoes of Barabbas? A convicted criminal—a robber, a murderer, a rebel—condemned to die by crucifixion. Even the most hardened of criminals shuddered at the thought of this most torturous form of death. On this day, possibly the day that you are scheduled to die, you are taken from your cell and rushed to the platform overlooking the frenzied crowd. Then, before you know it, and for reasons that you do not understand, they have chosen you to be released. You are not going to die today. This innocent Man will die instead. Though we don't like to admit it, that is our story. Like Barabbas, we are lawbreakers, convicted of transgressing God's law with our sins. Because of those transgressions, we are subject to death (Romans 6:23). But there is Jesus, standing in our place, paying our price, accepting our punishment. We are released from our guilt while He suffers in our place. That is our story! Barabbas represents us!

Why do you think that Jesus was willing to suffer for us?

DON'T FORGET TO PRAY AND HAVE A GREAT DAY!

 **⌛ THINGS TO PRAY FOR TODAY:**

DAY 326

 Today's Reading:
Luke 23:13–25

While Matthew and Mark's accounts of this event focus on other aspects, Luke focuses his attention on Pilate. This Roman governor had found no fault in Jesus and had no reason to see Him punished. He knew what was right and what should happen. Even if the Jewish accusations were correct, Jesus was only guilty of misleading the people. But they had demanded that He be put to death in place of a convicted rebel and murderer. To Pilate's credit, he tried again and again to reason with the Jews and argued for Jesus' release, but all of his arguments fell on deaf ears. However, lest we become too sympathetic toward Pilate, let us remember that ultimately he gave into the pressure of the situation and did what he knew was unmerited and unjust. The persistence and determination of the Jewish leaders had won out and Pilate "delivered Jesus over to their will."

What lessons are there to be learned from Pilate?

DON'T FORGET TO PRAY AND HAVE A GREAT DAY!

⏳ THINGS TO PRAY FOR TODAY:

DAY 327

Today's Reading:
Matthew 27:27–31

It is difficult to think about the humiliation and abuse Jesus endured on that day. Even before He was nailed to the cross, Jesus suffered immensely at the hands of the Roman soldiers. They were not acting out of hatred as were the Jewish leaders, for they did not know Jesus and had no feelings toward Him at all. The Romans had little regard for the Jews and viewed them as second-class citizens. To mock this Jewish man and by extension the entire Jewish nation, would have been an easy and natural thing for them to do. These soldiers were trained in the art of torture, and the humiliation that preceded crucifixion was as much for their amusement as it was for the victim's suffering. But to see Jesus—the King of kings and Lord of lords, a Man full of compassion and grace—standing before them, a crown of thorns pressed into His head, blood trickling down His face as they mockingly bow down before Him as if in worship, is a painful image to consider. And if that were not difficult enough, we are reminded that it was for us that He endured such abuse. Oh, what a Savior!

Why do you think the Roman soldiers mocked Jesus as they did?

DON'T FORGET TO PRAY AND HAVE A GREAT DAY!

⏳ **THINGS TO PRAY FOR TODAY:**

Day 328

Today's Reading:
Mark 15:16–20

In today's thought, I would like for us to consider what we do not read in this text. We do not read of Jesus retaliating in any way in response to the mocking and abuse. We do not read of Him responding verbally to the things that were said and done. We do not read of Him calling down an army of angels, as He told Peter was within His ability. In fact, we do not read of any attempt to defend Himself at all. Long before this day, Isaiah prophesied about it saying, "He was oppressed and He was afflicted, yet He opened not His mouth" (Isaiah 53:7). Throughout this ordeal, Jesus displays an incredible amount of strength and self-control by silently enduring the abuse and suffering. But how? How could He simply endure when He had the power to stop it, to punish the blasphemers, to free Himself from the pain, to demonstrate once and for all that He was without a doubt the Son of God? The simple answer is that God's will was His will. Our redemption and salvation were more important than His pride, freedom, or comfort. He willingly suffered because of His great love for us!

How hard would it have been for you
to be in Jesus' position and endure silently?

DON'T FORGET TO PRAY AND HAVE A GREAT DAY!

 THINGS TO PRAY FOR TODAY:

Day 329

Today's Reading:
John 19:1–16

John reveals that, before He was led away to be crucified, Jesus was scourged. This seems to have been part of Pilate's plan to secure Jesus' release, thinking the Jews would be satisfied to see Jesus suffer this agonizing beating at the hands of a Roman soldier. The instrument used for scourging was a short whip made of leather strips, each one with some material (such as bone or metal) attached to the end. As the flagellum was brought down against the tightly stretched skin of the back, each strand of the whip caused deep lacerations and excruciating pain. The Jews had a law that a man could not receive more than forty lashes with a whip. To assure that they did not violate that law, their practice was to stop at thirty-nine. But Jesus was not scourged by the Jews, but by the Romans who had no such law. Jesus was completely at the mercy of the soldier wielding the flagellum. As He stood before the Jewish crowd one last time, beaten and bloody, weakened by dehydration and loss of blood, the Jews mercilessly demanded that Jesus be put to death, adamantly declaring, "We have no king but Caesar!"

What is the significance of the Jews' statement:
"We have no king but Caesar"?

DON'T FORGET TO PRAY AND HAVE A GREAT DAY!

 THINGS TO PRAY FOR TODAY:

DAY 330

 Today's Reading:
Luke 23:26-31

As they make the short journey to Golgotha, many of the disciples of Jesus followed behind. Some of these disciples, women who had been faithful to Jesus during His ministry, were weeping and mourning for Him. Even in the midst of His suffering, Jesus speaks to them, warning them of the coming judgment upon Jerusalem. Jesus has warned about this event before (Luke 21:20-24) and now reiterates the certainty of its coming. Because of the hard-heartedness of the Jewish leaders and their rejection of Jesus, God would allow Jerusalem, the holy city, to be defeated. In less than forty years from that time, the city would be overrun and completely destroyed. Jesus had earlier given instructions to His followers on what to do in order to save themselves when they saw that event taking place. The destruction of Jerusalem, not His death, was the event that was truly worthy of mourning. Jesus' death, while terrible, represented victory. But the destruction of Jerusalem represented nothing but unbelief and defeat for the Jewish people.

How did Jesus' death represent victory?

DON'T FORGET TO PRAY AND HAVE A GREAT DAY!

⌛ THINGS TO PRAY FOR TODAY:

DAY 331

Today's Reading:
Matthew 27:32–44

Crucifixion was by no means a quick or easy death. Even in a weakened state as a result of scourging, victims of crucifixion typically lived for hours on the cross. For those who gathered at the crucifixion site, the event was essentially a spectator sport, a sickening form of entertainment. They would sit and watch as the condemned men, hanging from crosses, struggled to find the strength to draw each excruciating and laborious breath. The spectators would pass the time by hurling insults and mockeries at those being crucified, laughing and reveling in their suffering. The slow, agonizing death of crucifixion was by design as a punitive part of the experience. Typically, those who were crucified were condemned criminals, guilty of some grievous wrong against the Empire. In the eyes of the law or the people, they deserved no mercy and no respect. The cross was as much about humiliation and suffering as it was about the eventual death of the condemned. Jesus, of course, was an exception. He was not a criminal. He had broken no laws, nor had He harmed anyone. But His suffering and death was no less than the worst of offenders.

What do you think the worst part of crucifixion would have been?

DON'T FORGET TO PRAY AND HAVE A GREAT DAY!

⌛ THINGS TO PRAY FOR TODAY:

DAY 332

Today's Reading:
Mark 15:21–32

A Roman cross, the type that Jesus would have been hung on, was constructed in the shape of an uppercase T. The vertical part of the cross was permanently placed in the ground and the horizontal beam was removable in order to allow for easier placement and removal of bodies from the cross. It was common practice for the condemned man to be forced to carry that horizontal beam in a processional to the place of crucifixion. Jesus—suffering and weak from exhaustion, dehydration, and blood loss—fell under the weight of His cross. In His place, the soldiers chose a man at random from the crowd to carry Jesus' load. His name was Simon. We know nothing about him other than that he was from Cyrene, and that he was the father of Alexander and Rufus. Was he a disciple of Jesus? Did he even know who Jesus was? Maybe the bigger question is, how was he affected by this small, coincidental role in the death of Jesus? One thing that most do believe is that his sons, Alexander and Rufus, became Christians and are mentioned because they were known to the church in Rome. Could it be that carrying Jesus' cross changed the course of Simon's life?

How do you think that this event could have changed Simon?

DON'T FORGET TO PRAY AND HAVE A GREAT DAY!

⏳ **THINGS TO PRAY FOR TODAY:**

Day 333

 Today's Reading:
Luke 23:32–43

In this passage, Luke records the first words spoken by Jesus as He hung on the cross. They are not words of selfishness as He suffered, or of anger toward His killers. His words are words of compassion, love, and forgiveness. Even in His suffering, Jesus is thinking of others. His mind is firmly set on the reason for His suffering, the atonement of the sins of the world. As He looks down at those who are abusing and mocking Him, He sees through eyes of loving forgiveness a people who desperately need God's grace. He doesn't want them to be punished but to be forgiven. The same is true of the thief hanging beside Him. His promise of salvation to the repentant sinner is a testament to the love of God and the power of the cross. It was only through the suffering and death that Jesus was enduring that He could offer that forgiveness and salvation to the thief, and it is only through that suffering that you and I have the opportunity for our sins to be forgiven. In these first words of Jesus, we are reminded of the very reason Jesus was crucified—love, grace, and forgiveness.

What does it say about the character
of Jesus that He was willing to forgive?

DON'T FORGET TO PRAY AND HAVE A GREAT DAY!

 **⏳ THINGS TO PRAY FOR TODAY:**

DAY 334

Today's Reading:
John 19:17–24

An accusation. A title. A statement of truth. It was common for the Romans to place a placard above those being crucified with a statement of their crime and reason for execution. In Jesus' case, Pilate simply instructed that the sign read, "Jesus of Nazareth, the King of the Jews." It was not a crime, but it was the accusation that the Jews had brought against Him. But the Jewish leaders objected to the wording. They complained to Pilate that the wording should be changed to indicate clearly Jesus' blasphemy, but Pilate refused. It is clear that Pilate had chosen the wording carefully and deliberately and had no inclination to change it. The question is "why," and only two possibilities exist. One is that he was angry with the Jews for putting him in such a difficult position and forcing him to do their dirty work. He thus was using the sign as a way to embarrass and get even with them. The other is that Pilate, through his time with Jesus, had come to believe that He truly was the Son of God and was using the placard to state such a belief. We have no record that Pilate ever became a Christian, but his final statement concerning Jesus was a powerful one.

Why were the Jews so upset about the wording of Jesus' accusation?

DON'T FORGET TO PRAY AND HAVE A GREAT DAY!

⏳ **THINGS TO PRAY FOR TODAY:**

DAY 335

Today's Reading:
Matthew 27:46–56

They are, in my estimation, the saddest words in Scripture. "My God, My God why have You forsaken Me?" Despite all of the torturous suffering that Jesus has endured, all the pain, all the humiliation, all the brutality to his physical body, it is this cry of agony that pierces the midday darkness. Because of sin—my sin and yours, the sins of all the world and all of time—Jesus, while on the cross, experiences, for the first and only time, the separation from God that sin brings. He could, and did, endure all the physical suffering of the cross—the crown of thorns, the scourging, the nails in His hands and feet— without complaint, but none of those things could compare to the spiritual agony of being separated from God. In His torment, He cries out to God. As I consider this fact, I am confronted with the truth that so many of us are not affected very much, if at all, by the separation from God that our sin causes. We often go through life for weeks, months, even years, being separated from God by sin and showing no signs that that separation has had any effect on us whatsoever. Oh, that we yearned for togetherness and relationship with God as Jesus did!

Why was separation from God so troubling for Jesus?

DON'T FORGET TO PRAY AND HAVE A GREAT DAY!

 THINGS TO PRAY FOR TODAY:

Day 336

Today's Reading:
Mark 15:33-41

Throughout His life, Jesus had displayed a character that only validated His claims to be the Son of God. His words, actions, attitudes, and miracles reflected a wisdom and power that could only come from God. Now in His death, as in His life, Jesus' conduct and character is nothing short of extraordinary. The humility and self-control with which He endured suffering, the compassion that He displayed even toward those who were abusing Him, the trust and submission with which He approached His Father, and the dignified and courageous way with which He accepted death all serve to confirm that Jesus was and is Who He claimed to be—the only begotten Son of God. So remarkable was this man's death that even the unbelieving centurion in charge of the proceedings became a believer, exclaiming, "Truly this Man was the Son of God!" Even in His death, Jesus exalted and exemplified God in a way that brought glory to God and that testified of Him as Lord and Savior.

What were some extraordinary things about Jesus' death?

DON'T FORGET TO PRAY AND HAVE A GREAT DAY!

⌛ THINGS TO PRAY FOR TODAY:

DAY 337

Today's Reading:
Luke 23:44–49

If you ever doubted the glory of Christ or the significance of this event, surely the events that accompanied the suffering and death of Jesus are an overwhelming testament to both. As He suffered on the cross, the sun refused to shine, and as He breathed His last, the earth trembled. So monumental and powerful was the sacrificial death of Christ that the earth could hardly contain it and threatened to give way under its weight. But maybe the most significant happening was not the most noticed or remarkable. Luke tells us that, with Jesus' death, the veil of the temple was torn in two from top to bottom. This veil was symbolic of the separation that had long existed between God and man due to sin. In the tabernacle and temple, it had prevented man from coming into God's presence. But that veil had been thrown open, not by the hand of man, but by the very hand of God. Through His Son, He had defeated sin and taken down that partition, allowing us to come into His presence and have a relationship with Him. Hallelujah, what a Savior!

What does it mean to say that we can come into God's presence?

DON'T FORGET TO PRAY AND HAVE A GREAT DAY!

 THINGS TO PRAY FOR TODAY:

DAY 338

Today's Reading:
John 19:25-30

In this passage, John records several statements made by Jesus as He hung on the cross. A statement of concern for the physical needs of others—namely His mother and John. A statement of physical need for Himself: "I thirst." And then there is the simple statement just before His death: "It is finished!" On the surface, it may seem that Jesus is wording a statement of relief that His suffering and pain are finally ending, but the true meaning of these words is likely much deeper than this. If you replace the word "finished" with "completed," you begin to get an idea of what Jesus was truly saying. Since the garden of Eden, God had been working toward the redemption of mankind from sin. Now with the atoning death of Christ, God's plan to defeat sin and redeem man was complete. No more would man be powerless over sin. No more would Satan have the upper-hand. Jesus had paid the price and won the victory! God's plan of redemption was complete!

How was Jesus' death the completion of God's plan of redemption?

DON'T FORGET TO PRAY AND HAVE A GREAT DAY!

⏳ **THINGS TO PRAY FOR TODAY:**

DAY 339

Today's Reading:
John 19:31–37

Crucifixion was by design an extremely slow and agonizing form of death, often taking many, many hours to complete. The actual cause of death in crucifixion was typically asphyxiation as the victim's lungs, constricted by his posture, were unable to function properly and eventually filled with fluid. When circumstances merited, death could be expedited by breaking the legs of the victim, preventing him from pushing up with his legs to create space in his chest cavity for the lungs to expand. At the request of the Jews, this method was utilized on those who were crucified with Jesus. But with Jesus, it was not to be so. When the soldiers came to Jesus for the purpose of breaking His legs, they found that He was already dead, fulfilling the prophecies that had been foretold long before that no bones would be broken. John records these things, he says, "that you also may believe." Can there be any greater proof that these events were by God's will and design than to know that each detail of Jesus' death was accurately foretold by the prophets?

How do the prophecies prove that Jesus' death was God's will?

DON'T FORGET TO PRAY AND HAVE A GREAT DAY!

 THINGS TO PRAY FOR TODAY:

Day 340

Today's Reading:
Matthew 27:57-61

We will consider Joseph of Arimathea and his role in the story of Jesus over the next couple of days but, in this thought, we will focus on another group of people mentioned in this text. For much of Jesus' death, the women who were followers of Jesus occupy the background. But do not underestimate the importance of the fact that they were there. When many of Jesus' followers had stayed away, either out of fear or disillusionment, these most faithful disciples of Jesus had courageously stayed. They had accompanied Him from the Praetorium to Golgotha and had faithfully stayed with Him, witnessing the gruesome events of His crucifixion. And now after His death, as Jesus is removed from the cross and prepared for burial, some of those same women are there, continuing to watch carefully over their Lord and Master. What a beautiful example of devotion and commitment these women are!

What lessons can we learn from these women?

DON'T FORGET TO PRAY AND HAVE A GREAT DAY!

⏳ **THINGS TO PRAY FOR TODAY:**

Day 341

Today's Reading:
Mark 15:42–47

Mark records that Joseph "took courage" in going to Pilate to ask for the body of Jesus. As a member of the Jewish council, he was joined to the group that had conspired to destroy Jesus. Though he had been a disciple for some time, he had kept his discipleship quiet for fear of the council (according to John). Despite his faith, Joseph was controlled more by fear than devotion. He had stood by while Jesus had been abused and falsely accused by his brethren without revealing his faith. Though it was too late to stand up for Jesus to save His life, Joseph could stand up for Jesus in His death. But to ask for the body of Jesus and give it a proper burial would surely show his true colors. His discipleship would be revealed. He would no longer be able to stand silently in the corner and maintain a secret faith. And that revelation of his faith would certainly bring with it retribution from the Jews. He would pay a high price for his faith. Still, Joseph had hidden long enough. It was time for his faith to leave the shadows and become active. It was time for him to take courage for Jesus.

*Are there situations when we need
to learn from Joseph and take courage?*

DON'T FORGET TO PRAY AND HAVE A GREAT DAY!

 THINGS TO PRAY FOR TODAY:

Day 342

Today's Reading:
Luke 23:50–56

The Jewish council was the force behind Jesus' crucifixion. Their hatred and disdain for Jesus is undeniable. But as we read this passage, we might be surprised to learn that they were not unanimous in wanting to destroy Jesus. Joseph of Arimathea was a member of that council and a prominent member at that (according to Mark). But he was not consenting to Jesus' death. He was, as Luke describes, a good and just man as well as a disciple of Jesus, albeit a secret one. Though the deed was done, and Jesus was dead, Joseph desired to do what he could to honor the Son of God. His caring for the body of Jesus and providing a proper burial place was his noble attempt to show his love and care for the One that had shown such compassion and care for so many during His time on the earth. Joseph of Arimathea is another reminder that, despite all of Jesus' enemies, there were also many faithful and devoted disciples.

What risks did Joseph take in doing this for Jesus?

DON'T FORGET TO PRAY AND HAVE A GREAT DAY!

⏳ THINGS TO PRAY FOR TODAY:

Day 343

 Today's Reading:
John 19:38–42

A long with Joseph of Arimathea, John mentions another disciple of Jesus who helps in His burial. Nicodemus is first mentioned in John 3 and again in John 7. He is described in John 3 as a Pharisee and a ruler of the Jews. It is obvious from our first introduction to Nicodemus that he is of a different spirit than many of his fellow Pharisees. Although he struggled to understand Jesus' teaching, he had been open-minded and willing to listen. In John 7, he criticizes the quickness with which his brethren had judged Jesus without knowing all the facts. Nicodemus, through his interaction with Jesus and his witnessing of Jesus' life, had clearly become a disciple of Jesus. Like Joseph, he had kept his discipleship a secret for fear of the council, but on this occasion, he could no longer stand by and do nothing. Together, he and Joseph care for the body of Jesus and give Him a proper burial. Though we might be critical of these men for standing silently by and allowing Jesus to die, we certainly are inspired by the courage and devotion they displayed in this great act of love.

How did this act display the love of these men for Jesus?

DON'T FORGET TO PRAY AND HAVE A GREAT DAY!

 ⏳ **THINGS TO PRAY FOR TODAY:**

DAY 344

Today's Reading:
Matthew 27:62–66

D estroy this temple, and in three days I will raise it up" (John 2:19). While they might not have initially understood the words of this statement by Jesus, the Jews now clearly knew that He was prophesying about the temple of His own body. He had stated, both privately to His apostles and publicly in the hearing of the Jewish leaders, that after His death, He would rise again in three days. Ironically, these enemies of Jesus gave more credence to His promise of resurrection than did Jesus' own disciples. Matthew is the only one who reveals how there came to be a guard at the tomb of Jesus. The Jewish leaders had successfully destroyed Jesus and put down His blasphemous and rebellious "movement." Or so they thought. But they remembered those words of Jesus concerning His resurrection. They did not want His disciples to have the opportunity to further His fame and influence by faking His resurrection. So they petitioned Pilate for an armed guard to secure the tomb. Ironically, their actions would only serve to validate Jesus' resurrection.

How did securing of Jesus' tomb help validate His resurrection?

DON'T FORGET TO PRAY AND HAVE A GREAT DAY!

⏳ **THINGS TO PRAY FOR TODAY:**

Day 345

Today's Reading:
Matthew 28:1–8

The earth shook as the power of God was displayed, and an angel pierced the barrier between spiritual and physical. As the stone was rolled away revealing an empty tomb, it was also revealed that no seal or guard and no amount of effort or force could withstand the power of God and prevent the resurrection of Jesus. The prophets had foretold it. Jesus had promised it. The Jews had tried to prevent it. But as the sun rose on the morning of that third day, so did the Son. His resurrection was the final surge in His victorious battle over sin and death as it brought completion to God's plan of redemption. As Paul would later write, just as we are reconciled to God by Jesus' death, we are saved by His resurrection (Romans 5:10). As Jesus rose from the grave, He became the firstfruits of the resurrection and made sure the promise of resurrection for His people. No longer are we under the curse of sin and death. We have a blessed hope and glorious future because of our resurrected Savior.

Why was Jesus' resurrection important to God's plan of redemption?

DON'T FORGET TO PRAY AND HAVE A GREAT DAY!

⏳ **THINGS TO PRAY FOR TODAY:**

Day 346

Today's Reading:
Mark 16:1–8

A peculiar thing about this text is the specific mentioning of Peter. Certainly "His disciples" would have included Peter, but the angel tells the women to tell Peter specifically of Jesus' resurrection. Have you ever wondered why? When was Peter last mentioned in the gospels? Was it not when he stood in the courtyard and denied his Lord three times? As the rooster crowed, Peter turned and looked into the knowing eyes of Jesus and fled from that place weeping. He had turned and walked away from His Lord in shame and failure. But that was not to be the end of Peter's story. As the news is given of Jesus' resurrection, there is a special message intended for Peter. Beyond the news that He had risen, Jesus wanted Peter to know that he was on His mind. He was still wanted and loved. Jesus had not given up on Peter and wanted him to be a part of this special event. What a wonderful reminder of the love and forgiveness Jesus offers to each one of us.

What does this scene teach us about God's forgiveness and love?

DON'T FORGET TO PRAY AND HAVE A GREAT DAY!

⏳ **THINGS TO PRAY FOR TODAY:**

DAY 347

Today's Reading:
Luke 24:1-12

Throughout His ministry, Jesus' disciples had struggled to understand, believe, and trust. They had been devoted to Jesus and committed to their discipleship, but the concepts and principles Jesus taught and discussed were challenging to their understanding of religion and the world around them. Even His closest followers had failed to understand how Jesus' death could lead to the establishment of His kingdom, and they had been shaken by the tragic end to His life. After Jesus' death, His faithful followers retreated from the scene, filled with sadness and confusion. They had forgotten His promise to rise again and seemingly believed that His death was final. Even upon receiving word of the empty tomb, the apostles could not find it in themselves to believe. They were troubled, distraught, blinded by sadness and loss. But their mourning would soon give way to joy as they came to the realization that their friend and Savior had not been defeated by death, but had overcome.

Why do you think that Jesus' disciples
struggled to believe in the resurrection?

DON'T FORGET TO PRAY AND HAVE A GREAT DAY!

 THINGS TO PRAY FOR TODAY:

Day 348

 Today's Reading:
John 20:1–13

As you read the four gospel accounts of the resurrection, it may be confusing and concerning to you to realize that the writers seem not to be in agreement about the events that take place. These supposed discrepancies have been used by many to attack the credibility of the Bible and to argue against its inerrancy. So how do we reconcile these issues? Remember that the four accounts of the resurrection are like four different eye-witness accounts of any event (e.g. an auto accident). Each one sees the event from a different perspective and reveals different details. While each writer is inspired and guided by the Holy Spirit so that his message is true and accurate, each account will differ based on the writer's own experience, his audience, and his purpose of writing. The events that are recounted are a series of happenings that all fit together like pieces of a puzzle. Only by piecing them together can we see the full picture of what happened on that morning. John's account in today's reading is actually the first piece in that timeline of events and precedes all the other accounts chronologically.

Why do you think God has given us
different accounts of the same events?

DON'T FORGET TO PRAY AND HAVE A GREAT DAY!

 THINGS TO PRAY FOR TODAY:

Day 349

Today's Reading:
Matthew 28:9–15

Of the gospel writers, Matthew is the only one who mentions the guards at the tomb. While we cannot know for sure why that is the case, it may be that, in writing to a Jewish audience, Matthew was intent on pointing out the hard-heartedness of the Jewish leaders and the unscrupulous methods they employed to prevent people from believing in Jesus. The Jewish leaders had been responsible for seeing that the guards were placed at the tomb to keep any rumors of a resurrection from being born. Now as the guards report to the chief priests the extraordinary events that they witnessed at the tomb that morning, they are bribed with "a sufficient sum of money" to keep the truth quiet and to say instead the very thing that they had been charged with preventing—that Jesus' disciples had come and stolen the body. Initially, we are taken aback by the hard-heartedness and deceit of these who were supposed to be men of God. But beyond that, it is incredible to consider that, when confronted with such overwhelming evidence of the divinity of Jesus, these men were not humbled into belief and submission. How could this be?

What do you think prevented the Jewish leaders from believing?

DON'T FORGET TO PRAY AND HAVE A GREAT DAY!

 THINGS TO PRAY FOR TODAY:

Day 350

 Today's Reading:
Mark 16:9–13

T he theme of this short passage seems to be unbelief. Actually, it may be better termed disbelief than unbelief, for it was not a stubborn refusal to believe that the disciples of Jesus displayed, but rather a shocked inability to believe. Many of them had witnessed the horrible death suffered by their friend and Lord. They had watched as the spear was thrust into His side, causing blood and water to come pouring from His lifeless body. Mary had been there as Jesus' body was wrapped and laid in a tomb. How could He be alive? Their grief and sorrow had clouded their memories of His foretold resurrection, and their faith had suffered a devastating blow. In addition to mourning the loss of their friend, they were probably also grieving what seemed to be the loss of the hope He brought to them. Their heaviness of heart would not allow them to believe. But Jesus was risen, and hope was not lost, as they would soon see with their own eyes.

Why do you think it was so hard for
them to believe that Jesus had risen?

DON'T FORGET TO PRAY AND HAVE A GREAT DAY!

⏳ **THINGS TO PRAY FOR TODAY:**

DAY 351

 Today's Reading:
John 20:14-18

Much has been made of the fact that, on a few occasions, the disciples of Jesus did not recognize Jesus when He first appeared to them after His resurrection, suggesting that He possibly had a different body or form than before His death. The truth of the matter is that there is no concrete evidence that this is the case and in fact the evidence of Scripture points to the fact that Jesus body was the same as before His resurrection. We are clearly told that He was flesh and blood and had the scars of His crucifixion (Luke 24:39; John 20:25-29). In the case of Jesus' appearance on the road to Emmaus (discussed tomorrow), the disciples' eyes were miraculously restrained from recognizing Him. In the case of Mary in today's reading, the dimness of the pre-dawn light (together with her weeping) could have easily obscured her vision so that she did not initially recognize Jesus. Despite the reasons why, the fact that some did not immediately recognize Jesus does not take away at all from the truthfulness or power of His resurrection.

Why is it important that Jesus' resurrected
form be the same as before His resurrection?

DON'T FORGET TO PRAY AND HAVE A GREAT DAY!

⏳ **THINGS TO PRAY FOR TODAY:**

DAY 352

 Today's Reading:
Luke 24:13-27

The thing that stands out to me in this passage is probably not the most significant portion of the text, but it is very interesting. As these two disciples walk and talk about the events of Jesus' death, Jesus joins them and asks what they are talking about, and why they are so sad. Their eyes being restrained from recognizing Him, they are astonished that anyone who has been in or around Jerusalem did not know of the events of the last few days. Crucifixions were not uncommon in the Roman Empire, but so noteworthy and tumultuous were the events surrounding the crucifixion of Jesus that it was the talk of the town. So influential and impactful was Jesus' life, that His death and the way in which He died was significant. It speaks to the great effect Jesus had on the world during His short time here. His character, compassion, teaching, and example had been a changing force in His world. But the impact that Jesus' life had on His physical world, as great as it was, pales in comparison to the impact that His death and resurrection have had on all of humanity for all time.

How has Jesus' death and resurrection impacted your life?

DON'T FORGET TO PRAY AND HAVE A GREAT DAY!

⏳ **THINGS TO PRAY FOR TODAY:**

DAY 353

 Today's Reading:
Luke 24:28–35

P eople are often known and recognized for how they do what they do best (athletes, actors, artists, etc.). While I believe that the Bible teaches us that the eyes of these men were miraculously restrained from recognizing Jesus (in yesterday's reading), it is interesting to note their reaction to their eyes being opened to Jesus. "Did not our heart burn within us while He talked with us on the road, and while He opened the Scriptures to us?" While their eyes were restrained from recognizing Him, there was something about His teaching that touched their hearts, something powerful, something familiar. They later reported, "He was known to them in the breaking of bread." This is likely referring to the prayer Jesus offered in blessing the bread as He broke it. Jesus' teachings and prayers were unique and set Him apart from anyone who had ever been known. A few minutes spent with this Man revealed that He was, without a doubt, the Master Teacher and the risen Christ.

Why do you think Jesus' teaching and prayers were so unique?

DON'T FORGET TO PRAY AND HAVE A GREAT DAY!

 THINGS TO PRAY FOR TODAY:

DAY 354

 Today's Reading:
Luke 24:36–43

The appearances of Jesus following His resurrection are fascinating. They are sporadic, brief, and always seem to have a very specific purpose. On this occasion, as the two disciples from Emmaus are reporting to the apostles and others about their encounter with Jesus, He appears in their midst. This is Jesus' first recorded appearance to the apostles, and His purpose seems to be simply to validate the reports of His resurrection to them. Their response, even as Jesus stands before them, is one of disbelief. How could this be? It can't really be Jesus! It must be a spirit. But Jesus had risen and stood before them in flesh and blood. He invites them to look on His wounded hands and feet and to touch His flesh. Then in their presence He asks for food and eats. Jesus left no doubt, either in their minds or ours, that He was risen from the grave and was witnessed in the flesh after His resurrection.

Why is it important that Jesus was witnessed
in the flesh after His resurrection?

DON'T FORGET TO PRAY AND HAVE A GREAT DAY!

⏳ THINGS TO PRAY FOR TODAY:

DAY 355

Today's Reading:
Luke 24:44–49

This is the same occasion as yesterday's reading. Jesus has appeared to the apostles, not only for the purpose of validating His resurrection, but also to help them understand the purpose of His death and resurrection. His suffering, death, and resurrection were part of God's plan for redeeming mankind. They always had been. The law, the prophets, and the psalms all foretold it and looked forward to it. God had brought redemption and salvation to the world through the suffering of His Son, and now it was the apostles' turn to fulfill their purpose. As witnesses of the life, death, and now resurrection of Jesus, their duty and calling was to testify of Him to the world, to take the saving message of Christ to all nations, to preach repentance and remission of sins beginning at Jerusalem. This appearance of Jesus was not just a joyous reunion; it was a call to action!

Why was (is) the preaching of Jesus so important to God's plan?

DON'T FORGET TO PRAY AND HAVE A GREAT DAY!

 THINGS TO PRAY FOR TODAY:

DAY 356

Today's Reading:
John 20:19–23

This passage is parallel to what we read from Luke yesterday. These two passages represent John and Luke's accounts of the Great Commission that are better known from Matthew and Mark. John records that He breathed on them and imparted the Holy Spirit on them. This was most likely the opening of their understanding that Luke mentioned in His account yesterday. This was not the baptism of the Holy Spirit which would take place after Jesus' ascension (Acts 2), but rather an endowment of understanding of the Scriptures related to God's plan of redemption. The apostles had always struggled to understand Jesus' purpose and teachings, especially regarding His death, resurrection, and kingdom. Even now, as He stood before them in resurrected form, they struggled to believe and understand, but it was vital that they understand their mission. And so, with a miraculous gift of knowledge, He guides them into the understanding that they needed to accomplish their calling.

Why do you think the apostles needed
help in understanding their mission?

DON'T FORGET TO PRAY AND HAVE A GREAT DAY!

⧗ **THINGS TO PRAY FOR TODAY:**

DAY 357

Today's Reading:
John 20:24–29

Doubting Thomas. It is from this scene that Thomas inherits that rather unflattering label, but was he really doubting? As I read this text, I prefer to give Thomas the benefit of the doubt and see his actions in a much more positive light. First of all, it needs to be noted that Thomas reacted to the Lord's appearance in essentially the same way as did the other disciples (see Luke 24:36-43), but because Thomas alone was seeing Christ for the first time in this text, there is more of a spotlight on him. More importantly, I believe it was Thomas' devotion to Christ that prompted his response. He would not be duped into believing in a false Christ. He was devoted only to Jesus, and if he was to bow down before this man, he must know for sure that it was his Lord. Upon seeing the evidence, Thomas readily believed and proclaimed, "My Lord and my God!" Instead of labeling Thomas as a doubter, maybe we should be thankful for his example of devotion and love for Christ.

What do you take from Jesus' final statement in this text (v. 29)?

DON'T FORGET TO PRAY AND HAVE A GREAT DAY!

⏳ **THINGS TO PRAY FOR TODAY:**

DAY 358

Today's Reading:
John 20:30-31

What an experience it must have been to be in the presence of the resurrected Christ and witness all the signs and wonders He performed! How it must have bolstered the faith and fortified the strength of His disciples. In this brief summary statement, John informs us that what has been given to us in the gospels is only a small portion of the appearances and works of Jesus. There is much more that time and space would not allow to be recorded. But, John says, the things that are recorded have a very specific purpose: those who read them may believe that Jesus is indeed the Christ, the Son of God, and through that belief, they may be led into eternal life in His name. As Jesus' life, death, and resurrection were a demonstration to those of His own day of His identity as the only begotten of the Father and of His role as the sacrificial Lamb of God, so the recording of those events in the gospels serves the same purpose for all generations since. What a blessing the Word of God, and specifically the gospel of Christ, is to our lives!

Why do you think God chose not
to reveal all of Jesus' works to us?

DON'T FORGET TO PRAY AND HAVE A GREAT DAY!

⏳ THINGS TO PRAY FOR TODAY:

DAY 359

 Today's Reading:
Matthew 28:16–20

This is one of the texts that is often referred to as the Great Commission. Contained within this command of Jesus is a formula for bringing people to Christ that includes three distinct steps. The first is to "make disciples" of them. Certainly we can infer from this statement the idea of teaching them about Jesus so that they believe in Him and make a decision to follow after Him, thus turning away from and abandoning any other path in life (repentance). Once belief and repentance have been achieved, Jesus says to baptize them, bringing them into contact with Christ and His saving blood. But lest we think that baptism is the end of a person's journey toward Christ, He reminds us to continue to teach him, bringing him to a full knowledge and maturity in the Word of God so that he can "observe all" that Jesus had commanded. What a blessing it is to have the guidance and instruction of Christ as we strive to fulfill our calling!

Does the Great Commission still apply to us today? Why or why not?

DON'T FORGET TO PRAY AND HAVE A GREAT DAY!

 THINGS TO PRAY FOR TODAY:

Day 360

Today's Reading:
Mark 16:14–18

In Mark's account of the Great Commission, Jesus makes certain promises to those who believe concerning their working of miracles through His name. What are we to make of these promises? Are they still in place today? While these words of Jesus might cause some confusion and question in our minds, when the New Testament is examined in its entirety, a better understanding of this text is gained. Certainly throughout the book of Acts and the epistles, we see this promise of Jesus fulfilled in the lives of first-century Christians. In the absence of the completed New Testament writings, the Spirit worked through these Christians in miraculous ways to reveal and confirm the teaching and will of God in the church. But we are also told that when the written word was completed, these gifts would pass away, no longer being necessary (see 1 Corinthians 13:8-12). While we might tend to feel somewhat inferior for no longer having these miraculous gifts, we are in fact the more blessed for having the full revelation of God through His inspired word.

How did miraculous gifts in the first
century serve to reveal or confirm God's will?

DON'T FORGET TO PRAY AND HAVE A GREAT DAY!

⏳ **THINGS TO PRAY FOR TODAY:**

Day 361

Today's Reading:
John 21:1-14

"I am going fishing." For Peter, this was more than a leisurely day at the lake. Fishing had not been a regular part of Peter's life since he left his nets and family business to follow Jesus. The time since Jesus' arrest in the garden has been difficult, confusing, and discouraging for all the apostles, but maybe especially for Peter. Still haunted by his own failure in denying his relationship with Jesus, Peter is struggling to find his place and purpose in this new situation. Jesus' time with them since His resurrection has been brief and sporadic. No longer is He their constant companion. What are they to do? To go fishing was not necessarily a return to his previous life, but it was certainly a distraction and probably a temptation for Peter. He may not know what to do as a disciple without his Master, but he knew how to fish. Fishing was natural, comfortable. So he went fishing. But as Peter would soon learn, Jesus was not finished with him yet.

How could fishing have served as a temptation for Peter?

DON'T FORGET TO PRAY AND HAVE A GREAT DAY!

 THINGS TO PRAY FOR TODAY:

DAY 362

Today's Reading:
John 21:15-19

Three times Peter had been asked about his relationship with Jesus, and three times he had denied Him. That had been an event that Peter had struggled to come to terms with and overcome. Now as he stands before Jesus, His Lord and friend gives him three opportunities to affirm his love for Him. With the third question by Jesus, Peter becomes "grieved," probably because he wants so badly for Jesus to understand that his love for Him is true and so much greater than the fear that motivated his denials. And understand, Jesus did. I believe that in this scene there are three very important messages that Jesus is sending to Peter. The first is that He still loves him. Whatever failures might have taken place in the past had not affected the love Jesus had for His friend and disciple. Second, He had forgiven him. Though Peter was still struggling with it, Jesus wants him to know that it is in the past and has been forgiven. And finally, Jesus needs Peter to know that he is still useful and important to Him. He has a plan for Peter and needs him to fulfill that purpose for which he was called. What a beautiful passage of hope for anyone who has ever failed in their faithfulness.

How do you think this event helped Peter to overcome his failure?

DON'T FORGET TO PRAY AND HAVE A GREAT DAY!

⏳ **THINGS TO PRAY FOR TODAY:**

DAY 363

 Today's Reading:
John 21:20-25

At the end of yesterday's reading, Jesus reveals to Peter that he will die a martyr's death. You can imagine the shock and concern with which Peter receives that news. *Why me? Will I be the only one? What about the others?* Turning and seeing John, he asks Jesus, "What about this man?" Jesus' response contains an important lesson for all of us to learn from: "If it is my will that he remain until I come, what is that to you? You follow Me!" His simple message to Peter is to not worry about anyone else, but simply to focus on Jesus and faithfully follow Him. How often do we look around and wonder why someone else has it better than we do or why others aren't suffering while we are? In our minds, we might ask with Peter, "Lord, what about them?" But Jesus' message to us is the same. Don't worry about the lot of anyone else. "You follow Me." God has a plan and purpose for each of us. Our path may be different from that of others, but if we will simply follow Him, then we will surely receive the reward that He has laid up for us.

Why do you think we so often
want to compare ourselves to others?

DON'T FORGET TO PRAY AND HAVE A GREAT DAY!

⏳ **THINGS TO PRAY FOR TODAY:**

DAY 364

Today's Reading:
Mark 16:19–20

In Luke's account of Jesus' ascension (tomorrow's reading), he focuses on His leaving. Mark, on the other hand, focuses more on Jesus' destination as He ascends from the earth. The right hand of God, where Jesus sat down upon being received into heaven, was a place of honor and authority, and Jesus was deserving of both. As the sacrificial Lamb of God and the One who had defeated sin and overcome death, Jesus had been given "all authority" (Matthew 28:18). He was the Savior of the body, His church, which He had purchased with His own blood, and which was soon to come into being. He was King of kings and Lord of lords. And He continues to be all of those things. He is still seated at the right hand of God, all powers and authorities being subject to Him (1 Peter 3:22). And He continues to hold the power to overcome sin and death in all those who believe in Him and faithfully obey Him. Hallelujah, what a Savior!

Why is it important for us that Jesus
is seated at the right hand of God?

DON'T FORGET TO PRAY AND HAVE A GREAT DAY!

⏳ **THINGS TO PRAY FOR TODAY:**

Day 365

Today's Reading:
Luke 24:50-53

What is interesting to me about this passage is the reaction of the apostles to Jesus leaving them. As Jesus had previously warned and prepared them for His leaving, they had been troubled and confused. They had not wanted to accept or even consider the possibility that Jesus would leave them. But as we see them gathered at Bethany and witnessing the taking up of Jesus into the heavens, we do not see them grasping for Him or desiring to keep Him with them. We do not see them filled with grief or discouragement at His departure. Instead, we read that they were filled with "great joy," worshipping Him and then returning to Jerusalem as He had instructed them. They had grown in their faith and in their understanding of Jesus' purpose and their mission. They joyously celebrated their relationship with Christ and His triumphant return to His rightful place at the right hand of God. And they anxiously awaited the coming of the Spirit that Jesus had promised them. What a beautiful and fitting end to the story of Jesus' time in this world.

What do you think had contributed to the growth and understanding of the apostles?

DON'T FORGET TO PRAY AND HAVE A GREAT DAY!

 THINGS TO PRAY FOR TODAY:

A Final Thought

If you have followed this book as it was designed, then you have spent an entire year journeying through the life of Christ. Hopefully, that study has been one that has strengthened your faith and deepened your love for Christ. While this might mark the end of your year's study, it certainly should not be the end of your study of God's word or your journey with Christ. In fact, my hope is that this study has awakened within you a growing desire to know more about God's word and to be more devoted to Christ in your daily life. May God bless you as you continue to seek Him, and may we all strive daily to walk hand-in-hand with Christ.

"But thanks be to God, who gives us the victory through our Lord Jesus Christ."

—1 Corinthians 15:57